# Reservation "Capitalism"

Thanks Ron!

Bob Miller

# Reservation "Capitalism"

## Economic Development in Indian Country

## Robert J. Miller

NATIVE AMERICA: YESTERDAY AND TODAY
*Bruce E. Johansen, Series Editor*

PRAEGER

AN IMPRINT OF ABC-CLIO, LLC
Santa Barbara, California • Denver, Colorado • Oxford, England

**Library of Congress Cataloging-in-Publication Data**

Miller, Robert J.
    Reservation "capitalism" : economic development in Indian country / Robert J. Miller.
        p. cm. — (Native America : yesterday and today)
    Includes bibliographical references and index.
    ISBN 978–1–4408–0111–2 (hardcopy : alk. paper) — ISBN 978–1–4408–0112–9 (ebook)
1. Indians of North America—Economic conditions. 2. Economic development—United States.
3. Gambling on Indian reservations—United States. 4. Indian business enterprises—United States.
5. United States—Economic conditions. I. Title.
E98.E2M55  2012
338.9730089′97—dc23            2012000403

ISBN: 978–1–4408–0111–2
EISBN: 978–1–4408–0112–9

16  15  14  13  12        3  4  5

This book is also available on the World Wide Web as an eBook.
Visit www.abc-clio.com for details.

Praeger
An Imprint of ABC-CLIO, LLC

ABC-CLIO, LLC
130 Cremona Drive, P.O. Box 1911
Santa Barbara, California 93116-1911

This book is printed on acid-free paper ∞

Manufactured in the United States of America

# Contents

# Series Foreword

**R**obert J. Miller has news for anyone who believes that most Native Americans were forest-dwelling socialists. Although many Native American nations and tribes owned land in common, Miller develops a case that nearly everything else was privately owned, and often subject to a fierce entrepreneurial spirit. Practices varied among the several hundred peoples who earned their livings from the land before Europeans came, of course. Some, most notably peoples of the Northwest coast, were individualistic in ways that surprised even the immigrants. Most lived in settled villages; they were not running around the woods surviving solely off the bounty of nature.

In *Reservation "Capitalism": Economic Development in Indian Country*, Miller, author of *Native America, Developed and Conquered: Thomas Jefferson, Lewis and Clark, and Manifest Destiny* (Praeger, 2006) in this series, asserts that native peoples' economic situation will improve only when they quit relying on government to conduct their business and do more of it themselves. An example is provided by a minority of nations and tribes that have worked their way out of poverty by using casinos to supply capital for reservation nation-building. However, many of the native peoples who do not have access to a large urban gaming market remain mired in poverty.

Miller's study of the past—what was traditionally held communally, and what was private—is a prescriptive for the future. He sketches surprisingly vibrant pre-Columbian economic activity (especially with regard to wide-ranging trade). Cahokia, near present-day St. Louis, Missouri, was a major trade and manufacturing center that in 1250 CE (with a population between 20,000 and 50,000 people) was as large as London at that time.

Miller's account is direct and very well written, as it busts some myths, suggesting that the image of the "noble savage," the wild man of the woods, was used by immigrating European-Americans to justify the removal of native land and resources from their original owners on the model of Anglo real estate law's preference for "highest and best use." European-American immigration provoked population decline that destroyed infrastructure.

One of the rationales for removing the Cherokees and others was a mistaken belief that they could not properly use the land. Anyone who has studied the history of the time realizes that the Cherokees in 1830 were at least as affluent as their non-Indian neighbors. The native peoples of the Eastern Seaboard were mainly farmers who tilled their own plots and stored food in family caches. The Nootka peoples of the Pacific Northwest (including the Makah in present-day Washington State) privately owned houses, clam beds, beaches (and salvage rights on these beaches), as well as fishing locations. They recognized intellectual property such as carved images on their houses, ceremonial dances, songs, medicines, masks, and rituals. Many of these rights could be inherited. Accumulation of wealth was recognized (and distributed through potlatches).

"Poverty," Miller writes, "is not an Indian cultural or historical attribute." Native people "worked diligently and intelligently in past centuries to support themselves and appreciated living comfortably, as all humans do." He quotes Antone Minthorn, chairman of the Confederated Tribes of the Umatilla Indian Reservation in Oregon: "We need to make it acceptable in Indian country to be in business; it's not about rejecting culture, it builds sovereignty." Business income can be used to build lasting infrastructure and enhance language and culture, Miller writes. "Waiting for the federal government . . . has not been a successful strategy for the past two hundred years and is not going to change in the future." Says Miller: "Self-sufficiency is self-determination."

Even with a minority of reservations benefiting massively from casinos, the typical unemployment rate on an Indian reservation today is 50 percent, "a disaster for community building and preserving a nation and a culture," writes Miller. "Housing, roads, water, education, and other infrastructure . . . the basic services that most Americans take for granted are deficient on most reservations." What little money native people earn often does not stay in their communities. Because of "leakage," due to a lack of business infrastructure, capital that could be used to start businesses flows off the reservations. Miller urges a bottom-up evolution of private business to stem the flow.

Indian reservations are not lacking income sources. The problems often lie in gaining a fair return for these resources, and then developing business infrastructure to keep income at home. Government and corporations often have used extractive industries to remove not only resources; they also underpay for what is taken away. Native peoples have timber, minerals, oil, coal, gas, wind, solar, and uranium (which is so deadly that the Navajos have banned mining of it); leasable land for agriculture, ranching, and grazing; natural sites suitable for tourism; fishing rights; and water resources. In addition, business infrastructure is growing on many reservations, incorporating tribally owned and private businesses, government administration, and gaming.

Miller's book includes a separate chapter on Native American gambling has an economic motor. Gross revenues of gaming on Indian reservations are now more than $25 billion a year in the United States, with the 20 largest gaming facilities accounting for roughly half of it. On some reservations, unemployment has fallen to nearly zero because casinos and bingo halls are not only labor intensive, but also generate capital for many other business ventures. The Muckleshoot, near Tacoma, have generated more jobs (3,500 as of 2011) than enrolled members (2,200).

Miller surveys the potential for all sources of income, and offers incisive analysis of statistics indicating that income is now growing faster for American Indians than for any other U.S. ethnic group—with the largest gains, surprisingly, according to Miller, on reservations without substantial income from gambling. The state of impoverishment on some reservations is so intense to begin with that recent gains are only beginning to catch up with society-wide averages.

This book is full of valuable statistics and (just as necessary) intense examination of how solid the statistics may be, and what they mean in a broader context. It also contains a detailed examination of obstacles to business development on reservations of a practical, on-the-street level, such as difficulty obtaining loans due not only to a lack of collateral but also the fact that reservation property is often held in federal trust. (Some tribes act as banks, in effect, offering loans to their members.) All of this makes this book very useful to businesspeople looking to start ventures on reservations, as well as economic planners in tribal governments and federal agencies. Where legal expertise is required Miller is able to offer it because he is a professor of law, with real-world experience in this area.

This is an incisive treatment of an important issue that is basic to the future of Native America. I am honored to include this book in "Native America: Yesterday and Today."

*Bruce E. Johansen*
*Series Editor*
*Omaha, NE*
*May 2011*

# *Foreword*

The narrative of the Native American story is rich, tragic, complex, and polarizing. Its history provides extraordinary accounts of grandiose legends, rich tradition, tragic displacement, and extraordinary loss of life and livelihood. Further, it cannot ignore the oftentimes tense and troubled relationship between Indian people and the U.S. government.

Each aspect of this complicated history can help explain the current condition of Indian Country, where a vibrant culture continues to face extreme economic distress. A condition where economic deprivation brings near third-world social, health, and economic status. But past does not have to be prologue. History does not have to dictate the economic and social future for twenty-first century Native American generations.

Native American affairs have always been an important policy concern of mine beginning well before my career in politics. As a native South Dakotan, I have witnessed the economic struggles that plague Indian people and considered it a great privilege to work on both policy and projects during my time in Congress. In so doing, I have had the good fortune to experience their proud and unique culture, and have been blessed to call many within the community "le mita cola," my friend. It is for these reasons I remain dedicated to their future and to the goals of improved health care and economic prosperity. And even though I no longer serve in the U.S. Senate, the building of a stronger future of Indian Country remains an important part of my life's work.

Tragically, the problems today relating to health care, housing, unemployment, suicide, public safety, and education are every bit as monumental as they were when I entered Congress more than a quarter century ago. The numbers are staggering. New efforts to find new solutions are essential to survival and to the dignity for all Indian people that was promised in each and every one of the treaty obligations of the United States.

Economic development is one of the central challenges in Indian Country for a number of reasons. Past relationships and experiences among the U.S. government, state governments, and Native American tribes have created a precarious foundation for achieving economic prosperity. Furthermore, unending disputes over land rights, natural resources, gaming regulations, sovereignty, and jurisdictional matters have exacerbated improved economic development efforts. Additionally, geographic isolation has compounded the challenge for many Indian nations of the Great Plains and the West. Yet, while each of these factors creates understandable skepticism about prospects for future success, I remain inspired by those who believe in the wisdom of Nelson Mandela, who once asserted that many things seem impossible until they are done.

In his book *Reservation "Capitalism": Economic Development in Indian Country*, Robert J. Miller offers solutions to many of these central problems. Professor Miller's book offers a compelling and descriptive account of Native American history and the titanic struggle for economic success. By eloquently and powerfully describing economic conditions through history, as well as the troubled relationship between Native American and non-Indian governments, he sets the stage well for a thoughtful series of persuasive and long overdue solutions including reforms in the tribal court system, gaming laws, and the current government-to-government relationships. Additionally, he offers compelling arguments for the creation of vibrant small businesses within the tribal community.

Many of Professor Miller's readers will share his strong belief in self-determination and his call for renewed vigor in the fight for a brighter future and more prosperous life for the next Indian generation. It is a future where a dynamic culture and thriving economy can coexist. A future that recognizes that not only are these two not mutually exclusive, they can in fact lead to a unique and flourishing partnership.

Professor Miller's passion and his belief in the ability of Indian nations to experience a future filled with hope and with promise is substantiated with illustrative examples of tribes who have already achieved their economic freedom. I share his conviction that fighting for that freedom now for those tribes who have yet to achieve it may be the most important goal for this generation of Native American leadership.

For those willing to commit to the heroic effort required, Professor Miller offers sound strategic advice.

*Tom Daschle*
*Former U.S. Senate Majority Leader from South Dakota*

# Acknowledgments

I dedicate this book to my parents, James B. Miller and Hazel L. Miller (Captain). My dad taught me everything I know about small family businesses during the time I worked for him from 1968–1987 at Jim Miller's Used Cars, Inc., in Portland, Oregon. He created and operated his business for nearly 52 years from 1946 to the very day he died in 1997. My mom taught me about economics, budgeting, and the value of a dollar. She provided the seed money to start our family business by working in the Portland shipyards during World War II as a riveter and welder, and she also did the bookkeeping for the company for its first seven or eight years of existence. I owe them everything I am today.

I also gratefully acknowledge all the people who made this book possible and assisted me and supported me in seeing it to completion: Molly Smith, Leslie Miller, and Amanda Breunig. I thank Professor Alex Skibine, Steve Bahnson, and Jean Edwards for reading and commenting on earlier drafts of the book.

I also thank the people who generously gave me their time in interviews and personal conversations: Chief Glenna Wallace, Second Chief Jack Ross, Chairman Antone Minthorn, Chairman Clifford Lyle Marshall, Chief Charles Enyart, Danny Captain, Howard Birdsong, Danny Jordan, Jolanda Ingram-Marshall, Chairman Duane Sherman, Gary George, Kathleen Flanagan, Bill Tovey, Roberta Conner, and Tom Hampson.

I also thank Lynn Williams of the Lewis & Clark Law School Library, who endured years of countless requests from me for various research sources.

# CHAPTER 1

# *Introduction*

**P**rior to contact with Euro-Americans, the Indigenous peoples and nations of North America owned, controlled, and used all the natural resources and assets of its lands and waters. Today, American Indians only own 1 percent of those lands and resources. Somehow all of these valuable resources passed into the hands of nonnative peoples and governments. This transfer of wealth and other events have led to a situation of extreme poverty for the native peoples of North America.

American Indians are today the poorest of the poor in the United States. We will examine how the prosperity that America's Indigenous peoples enjoyed for centuries passed from their ownership and how it was replaced by crushing poverty, hardship, despair, and social problems that affect reservations and Indians in the United States today. We will mostly concentrate, however, on how Indians and their tribal governments are fighting to correct this situation and to address their economic issues. We will also examine tools that tribes and Indians can use to help them in this important struggle to reach a level of economic prosperity that sustains their lives, families, communities, and cultures, and that enables them to better exercise self-determination, self-sufficiency, and self-governance.

The subject of this book is absolutely crucial because reservation and urban Indians suffer from the social pathologies that accompany poverty. These problems need to be addressed and solved. American Indians and tribal governments have the right to enjoy the same prosperity and security as other Americans.

A common stereotype today is that Indians must be rich due to tribal gaming. In reality only a few tribes have made large amounts of money from gambling while the rest of the 565 federally recognized tribal governments in the United States still suffer from long-entrenched poverty. American Indians on reservations suffer unemployment rates from 20 to 80 percent and have the highest substandard housing rates in the United States.

During the U.S. recession of 2008 to 2011, unemployment was an average of 10 percent in January 2010 (reduced to 9.1% by May 2011) and was at its highest at nearly 11 percent in Detroit, Rhode Island, and Oregon. Those are worrisome figures. Moreover, when Detroit's unemployment was only at 8.2 percent, it was considered a disaster and was blamed for Detroit having a "struggling economy [and] an environment characterized by social breakdown."[1] In addition, one economist commented in 2011 on Oregon's anticipated long-term 9 percent unemployment rate: "To live with 9 to 10 percent unemployment for a number of years is just unfathomable to me."[2] But compare those 8.2 percent and 9 percent unemployment figures to the 20 to 80 percent unemployment rates on Indian reservations. And while that is the range of unemployment on reservations, a 2001 U.S. Department of Treasury report, and other federal reports, state that the average unemployment on all reservations is 50 percent. Is it any surprise that poverty is rampant and that there are numerous social problems on reservations?[3]

A society simply cannot function with 20 to 80 percent unemployment. It is a recipe for disaster for community building and for preserving a nation and a culture. Those daunting figures only hint at the economic problems that exist in Indian Country and why it is so important to improve that situation.[4]

The economic news in Indian Country is no better when we talk about housing, roads, water, education, and other infrastructure issues. The basic services that most Americans take for granted are deficient on most reservations. Adequate roads and housing, clean water and sanitation, telephones and electricity are in short supply on many reservations. A 2001 Department of the Treasury report stated that more than 66 percent of reservation roads were unimproved earth and gravel, and that annual fatality rates on those roads were more than four times the national average. Moreover, only 47 percent of reservation Indian households had telephones, compared to 94 percent for nonnative rural Americans. One quarter of tribes did not have 911 emergency services. And only 9 percent of rural Indian houses had personal computers and only 8 percent had Internet access.

Furthermore, only 14 percent of Indian lands even had a financial institution in their community. More than one in six American Indians had to travel over 100 miles to find a bank or an automated teller machine, and one third of Indians had to travel at least 30 miles to reach an ATM or bank. In 1990, the Navajo Nation reservation, which is as large as America's 40th largest state, had only three bank branches and one ATM.

As of 2008, up to 35 percent of Indian homes lacked adequate water and 10 to 15 percent of Indian homes did not have plumbing. On some reservations nearly half the homes did not have electricity or phone service and the Department of Energy reported in 2000 that 14.2 percent of Indian homes on reservations had no access to electricity, compared to just 1.4 percent of all U.S. households.

Many reservation communities also suffer from the highest infant death rates, malnutrition rates, shortest life expectancy rates, and the lowest levels of formal education for any U.S. group. In 1999, President Bill Clinton compared three reservations that he visited to third-world countries.[5]

These facts demonstrate the magnitude of the problems and the importance of tribal, federal, and state leaders and Indians addressing these issues. I suspect that most Indians are tired of hearing these numbers recited and must really be frustrated about living in these kinds of conditions. Indian peoples and tribal leaders want to correct these situations and they expect and hope that others will assist them.

Consequently, expanding and creating new forms of economic development and activities in Indian Country is probably the most important political, social, community, and financial concern that Indian nations, tribal leaders, and Indian peoples face today. Tribal governments and Indians need to create jobs and economic activities on their reservations and for tribal citizens who live off reservations. How much longer can reservations sustain their communities and cultures in the face of these serious economic challenges?

One obvious problem that inhibits the development of economic activity in Indian Country is the almost total lack of functioning economies. An economy and economic activity, as these terms are used in this book, are defined in Webster's as the structure and organization in a specific region or country for the production, distribution, and consumption of goods and services. This kind of activity and the interrelated business conducted between consumers and publicly and privately owned business entities is absent on most reservations. In fact, real economies do not exist on almost all of the 300 Indian reservations in the lower 48 states and in the more than 200 Alaska Native villages. For example, few reservations have large grocery stores or retail outlets and there is an almost complete absence of businesses where people can spend money on the necessities and luxuries of life. Many factors contribute to this problem. Most reservations are in rural areas and they face the same economic challenges as other rural areas in the United States. There are very few privately owned businesses on most reservations and, in fact, Indian peoples own private businesses at the lowest rate per capita for any ethnic or racial group in the United States. In addition, the businesses American Indians own produce less income on average than others. The absence of economies and a sufficient number of small businesses also seriously impacts the growth and development of new economic activities in Indian Country. The financial news for urban Indians who live off reservations is not much better. Urban Indians have jobs, incomes, family wealth, and home ownership rates far below U.S. averages and they are three times more likely to be homeless than the average American.[6]

This book focuses on the subject of developing tribal and Indian-owned economic activities and creating functioning economies in Indian communities. The absence of a significant number of private businesses on reservations negatively impacts the potential of creating vibrant economies, because jobs and economic activities are primarily located elsewhere. The importance of developing privately owned businesses in Indian Country is demonstrated by the fact that small business is the primary ingredient of the U.S. economy. Statistics show that as of 2001 small businesses created 93 percent of the new jobs nationwide. The economy of Oregon, for example, reflects the significance of small business. Family-owned small businesses make up 90 percent of the state's economy, create 78 percent of all new jobs, and pay more than 65 percent of all wages. When we compare these facts to the almost complete absence of small businesses and functioning economies in most of Indian Country, it is no surprise that poverty exists on reservations.[7]

Furthermore, the lack of small businesses and economies on reservations leads to a well-known economic problem called "leakage." Economists define leakage as a situation where money leaves or leaks away from the local economy of a town, city, county, or state sooner than expected and sooner than is optimal. Ideally, it is stated that money should circulate in the local economy where it was received or earned five to seven times before it spins out of that community. Leakage usually occurs because consumers cannot buy the goods and services they desire in their local areas. Rural areas, Indian reservations, and tribal governments well understand this problem.[8]

A central premise of this book is that tribal governments and Indians can greatly benefit their communities and help alleviate poverty and its problems by working to create functioning economies composed of a mix of tribally owned and privately owned businesses. Tribal governments need to attract more Indian and non-Indian businesses and investors to reservations, operate more tribal businesses and related programs, and increase the entrepreneurial activities of tribal citizens, all with the goal of increasing the number of tribally owned and privately operated Indian and non-Indian businesses in Indian Country. These actions will help create functioning economies and help redress the problem of money leaking from reservations and Indian communities. Reservation economies that can create and attract decent jobs and build adequate housing will also greatly benefit their communities and cultures by allowing Indian families to live and work on their reservations, where they can participate in and help perpetuate their cultures, communities, and languages. Many tribal citizens are eager to move home to their reservations if only they can find decent housing and employment.[9]

It also bears emphasizing that poverty is not an Indian cultural or historical attribute. As I will discuss, tribes and Indians worked diligently and intelligently in past centuries to support themselves and they appreciated living comfortably, as all humans do. Similarly, tribes and Indians today do not want to continue to live on the edge of existence. One Navajo Nation chairman affirmed this point: "Traditional Navajo values do not include poverty."[10] And the chairman and CEO of the Oneida Nation of New York commented: "We had tried poverty for 200 years, so we decided to try something else."[11] Poverty is not an Indian cultural trait.

Many other Indian leaders and commentators agree. The chairman of the Confederated Tribes of the Umatilla Indian Reservation in Oregon, Antone Minthorn, stated in 2008 at an Indian business conference: "We need to make it acceptable in Indian country to be in business; it's not about rejecting culture, it builds sovereignty."[12] In fact, instead of injuring culture, private business ownership is an expression of Native American traditional values and supports tribal cultures. After all, as one tribally created business organization states: "economic development is a tool to achieve cultural integrity and self-determination with tribal sovereignty."[13] This organization also argues that increasing economic development on reservations supports tribal cultures because "contemporary American Indian sovereignty depends directly upon a successful rekindling of [Indian] entrepreneurial spirit."[14] Furthermore, one of the leading studies of tribal economic development, the Harvard Project on American Indian Economic Development, has concluded that it is "not necessary to stop being tribal or 'traditional' to develop economically."[15] And Bill Yellowtail, of the Crow Nation and an ex-Montana state legislator, adds that "we must give Indians permission to pursue that age-old . . . paradigm of entrepreneurial self-sufficiency."[16] This is absolutely true because "developing reservation economies is vital to sustaining and developing Native American cultural identities."[17]

Some people, though, question whether economic development and creating reservation economies will injure Indian cultures. I will discuss this issue in several chapters of this book. It suffices here to make two points. First, as stated above, many tribal leaders, historians, and commentators agree that economic development and business activities are not at odds with historic and traditional tribal cultures and economies. In addition, tribal governments and American Indians do not have the option to do nothing about their economic conditions. Clearly, it does not serve the long-term success and preservation of native cultures and communities when Indian families are mired in poverty, and lack adequate and nutritious food, decent housing, beneficial work, quality education, clothing, transportation, and other daily needs. How will Indian cultures and communities continue to survive in the midst of desperate poverty? If Indian peoples cannot afford to live on their reservations, how will they perpetuate their reservation-based communities and tribal governments? How will they pass their cultures and languages on to new generations and how will they expose their children to tribal elders and to religious and traditional leaders? If Indians and tribal governments do not have the resources to send their citizens to quality schools and colleges, who will study and perpetuate tribal nations, cultural traditions, and tribal languages? How will tribal leaders and reservation inhabitants build lasting governments and communities without the economic resources and infrastructure that life requires?

The answers to these questions seem obvious. Tribes and reservation populations need to reach some basic level of economic stability and prosperity to be self-sufficient and independent, and to perpetuate and strengthen their governments, communities, and cultures. I do not see any alternative.

I also do not think that tribes and Indians should suffer in poverty and its related problems while they wait for the federal government to address these issues. That is not self-determination and self-governance; that is dependence. Waiting for the federal government to fix tribal economic and social problems has not proven to be a successful strategy over the past two hundred years and it is not going to change in the future. As Sam Deloria recently wrote about Indian education: "the federal government can't give our young people hope and pride: we have to do that ... High-level people in Washington can help ... but we can't look to them to do our jobs."[18] Instead of waiting on others, tribal governments and Indian peoples can only rely on themselves to address and solve their economic issues. Tribes will need all the help they can get, so they will continue to look to the federal government for assistance, and especially for the United States to fulfill its treaty promises and trust duties for tribes and Indians. But in the long run, tribal governments and Indians will have to do most of the work. They have to preserve and perpetuate their own cultures and communities. As many commentators agree, tribes and Indians can do this by building economically secure, self-reliant, and self-sufficient communities. In fact, Professor Dean Howard Smith, a native person and tribal economic planner, said that tribal and individual Indian economic development is not just about making money. Instead, it is designed to strengthen reservation communities by making them viable places to live, and he says it is "necessary" for "maintaining cultural integrity" and "sustaining and developing Native American cultural identities."[19]

Indian citizens and tribal governments have endured intolerable economic situations in Indian Country for far too long. The federal and state governments as well as the American public have also tolerated this situation for far too long. It is time for tribal, federal, and state governments, and Indians and U.S. citizens, to do something about it. It is time for tribes and American Indian peoples to use their historical entrepreneurial spirit to solve the economic and poverty-related issues they face.

\* \* \* \* \* \* \* \* \* \* \* \* \* \* \* \* \* \* \* \* \* \* \* \* \* \*

In the following chapters, we will examine several economic subjects and ideas. In Chapter 2, I dispel the mistaken idea that American Indians did not understand and protect property rights and did not use economic systems and principles. For the past hundreds and thousands of years, Indian peoples, governments, and cultures worked hard and intelligently to support their lifeways by labor, manufacturing, trade, agriculture, and hunting and gathering. Indian societies, cultures, and governments supported these economic efforts and they protected the property rights that were thereby created.

In Chapter 3, we will look at how 99 percent of the land and assets in the lower 48 states were lost from tribal and Indian control and how tribal communities and governments fell into dire poverty and dependency on the United States. Obviously, this situation has not worked out to the benefit of tribal governments and Indians.

In Chapters 4 and 5, we survey the current economic development that is occurring on reservations and examine more closely the economic and business activities of three tribes in Oregon, California, and Oklahoma to illustrate the varied and diverse paths and opportunities tribal governments and individual Indians are using to create beneficial economic development. We will also examine the $26 billion a year phenomenon of tribal gaming.

Chapters 6 through 8 examine strategies that tribal governments and Indian communities can pursue to improve their economic conditions on and off reservations and to attract investments and create privately owned businesses. Attracting new investments to reservations is crucial, and much needed as the U.S. Department of the Treasury estimates that there is a $44 billion gap between current and potential investments in Indian Country as compared to the U.S. economy in general. If tribal governments and Indian individuals can take the necessary steps to correct this investment shortfall, it will go a long way towards assisting economic expansion and development in Indian Country.

\* \* \* \* \* \* \* \* \* \* \* \* \* \* \* \* \* \* \* \* \* \* \* \* \*

We will not discuss every economic theory or topic surrounding development and business in Indian Country. That subject is too large for one book. Also, I am not an economist and this book is not intended to be a primer on every economic principle or theory that might apply to Indians and tribal governments. I will refer to applicable economic principles but will instead focus on practical questions and solutions. I will lay out the issues I have encountered, researched, and written about, and will discuss some promising avenues that tribal governments and individuals can pursue to improve their financial situations.

I will also highlight the importance of this issue for the United States, the states, U.S. citizens, and especially for American Indians and tribal governments. All of these entities face problems and challenges caused by the poverty and accompanying social problems prevalent in Indian Country. The United States and state governments are adversely affected when they fail to serve the needs of all their citizens, and when they fail to involve all their citizens in America's prosperity. But far more important to Indian families, communities, and cultures is that all of Indian Country is injured when Indians live in poverty and substandard housing, and lack adequate education and health care. These issues keep Indian peoples from having the time, health, and resources to sustain and expand their communities and from studying and practicing their traditions, cultures, religions, and languages. In fact, studies and experience have shown that actual health and community benefits follow from even small improvements in tribal and Indian financial conditions. These concrete results include tribal families being able to live and work on their reservations, improved child mental health, longer life expectancy rates, lower infant mortality rates, and higher educational attainment rates. Tribal governments also have used increased revenues to build day care centers, medical and dental centers, cultural programs, and a wide variety of projects. Obviously, these kinds of results create benefits for tribal communities and cultures.[20]

I believe that beneficial economic development will spread to tribes, reservations, and Indian families only if Indians and tribal governments create that result for themselves and their communities. In undertaking these efforts, tribal governments and communities will for the most part carefully respect and honor their own cultures, traditions, and religions while they are improving their economic situations. Self-sufficiency and self-governance in economic development, as in every other field, is the best path for tribal governments and American Indians to attain real self-determination.

# CHAPTER 2

# *Historic American Indian Economies and Property Rights*

To understand modern-day American Indian economic issues, we must start with an accurate understanding of the history of Indian economies and economic activities, and with a general knowledge of the property rights systems that Indian cultures created throughout hundreds and thousands of years. Thus, in this chapter, we explore in some detail how Indian societies developed, appropriated, and divided assets, and how they worked to acquire material goods and property rights. We also briefly examine the legal property rights regimes these cultures created to define and protect the material goods Indians worked to create and acquire. In essence, this chapter considers the economic history of Indian Country and debunks the erroneous idea that Indian societies did not historically, and do not today, appreciate and recognize principles of entrepreneurship, private business, and private property.

It is clear that the Indigenous nations and peoples of North America supported themselves for thousands of years with all sorts of private economic activities. Many Indians engaged in hunter-gatherer activities, but a majority of tribal communities worked in private family groups and through individual efforts to grow and gather their daily subsistence needs and to organize communal and family manufacturing projects to sustain their lives. Indians did not survive in North America for millennia just by living off the natural bounty of the forest. In fact, as one historian noted, in the 1600s the Indians in New England produced 65 percent of their diet from agriculture. Clearly, then, Indian peoples and tribal governments worked in an organized and intelligent fashion to create the foods and material goods necessary to maintain their lives and their communities. They also developed, as do all societies, property rights systems to protect the assets and items that individuals and families created. As one professor noted, "aboriginals everywhere have had sophisticated property rights and trading tradi-tions"[1] and when Europeans arrived in what is now the United States that the Indian peoples were primarily reliant on agriculture and not on hunting and gathering. Another professor also states that in pre-colonial times Indigenous societies were not universally hunter-gatherer societies but that instead corn, beans, squash, and grains were prevalent across the continent, as was long-distance trade, specialized labor, and manufacturing.[2]

In addition to the common misunderstandings about traditional American Indian economies and property rights, throughout history Euro-American settlers and government officials downgraded, ignored, and actually lied about how Indians and tribes supported themselves, defined property rights, and operated their economies. This may have been due to innocent ignorance because one culture always has trouble understanding another and the differences in beliefs and customs. Perhaps our colonial and U.S. ancestors just did not understand Indian property and economic systems.

On the other hand, there is a darker explanation as to why Euro-Americans "misunderstood" Indian economies and property rights. It was perhaps a pur-poseful strategy in which Euro-Americans chose to ignore Indian property rights and economic abilities because they wanted to justify taking those rights and assets for themselves. In fact, a famous definition of racism states that an essential element of a racist attitude is to stress real or imaginary differences between peoples and cultures and then to assign arbitrary values to these alleged differences. Euro-Americans engaged in exactly this kind of conduct when they overlooked and misunderstood American Indian property systems.

An example of this kind of purposeful ignorance is demonstrated by U.S. Supreme Court Chief Justice John Marshall in an 1831 case in which he charac-terized the Cherokee Nation as living in abject poverty and as relying on the United States for its daily food and clothing. This statement was false because the Cherokee were quite prosperous with at least half of Cherokee households producing substantial surpluses of agricultural products for trade and with many families even being slave-owning cotton plantation owners in Georgia in the 1820s and early 1830s. The Nation had even organized itself under a constitution written in English that created a three-branch system of government patterned on the U.S. government, and had enacted all manner of laws and established its own court system and a newspaper published in English and Cherokee. Yet this was the Nation that Chief Justice Marshall said was in dire poverty and needed the United States to survive. That statement was not true. Consequently, perhaps misrepresentations about Indian property rights and economic conditions were just excuses used to justify taking those rights.

The federal policies that forced the Cherokee and dozens of other tribes to remove westward resulted in the loss of their farms, improvements, homelands, and valuable assets that then came into the possession of non-Indians. In fact, the advocates for Indian removal "deliberately understate[d] the extent of eco-nomic progress in the Eastern Cherokee Nation."[3] As one professor points out, the political ends of Indian policies inevitably served the interests of non-Indian groups. And, as another commentator noted: "colonials liked to regard the Indians as members of a nomadic hunting race with no fixed habitation . . . [and used it] as an excuse for taking Indian land."[4] We should not make the same mistake today of misunderstanding or ignoring the truth about the history of American Indian economic and property rights systems.[5]

Our review of Indigenous economies and property rights systems is of necessity brief because we are attempting to highlight the economic activities and situations of hundreds of diverse tribal governments and communities that inhabited what is now the United States over centuries of time. We will only scratch the surface of the complexity, differences, and significance of the economic activities of these widely divergent groups. We will see clearly, though, that native peoples understood, appreciated, and lived by principles that today we call private property rights, entrepreneurship, and free market economics in which individuals voluntarily participate in the manufacture of excess crops and goods and engage in trade mostly without governmental direction or control.

## INDIAN PRIVATE PROPERTY RIGHTS

European colonists and U.S. settlers misunderstood and ignored tribal economies and property rights, and even today there is little understanding of historic, traditional, and modern-day Indian cultures and the private property rights and economic activities they created. Indian tribes and peoples were not socialistic societies where everything was jointly owned and shared by the community. This misperception seems to be based almost exclusively on the idea that most Indian nations considered that land was communally owned by the tribe. But as historians have noted, all Indian assets except for land were privately owned, and "truly communal property was scant" among Indians.[6] Somehow, though, Euro-American colonists came to believe that Indians did not believe in or understand private property and related economic principles.[7]

As in all societies, American Indians and their governments had to provide for their daily needs. Indians did not just frolic through the woods living off the surplus of the wilderness. Instead, almost all native societies were actively involved in managing their landscapes, for example, by setting fires at regular intervals to develop specific kinds of forests, to clear land for deer and buffalo, and to allow wild and domesticated plants to flourish, and in organizing their agriculture, building irrigation systems, domesticating wild plants, producing food, tools, clothing, shelter, and other items for personal use. Also, Indian peoples across North America regularly traded goods near and far for survival and comfort. The majority, if not all, of the extensive trade that took place throughout the continent and for over a thousand years was conducted in free market situations where private individuals voluntarily came together to buy and sell items they had manufactured or amassed and which they exchanged by barter and even sold for exchange mediums that we would call money or currency. Today, for example, we call a dollar bill a "buck" because Mississippi Valley Indians used deerskins as currency in the 1700s.[8]

In fact, it appears that the only major difference between Indigenous principles of property and Euro-American concepts was in how those societies viewed the private ownership of land. With only one major difference in the treatment of private property and economic activities, one might be puzzled why Euro-Americans seemed confused about tribal property rights and business activities. As already mentioned, perhaps the actual purpose was to discount and intentionally ignore Indian property concepts to better justify taking those rights and assets.

# Land

At the time of contact with Europeans and Americans, the majority of Indians lived permanently or semipermanently in towns and villages and supported themselves primarily through various farming activities. In the eleventh through the thirteenth centuries, for example, some American Indian cities were larger and controlled by more sophisticated societies than European countries of the time.[9]

Even tribal groups that might be considered nomadic followed "seasonal rounds" in which they moved to identical locations year after year to utilize their food sources. For example, tribal peoples would move to take advantage of seasonal salmon runs, buffalo migrations, and ripening wild crops. Many of these tribes also planted domestic crops and returned to harvest them as part of their seasonal rounds. These "nomadic" peoples recognized property rights in foodstuffs, the hunting and gathering territories they owned, the crops they planted, and the home sites they returned to year after year.

Most of the land Indians hunted, lived on, and farmed, however, was considered to be tribal land. It was owned by the tribal government and by the citizens in common. Even though the governance structure and the tribal community was considered to own tribal territory, almost all American Indian tribes recognized various forms of permanent and semipermanent private rights for individuals and families in communal lands. The fact that land was communal property of the tribe did not prevent individual citizens, families, and clans from acquiring and exercising rights to use specific pieces of land. A right to use lands that belong to another is called usufructuary rights. Under Anglo-American property law, and also under tribal property rights systems, usufructuary rights are private property. Among the Choctaw of Mississippi, for example, each family had its own small plot near their cabins and "most Choctaws had specific fields marked out within the communally prepared town lands. . . . A family . . . could take any uncultivated lands they thought suitable and hold it as long as they used it."[10] Pawnee women planted their corn, beans, melons, and squash in one- to three-acre plots that were assigned to them by chiefs. They were entitled to these plots as long as they wished, but the plots reverted to the tribe upon the woman's death. Consequently, these Indians acquired and exercised ownership rights, private property rights, to specific pieces of land even though the lands were held in common by the tribal government. In many other tribes, individual Indians and families that began farming, hunting, or trapping on any unused land in effect made those communal lands their own private property when they began individually developing and working it.[11]

There are numerous examples of these types of private property rights in communal lands among a diverse group of tribal communities from all over the United States. Indian private use and ownership of land is demonstrated in the Pueblos of the American Southwest, where private farming rights were allotted to individuals by tribal leaders even though the tribe continued to hold communal title to the land. Commentators have characterized these rights of families and individuals among the Pueblos and Hopis as a private property right to use the tribal lands and to own any improvements they built on the lands. These private rights applied even to the sophisticated irrigation systems that the people built communally to serve all the tribal lands. The Pima Tribe, for example, worked communally to build extensive irrigation systems, yet the village headmen would then assign specific farming plots to individuals and the plots became the permanent property of the assignees and their heirs. The ancient Hohokam people built, maintained, and shared irrigation canals over 2,000 years ago near Phoenix, Arizona, and were still practicing crop irrigation when the Spanish arrived in the 1500s.[12]

Furthermore, many eastern and southeastern tribes produced the majority of their subsistence by farming and not from hunting and gathering. While the lands they used belonged communally to the tribe, individuals and families held usufructuary rights to specific lands. The Creek and Cherokee peoples from the American Southeast farmed their own plots and put the crops they harvested into their privately owned storehouses. Moreover, garden plots among Indians of New England and Virginia "were either owned outright by families or held in usufruct by them."[13] The Havasupai Tribe in Arizona also considered that communal tribal lands were privately owned by individuals as long as the land was put to a productive use. All tribal groups that practiced agriculture "definitely recognized exclusive land use."[14]

The Navajo of the Southwest also demonstrate how American Indian cultures considered and still consider today that agricultural lands are individual property which individuals or families claim by using the land. This is true even though the ownership of the land is vested in the community and tribe as a whole. Various modern-day Navajo court cases clearly state that this type of land "ownership" was and still is recognized by Navajo people and their laws. "While it is said that land belongs to the clans, more accurately it may be said that the land belongs to those who live on it and depend upon it for their survival."[15] The Navajo Supreme Court also stated in 1986: "Land use on the Navajo Reservation is unique and unlike private ownership of land off the reservation. While individual tribal members do not own land similar to off reservation, there exists a possessory use interest in land which we recognize as customary usage. An individual normally confines his use and occupancy of land to an area traditionally occupied by his ancestors."[16] In 1991, the Court added, "Traditional Navajo land tenure is not the same as English common law tenure, as used in the United States. Navajos have always occupied land in family units, using the land for subsistence."[17]

In addition, tribes and Indian cultures recognized other private property rights in land than just agricultural rights. Tribes in the West that relied heavily on fishing naturally developed personal and private property rights that demonstrated the importance of this resource. Columbia River salmon fishing sites that consisted of man-made wooden platforms or well-located rocks were assets that were individually and family-owned properties and were passed to their descendants by established inheritance principles. Other people were only allowed to fish at these sites with permission. But even that permission could be revoked at any time if the property owner was not catching enough fish. Other cultures also developed principles of private property that controlled fishing sites located on tribally owned lands and included the right to exclude others from these communally owned lands. These kinds of property rights were firmly established in many Oregon and California tribes, for example. Owners could pass their privately owned rights on by inheritance and these fishing sites could be rented out or sold by the owners. Historians are well aware of these facts and one commented that "Indians had well developed legal systems that emphasized individual rights and individual ownership."[18] A U.S. judge even wrote in 1974: "Generally, individual Indians had primary use rights in the territory where they resided."[19] In addition, the Chairman of the Hoopa Valley Tribe told me in 2009 that many fishing sites on the Hoopa Reservation, which is communally owned by the Tribe, are still held today as private property by Hoopa individuals and families.[20]

The Inuit peoples and governments in Alaska and Canada and other tribes also exercised and enforced precise concepts of private property ownership regarding tribal hunting and fishing territories. Some Canadian tribes controlled overhunting by assigning tribal hunting territories to individuals and granting the owner exclusive use. For instance, the Canadian James Bay Cree Tribe and the Montagnais recognized individual ownership of fishing sites and that other persons did not have a right to use these privately owned sites. Tribes which became involved in the European fur trade also developed individual private property rights in specific rivers and streams to control overharvesting, and even allotted hunting territories to specific individuals: "usufructuary rights to trap in specific territories became established."[21]

The Nootka people of the Pacific Northwest, which includes the Makah Tribe of Washington, "carried the concept of ownership to an incredible extreme."[22] In Nootka cultures and property law, individuals held as "privately owned property" their land and houses, clam beds, beaches, the salvage rights on those beaches, river fishing spots, and even fishing spots and sea lion rocks in the ocean! The Tlingit Tribe of southeast Alaska also created, recognized, and protected private property rights in salmon streams, hunting grounds, and sealing rocks, and protected the accumulation of wealth by individuals. Most of these rights were inheritable, too.[23]

Tribes also recognized many other forms of personal property in land. In the vast majority of tribes, individuals or families privately owned their housing and their home sites. In addition, many tribes recognized exclusive property rights to valuable producing plants such as berry patches, and fruit and nut trees. The property rights recognized in these assets were considered inheritable and some could even be bought and sold.[24]

Consequently, it is clear that most American Indian tribes and cultures recognized and protected a wide range of individual and family private property rights in land, even though the lands were owned in common by the tribal community. These tribal property systems encouraged the entrepreneurial, individually directed, and privately owned operation of food production and manufacturing activities on specific pieces of land. Individuals and their families owned the products of their labors as private property and left them to their descendants under well-established tribal laws of inheritance.

## Private Property Other Than Land

Almost every American Indian tribe and culture also recognized and protected various forms of private property in assets other than land. In an early form of what is called intellectual property, copyright, and trademark law, in some tribes, families privately owned the exclusive rights to use certain carved images on their houses, in ceremonial dances, marriage ceremonies, names, stories and legends, songs, medicines, masks, and rituals. These items were all inheritable and passed to their descendants. Similarly, individuals in the Tlingit Tribe privately owned their totem pole symbols. All Indians, of course, privately owned as personal property their animals, clothing, cooking utensils, housing, tools, weapons, canoes, handicraft and trade goods, and the foodstuffs they produced. These items were private property that were produced and owned by individuals and families. They were not tribal or communal property. Generally, Indians personally owned all their possessions except for land. From the Inuit/Eskimo people of Alaska to the Havasupai of Arizona, items of personal use were "clearly owned by the individual."[25]

The ownership of horses, one of the most valuable pieces of personal property, well illustrates how almost all Indigenous cultures viewed private property and business endeavors. After the Spanish brought horses to the Americas, some sedentary agricultural tribes adopted seminomadic lifestyles in which increased buffalo hunting played a prominent role. Horses were always items of personal property that were privately owned by individuals and never communally owned. The Umatilla tribal chairman explains that in 1855 the Cayuse people owned 20,000 horses. Many individual Cayuse owned up to a thousand horses each and they would leave their herds to their children under tribal inheritance rules. Furthermore, among the Pawnee the horse became a necessity and "took its place as a peculiar form of property ... [that] began to denote wealth and created the beginnings of a social standing somewhat apart from the older distinctions of birth, knowledge, and skill. Horses were personal property, and they remained unevenly distributed."[26] In fact, private property rights in horses were so strongly protected in many tribes that an individual retained rights to a specific horse even if it was lost to another tribe and later recaptured. Well-trained buffalo horses were very valuable private assets, and, interestingly, Indians even engaged in the entrepreneurial activity of leasing out their horses. Horses would be rented for up to one half of the game killed or loot captured by the lessee. In addition, the Indian principles of entrepreneurship and private property rights gained by private initiative are well demonstrated by the fact that even in communal hunting, raiding, and warfare situations, where one might assume that a tribal community would share the catch and spoils equally, most tribes recognized and protected individual and private property rights in captured items. Also among the Pawnee, buffalo meat was apportioned according to who killed the animal, although a man without a horse could butcher a downed animal and get half of the meat. Consequently, the capture of assets such as buffaloes, whales, horses, and the spoils of raiding created private property rights.[27]

Buffalo and whale hunting provide further examples of tribal private property rights. These food production activities provided the main subsistence for Plains Indians and other tribes for centuries and for many coastal American tribes. These activities also made many individuals wealthy. The wealth created by success in these activities was demonstrated by large families, accumulation of material items, and tribal influence. Individuals worked hard to acquire the skills and assets to succeed in these endeavors. Indians from a wide variety of tribes also engaged in specific occupations or professions other than hunting in which they sold their personal services and thereby gained private property rights from their efforts. The Makah Tribe had specific career paths and occupations to which persons aspired, because there was "some degree of specialization into whale hunters, seal hunters, doctors, gamblers, warriors and fishermen."[28] In other tribes, people specialized in professions such as healers, shamans, craftsmen, manufacturers, singers, and songwriters and were hired for fees rather than as a part of barter transactions. These private and voluntary economic endeavors provided income and material support for the individuals and their families, because they were paid for their services with trade goods or items of currency and they kept the payments and goods they received and produced from their occupations as their private property.[29]

## Wealth Accumulation

Another intriguing aspect of native private rights is that certain tribes and many Indian peoples engaged in wealth accumulation. These kinds of private activities and pursuits were important to Indian peoples in historic times for the very same reasons we pursue wealth today. Wealth accumulation among Indians led to ample leisure time, manufacture of art and handicrafts, the practice of elaborate social and religious ceremonies, and even public displays of wealth. This idea is no doubt completely contrary to stereotypical notions of communal Indian societies.

As already pointed out, most if not all tribes recognized private property rights in the production and accumulation of food and personal material objects. Indians and their families worked hard and often at very dangerous activities to acquire the material goods they needed to make their lives easier and more secure. Buffalo hunters, traders, farmers, fishermen, and whalers could be very prosperous businesspeople and they often accumulated considerable amounts of privately owned assets and wealth. All tribal communities understood the value of amassing economic surpluses. For many Indians, their work and ingenuity provided an ample source of life's necessities and their "economic year"— that is, the time it took them to produce all their annual food and subsistence needs—was only about four to five months. That short economic year left plenty of time for leisure, culture, and ceremony. In contrast, most Americans today have an economic year of 50 weeks because we only get two weeks of vacation.[30]

Furthermore, in some tribes, individuals did not keep their wealth a secret and in fact they even put it on display. The Pacific Northwest coast Indians "had cultures that valued status and wealth."[31] These people would publicly demonstrate their wealth by pouring valuable whale oil in the fire or even over their guests at gatherings. At ceremonies, citizens of some tribes engaged in ostentatious displays of their wealth by destroying very valuable copper objects and by freeing slaves. Other Indians accumulated valuable dentalia seashells, which were used as money, and women would wear great strands of dentalia to demonstrate the family wealth. This is similar to how people today wear gold and silver jewelry. Some Indians even hoarded and buried their dentalia and they would dig them up occasionally to admire them.[32]

An interesting demonstration of how tribes accumulated, displayed, and used wealth is presented by the potlatch, an aspect of the Pacific Northwest coast cultures. Potlatching is the social, economic, and even competitive gifting of enormous amounts of goods at feasts that chiefs and rich families would give for other families, clans, or tribes. The "purpose [was] of gaining fame and standing."[33] Potlatching required extensive amounts of productive work to create and gather the wealth needed to then give it away. The accumulation of wealth was an absolute necessity to host potlatches. The potlatch demonstrates that Indians understood wealth and its uses and value in their societies, even if it was for giving away to help others or to gain social standing. U.S. and Canadian officials did not understand potlatching and they tried to outlaw the practice because they thought it caused poverty to the host family. But according to these native cultures, this was an economic, social, cultural, and valuable way to use extra wealth. This is no different than how U.S. society today chooses to spend money on activities we desire, which includes giving extra wealth to social and charitable organizations for tax deductions and because our society values that kind of generosity. The Pacific Northwest native cultures did the same thing through potlatching.[34]

In sum, this brief overview clearly demonstrates that tribes and Indian individuals conceptualized and established private property regimes and ownership rights. Indians and tribal governments understood and protected the ownership of private property in land, river and ocean fishing sites, hunting sites, nut and fruit trees, and in personal property such as horses, manufactured items, and professional services. Indian peoples thus created and acquired individual property rights by investing their human capital, their labor, and their physical capital of tools and assets to manufacture foodstuffs and other items. They developed their lands and resources by cultivating and protecting them, by protecting and using hunting and fishing sites, and by making various products and trade goods. European colonists and early Americans saw these property rights regimes at work and they benefited from them by trading with tribes and Indians and using tribal products. But they misunderstood these Indian economies and their laws on private property. In contrast to what Euro-Americans chose to believe, almost all Indian tribes and peoples were very well acquainted throughout history with using private property rights and private entrepreneurial economic activities to support their families, societies, and cultures.

## HISTORIC TRIBAL ECONOMIES

The words "economy" and "political economy" are defined as the production, distribution, and consumption of goods and services. They also mean the "administration of the concerns and resources of any community or establishment with a view to orderly conduct and productiveness" and "managing the resources of a nation so as to increase its material prosperity."[35] Tribal governments have played a role in these types of activities in the past and in the modern day.

## Tribal Economic Management

Throughout history, tribal leaders governed and managed economic affairs in their territories. Some tribal governments exercised various levels of control over their communally owned lands and assigned private rights to use tribally owned assets. Tribal governments also led military actions to defend their territories and even to take the lands of other tribes. Much of this activity was designed to acquire and control valuable farming and hunting areas. In addition, tribal authorities often organized economic activities regarding land to benefit the tribal community as a whole. Male and female leaders organized and led projects such as building irrigation systems, assigning hunting and farming areas to individuals, and determining hunting, planting, and harvesting times. Tribal citizens could be punished for violating these directions. Native governments were also astute enough to try to protect their resources by controlling the overuse of hunting, fishing, and trapping rights.[36]

Farther back in history, some tribal leaders exercised very extensive and even autocratic authority over economic affairs and organized labor to build impressive cities and temples, public works projects such as irrigation canals, and to support large populations. For centuries, Indian cultures in the Mississippi valley from the Gulf of Mexico to Minnesota, and in Colorado, New Mexico, and Arizona built cities and ceremonial structures, and supported large populations with established agriculture from perhaps 3000 BCE forward. The Ancestral Puebloans at Chaco Canyon in northwestern New Mexico and at other locations built hundreds of miles of paved roads 30 feet wide, connecting Chaco and its enormous residential and ceremonial houses to outlying farming towns. The Chaco government also created a manufacturing center where raw materials, such as turquoise, were mined and manufactured into utilitarian goods and ornamental objects as jewelry. Some archeologists believe that "turquoise may have been a medium of intercultural trade" and that Chaco was "the mint."[37]

Distinct cultures flourished in the Mississippi valley and points north and east in ancient times, including the Adena culture from about 500 to 100 BCE in central and southern Ohio and the Hopewell culture in Ohio from around 200 BCE to 500 CE. These cultures constructed large urban areas and supported large populations. They and many other ancient American Indian peoples were known as mound builders because they built thousands of earthen mounds, some of them among the largest human structures in the world, from roughly 3400 BCE to the early 1700s. The mounds were used for burials of elites and for ceremonial purposes. Some of the mounds were built with a sophistication demonstrating geometrical and astronomical knowledge, and some earthen and wooden structures appear to have served as solar calendars. Sometime after 3000 BCE, long-distance trade networks developed to serve these cultures, and trade developed in all kinds of items including stones, shells, and minerals. Around this time, people began to use copper from the Lake Superior area to make various tools and beads. Other minerals like galena and hematite were also significant trade items all along the Mississippi, as were chalcedony, quartz rock, and flint. Hundreds of pounds of obsidian were also imported all the way from Montana to Ohio. Jewelry and luxury items were produced and traded, and silver from Ontario, chert, ceramic figurines, carved soapstone pipes, mica, shell beads, animal teeth, and turtle shells were accumulated by these cultures. The oldest pottery found anywhere in North America, including Mexico, is from South Carolina and dates to 2515 BCE. Other pots dating to 2000 BCE have been found along Florida's Atlantic coast, and clay objects from 1300 BCE have been found in the lower Mississippi valley. According to Florida shell middens from 2000 BCE onward, people appear to have lived in the same place year round and cultivated corn and other crops. Archeologists also claim that as early as 4500 BCE, American Indian ancestors were tending wild plants and by 2000 BCE they began domesticating them. Later,

American Indians domesticated and developed many other plants including marshelder, knotweed, maygrass, and little barley.[38]

We should also note the American Indian culture that created Cahokia, a U.N. World Heritage site located eight miles from St. Louis, Missouri. The Cahokia Mississippian culture was a very sophisticated society based on agriculture that existed roughly from 700–1300 CE, and reached its peak in 1250–1300. Cahokia was the preeminent civilization of eastern North America and the largest north of Mexico. By 1250 CE, the city of Cahokia was larger than London, with a population estimated at 20,000 to 50,000. The people of Cahokia built hundreds of mounds, but their largest, 30 meters tall and 316 by 240 meters at its base, is the world's largest earthwork and still stands today. It covers 14 acres. By comparison, the Great Pyramid of Cheops in Egypt only covers 13 acres. Furthermore, Cahokia was surrounded by a wooden wall and contained an American Stonehenge made of wood, which appears to have been a calendar used to determine the solstices, equinoxes, and other important dates. The citizens of Cahokia used long-distance trade to import raw materials and manufactured products from all over North America. Citizens performed specialized labor, and artisans manufactured pottery, baskets, leather clothing, stone tools, and ornamental objects like shell beads and sheets of copper. They cultivated corn and beans from about 800 CE forward. They also began producing and trading salt around 900 CE. Cahokia and other Mississippian societies were divided into ranks or classes and practiced elite burials with valuable goods being buried with the deceased. French accounts from the early 1700s about the Natchez culture indicate that it was ruled by a royal lineage that claimed descent from the sun and that the leading citizens were carried about in litters by commoners. Spanish explorers were also impressed by these Southeast American cultures and the size of their populations, the abundance of corn, and their technical capabilities.[39]

These historical native governments and cultures also mobilized labor to build impressive public works and food production systems, and to control trade and the distribution of water. These civilizations were structured and organized on economic grounds and their governing bodies had significant control over their people. They taxed their citizens and somehow organized or coerced labor for public works projects. Other tribal governments also mobilized group assets and would hold public monies and crops for future needs. The Cherokee, Creek, and other tribal governments taxed tribal citizens part of each crop, and this grain was kept in a tribal treasury for future public needs.[40]

Other American Indian tribes throughout history organized manufacturing endeavors to produce specific items for sale. Tribal peoples would occasionally engage in the same economic activity at the same time and appear to have worked under the direction of the tribal government. Some tribes were famous for manufacturing certain items, like wampum, which is a seashell that was often woven into belts of shells and used as money and for other purposes, and pipes that were sold and traded across North America, and pottery or blankets. These tribal peoples labored as a group to serve a specific market niche that they and their government had worked to develop. Furthermore, other tribes took even more drastic steps to control their economic interests and engaged in armed conflicts to expand or control trade routes and trading partners. Tribes were also known to relocate villages to be closer to trading partners or to exclude other tribes from interfering in the trade.[41]

Indian governments and leaders were also very knowledgeable about the economic possibilities and advantages of controlling trade routes and the Euro-American traders. Many tribes charged traders tolls to cross tribal lands or to use rivers. Other tribes were eager to donate land for trading posts so that they could be near the supply of goods and control the trade. Often tribal governments sought economic advantages by getting non-Indian traders to deal only with their tribe so that they could then become the middlemen for transactions with other Indians and tribes. Specific tribes created markets and set the prices for the transfer of Indian and non-Indian goods. These tribes went to great lengths to keep their trading partners separate so that they could profit from being the wholesaler or middleman in these business deals. To maintain monopolies over trade, tribal leaders often tried to prevent Euro-American traders and other tribes from dealing directly with each other. These kinds of monopolistic positions were taken by numerous tribes all across the modern-day United States. In fact, nearly all tribal governments pursued policies to gain advantages in trade and in their attempts to make profits.[42]

These few examples from diverse tribes and different times and parts of what is now the United States demonstrate that tribal governments and leaders understood economic principles. Many tribal governments took steps to control their economies and increase the prosperity of their people and were actively involved in economic management.

## Tribal and Individual Trade

Almost all Indian tribes and peoples engaged extensively in trade, exchange, barter, and buying and selling of goods from time immemorial. Indians traded and sold surplus food and manufactured items to other peoples near and far in mutually beneficial exchanges. Some Indians and even specific tribes developed particular manufacturing skills and would produce and sell or trade surplus items to others who were proficient at making other items in return. Indian peoples long made goods for sale and traded them at large fairs or markets that were held at regularly scheduled locations and times across North America. These trading activities were almost completely controlled and motivated by private property rights and individual initiative. The well-established principles of trade and the trade networks that developed demonstrate the recognition, protection, and respect Indian cultures gave to private property rights and entrepreneurial activities.[43]

## Native Trading Networks

Indians and their governments participated in extensive trade networks that criss-crossed North America. Tribal governments and individuals traded a wide variety of goods that they had grown, gathered, or manufactured to other peoples. These goods were often then traded again to other people hundreds or even a thousand miles away from their original source. For example, seashells from the Gulf of Mexico, the southeastern Atlantic, the Gulf of California, and the Pacific Ocean have been found a thousand miles away. This extensive distribution of trade items occurred in times when travel and transportation of goods over even short distances was an arduous task. In fact, Indians engaged in much of this wide-spread trade when the dog was their only pack animal.[44]

Tribes and Indians also mined and traded a variety of minerals to distant loca-tions. As mentioned, copper from the Great Lakes, Rocky Mountain obsidian, salt, and other minerals have been found in substantial quantities hundreds and even a thousand miles from their point of origin. Often, these items had also been manufactured into ceremonial and luxury items. Southwest tribes, for example, manufactured and traded turquoise, jewelry, and masks they made from materi-als they mined to people in Mexico for birds, feathers, and copper bells, and to people from the Gulf of California for shells. In addition, these extensive and well-established tribal trading networks spread newly arrived Euro-American goods to many Indians long before they actually encountered their first Euro-Americans. Tribal governments and individual Indians had no problems incorpo-rating the Euro-Americans and their new goods into the native trading networks. Indian peoples and tribes willingly engaged in trade and extended their activities to these new trading partners and goods as both sides became customers and traders in common. Just as with all peoples, Indians were interested in procuring new items for their functional and luxury potentials.[45]

## Tribal Markets

Many tribes and Indians regularly hosted and attended regional trading markets that were located across the modern-day United States. The markets were in existence from prehistoric times until long after Europeans arrived. Trading for necessary and luxury goods was a fundamental feature of life. In the 1740s, for example, a German count was so impressed by the market the tribes maintained in eastern Pennsylvania, and by the amount and diversity of goods for sale, that he stated it was "like the Hague in Holland."[46] From 1803 to 1806, the Lewis and Clark expedi-tion marveled at several tribal trading fairs they encountered. In 1805, for instance, Lewis and Clark witnessed firsthand the great market near present-day The Dalles, Oregon. They were amazed at the fish storage technique, the tons of dried fish the Indians sold, and the amount of other trade in which the Indians engaged.[47]

These tribal markets were held at regularly scheduled times and places and large numbers of Indians from a wide array of tribes would come together every year or more often to trade. These established markets were so important that tribes, and later even the Spanish, would call truces to hold the markets. Again, Lewis and Clark observed the importance of trade when they spent the winter of 1804–1805 in the Mandan and Hidatsa towns in what is now North Dakota. They observed that many enemies of the Mandan and Hidatsa came to trade for abundant Mandan corn and other crops. Trade was so important and integral to these communities and their economies that enemies would be temporarily and ceremonially adopted into the tribe to engage in trade.[48]

## Traditional Indian Business Skills

Tribal governments and Indian peoples also developed regularized business and trading practices and principles long before contact with Euro-Americans. After first contact, Euro-American traders quickly learned that Indians were astute and experienced businesspeople. Indians were sophisticated traders and were proficient at operating their business affairs and at manipulating economic factors. Indians were well aware of the value and prices of the goods they wanted and they negotiated vigorously. They also realized that Euro-American traders could not afford to return home with goods they had transported to the frontier, and Indians took advantage of this situation.[49]

In addition, some Indian businesses and regional markets used standardized measurements, and some Indians gave guarantees and had well-established rules of trade. Some native businesspeople extended credit, and many Euro-American traders sold goods to Indians on credit. Hence, most natives were familiar with credit and loan and repayment principles. Some Indians even engaged in lending money and goods and charged interest on these loans. Obviously, many Indians were sophisticated in the practice of business activities.[50]

As mentioned, many tribes and Indians across North America understood the economic value of gaining monopolies, controlling trade routes, and becoming the middleman in transactions to earn profits on the resale of goods. Tribal governments fought vigorously both politically and in actual warfare to maintain these advantages and to control the trading that occurred within their territories. They understood profits and how to manipulate markets to their advantage.[51]

Tribes and Indians were also readily adaptable to the new economic activities and trading partners that arrived from Europe. The fur trade and European trade goods brought new activities and goods to North America. Many tribes and Indians voluntarily participated in the entrepreneurial fur trade and the trade in European goods. Various tribal practices and principles of property ownership were influenced by and adapted to this new commercial activity. That is normal with any people, in any time, and in any culture. Luxury goods quickly became necessities, as they do for everyone, and Indians worked hard to secure the goods that they desired.[52]

The foregoing demonstrates that Indians and tribal governments understood the principles of entrepreneurship and profit-driven trading activities, and they willingly, actively, and intelligently engaged in these pursuits throughout history.

# Tribal Currencies

Many Indian peoples and tribes also used forms of currency as a medium of exchange instead of only using a barter system where goods are directly traded for other goods. In various parts of what is now the United States, Indians used wampum (manufactured belts of seashells), beads, Hudson Bay Company blankets, turquoise, dentalia shells, deerskins, and other valued items as money or currency to transact business with other Indians and with Europeans. Wampum was even used for a time to pay tuition at Harvard and as cash in the Dutch colonies in Pennsylvania and New York. Moreover, some Indians engaged in money lending and loaned these currencies out at interest. Various tribal communities also used the wealth they accumulated in currencies to buy goods, to give to the poor, to settle disputes, and even to atone for criminal acts.[53]

Wampum was used as currency by many tribes in pre-contact times and after, and it was used by Europeans to buy and sell goods. The value of wampum as money was recognized by Europeans. In 1744, the governor of Pennsylvania said that traders cheated Indians out of their furs "and their wampum, which is their Money."[54] Some tribes made manufacturing wampum a tribal business and others were economically compelled into making wampum to trade for European goods. Wampum even suffered from inflationary valuations as currencies often do.[55]

In the Pacific Northwest, dentalia, a shell harvested from Vancouver Island, was used for personal adornment, like silver and gold jewelry, and also as a medium for trade as money. Dentalia was personal property and was highly valued. Some Indians hoarded and protected these shells to preserve their personal wealth. Citizens of several tribes would tattoo their arms or legs for measuring the length of strings of dentalia to determine their value. Many Indians and non-Indians used dentalia and other tribal currencies exactly as we use money today.[56]

The use of items as currency by American Indians and the existence of an active market of buying and selling products using various terms of credit and regulations demonstrates the long-standing experience Indian peoples and tribes have had with economic activities, trade, and profits. This historical discussion, brief though it is, demonstrates that Indigenous tribes and peoples understood and protected a wide variety of private property rights and individual economic activities that approximate the private, free market, entrepreneurial activities we are familiar with today. Indians worked to accumulate wealth and to protect the private rights they created in goods and currencies. In fact, as reported in a U.S. congressional hearing in 1934, "in the vast majority of cases Indian economic pursuits were carried on directly with individual rewards in view."[57] Consequently, private entrepreneurship and the idea of working to create and accumulate private property and profits to support yourself and your family are not new ideas to Indian cultures. These are the very activities that Indian individuals, families, and tribal communities have used to support themselves for centuries.

# CHAPTER 3

# Euro-American Impacts on American Indian Economies

In contrast to the sustainable economic and property rights regimes that Indians and tribal governments developed over hundreds and thousands of years before Euro-American contact, today Indians and Indian communities are mired in poverty and do not possess functioning economies. How did tribal governments and communities evolve from controlling most of the land and assets of the continental United States and being relatively prosperous to today being the most impoverished communities?

One obvious answer is that this was the express intention of Euro-American colonists and political leaders. European explorers, traders, and colonists who came to what is now the United States were primarily interested in acquiring Indian lands and assets. Under English and then U.S. governance, immigrants were enticed to America by visions of free land. These new settlers justified what they wanted to do by claiming that the lands in America were empty and available for their ownership. The Latin phrase *terra nullius*, or empty land, was a very common argument used to justify what colonists wanted: land. In fact, the American colonists' favorite philosopher, John Locke, developed his theory of how vacant land was turned into individual private property when he was writing about America and when he was the secretary for the Carolina colony and helping to draft its constitution.

The English also argued that God was on their side and then Americans made the same argument under the principle of Manifest Destiny. In fact, in 1620, King James I of England was delighted that smallpox was killing enormous numbers of Indians in New England, because he wrote, "by God's Visitation raigned a wonderfull Plague . . . amoungst the Savages and brutish People" to make room for the English.[1] Moreover, Massachusetts Bay governor John Winthrop stated in

1634 that by bringing smallpox epidemics to Indians "God hathe hereby cleered our title to this place."[2] Winthrop saw the plague "as an opportunity for claiming new land."[3] Furthermore, the colony justified taking land from Native Americans because the natives had not "subdued" the land and thus had no "civil right" to it. And in 1677, the New England minister Increase Mather expressed surprise that Indians fought to keep their homelands. He wrote that Indians "fought to dispossess us of the land, which the Lord our God hath given to us."[4] These same attitudes were demonstrated under American Manifest Destiny by Missouri senator Thomas Hart Benton when he was asked if American expansion would cause the extinction of natives: "I cannot murmur at . . . the effect of divine law. . . . The moral and intellectual superiority of the White race will do the rest."[5] A Wyoming newspaper stated in 1870: "The rich and beautiful valleys of Wyoming are destined for the occupancy and sustenance of the Anglo-Saxon race. . . . The Indians must stand aside or be overwhelmed. . . . The destiny of the aborigines is written in characters not to be mistaken . . . the doom of extinction is upon the red men of America."[6]

America's Founding Fathers and politicians used these philosophies for almost 200 years in dealing with Indian nations and in enacting laws to control Indian economic activities, lands, and resources. The United States used the international law called the Doctrine of Discovery to claim authority over the lands, assets, and rights of Indian tribes and peoples.[7] The United States often granted ex-soldiers and settlers future rights in Indian lands that the United States had not yet purchased, because everyone just assumed that it would acquire those rights one day. General George Washington was one of the originators of that idea. In September 1783, he was asked by Congress how it should deal with the tribes that had supported the British during the Revolutionary War. Washington advised Congress not to wage war against the tribes because he said Indian lands would naturally fall to the United States whenever it needed them. He compared Indians to the "Wild Beasts of the Forest . . . both being beasts of prey tho' they differ in shape" and called them "Savage as the Wolf."[8] Washington said that just as the animals and wolves retreated from the advance of the Americans, so too would Indians.

Washington and Thomas Jefferson and others were content initially to wait to buy tribal lands because the United States was too weak militarily to just take them. In fact, the federal government engaged in treaty relations with tribes from 1778 to 1871 primarily to buy Indian lands and to keep the peace. Instead of outright warfare, presidents and federal and state officials worked aggressively to remove Indian nations from their original territories so as to acquire their lands and assets for Americans. Interestingly, the favorite scripture of early colonists and the Founding Fathers reflected their thinking on why they deserved to acquire Indian lands. Genesis 1:28 was often cited by English and American settlers to justify their God-given right to Indian lands: "Be fruitful, and multiply, and replenish the earth, and subdue it. . . ." They reasoned that since Indians did not "subdue" the earth by cultivating it, then they did not deserve it, but that

Euro-Americans did. The colonists, of course, overlooked the fact that most Indian communities engaged in extensive agriculture to produce the majority of their diet.[9]

In this chapter, we will briefly examine how American Indians and tribal governments lost the ownership of almost all their lands and assets and became economically dependent on the United States. It should be no surprise that these losses, and 200 years of political, social, and economic domination by the United States, contributed to poverty and problems for Indian communities. In this way, we will better understand the decline of Indian societies from healthy and self-sustaining communities into mostly impoverished communities today.

## DEPENDENCY THEORY

Dependency is the leading theory offered by many experts in economics, American Indian studies, and political science to explain the economic situations of modern-day Indians. The seminal work on this subject is Richard White's *The Roots of Dependency*. He quotes a Brazilian economist for the definition of dependency:

> a situation in which the economy of certain countries is conditioned by the development and expansion of another economy to which the former is subjected. The relation of interdependence between the two or more economies, and between these and world trade, assumes the form of dependence when some countries (the dominant ones) can expand and be self-sustaining, while other countries (the dependent ones) can do this only as a reflection of that expansion, which can have either a positive or a negative effect on their immediate development.[10]

The development of this theory is credited to Latin American economists. Their ideas spread to other parts of the Third World and are also used to analyze the economic conditions of American Indians.[11]

Dependency analyzes the process in which peripheral, "satellite," or underdeveloped regions are incorporated into the core, "metropolis," or developed economic areas. The theory states that developed core areas benefit more from international trade than do the peripheral areas because the development of the dependent or peripheral areas is conditioned by the development of the core, metropolis centers. This dependence leads to the transfer of surpluses from peripheral countries to the economically developed countries and benefits the developed economic areas but actually retards the development of the peripheral areas. Dependency theory also looks at how the political, economic, and social systems of the peripheral areas are distorted by being incorporated into the core or metropolis.[12]

We should distinguish between the words "dependence" and "dependency." Almost all countries are dependent, or really interdependent, on other countries for trade and imports and exports. But the word "dependency" describes a particular condition that peripheral areas, primarily Third World countries, suffer when they engage in international trade and become nearly subservient to the stronger economic areas and remain underdeveloped and impoverished. Theorists have identified other consequences that arise from dependency: 1) economic activities in the peripheral regions are essentially controlled from the outside; 2) peripheral regions lack economic diversity and choice; 3) they suffer distortions in economic, social, and political conditions; 4) their subsistence systems collapse; 5) they come to rely on the economic core areas; and 6) social vacuums result in the establishment of new dependent institutions and economic practices. Anyone familiar with Indian Country and its history, and federal Indian law and policies, will recognize many of these factors.[13]

In *The Roots of Dependency*, White attempts to prove how dependency arose for the Choctaw Nation, Pawnee Tribe, and Navajo Nation from their interactions with the French, Spanish, English, and Americans. His conclusion is that the growth of the world economic system and market relations adversely affected these three tribes and that the "collapse of their subsistence systems and their integration into world markets brought increasing reliance on the capitalist core, lack of economic choice, and profound political and social changes. . . ."[14] As a result, tribal communities that had fed, clothed, and supported themselves for thousands of years gradually began to rely on non-Indians for manufactured goods, clothing, and food. White states that the voluntary trade exchanges these tribes undertook with Euro-Americans occurred at first on equal terms but that soon non-Indians dictated the terms, and that dependency and poverty ensued. He emphasizes, however, that dependency resulted "not from a single material and economic process that obliterated or subordinated all else, but rather from a complex interchange of environmental, economic, political, and cultural influences."[15]

The dependency theory in general, and as applied to American Indians, has been criticized. In a 1999 book, Professor Brian Hosmer examined how the Menominee Tribe of Wisconsin and the Metlakatla Indian Community of Alaska voluntarily participated in major economic activities because they viewed economic modernization and new economic relations as a positive way to maintain their independence. Hosmer concludes that these communities made a success out of their endeavors and preserved their independent and self-sustaining societies. He criticizes the dependency theory because it ignores the complexity of culture, starts from the idea of European superiority, and pays scant attention to Indigenous social and cultural factors. He thinks dependency is the reverse of acculturation and assimilation theories because it suggests that underdeveloped, backward people will stay that way forever. "Therefore, dependency, while ostensibly an effort at considering the 'other side' of the contact equation, often amounts to an analysis of white domination of Indians, not of how Indians reacted to challenging situations."[16] He also points out that dependency is criticized for implying that prior to European contact, Indigenous societies existed in a state of equilibrium. I agree that implication is a mistake. American Indian cultures and economies changed in many ways over hundreds and thousands of years. Indian cultures, like all cultures, change over time and in reaction to many different stimuli, both good and bad.

Professor Patricia Albers critiques dependency because "dependency literature operates at levels of abstraction where individual actors are hidden by the workings of larger systems. As a result, American Indians appear as pawns to forces and formations outside their control, and . . . it denies American Indian people agency."[17] Professor Colleen O'Neill also notes that dependency theory is "rife with internal tensions and contradictions" and that its "universal assumptions about the relationship between capitalism and Native American culture . . . obscured the role of indigenous people in crafting alternative strategies or pathways of development."[18]

## THE HISTORY OF INDIAN DISPOSSESSION

Most tribal governments and communities had been in existence for at least hundreds of years before first contact with Euro-Americans, and they were healthy, with large populations of fairly prosperous people. European explorers along the Carolina coast in 1523 said the area was "densely populated" and others noted that the salmon fishing peoples of the Pacific Northwest were well nourished and robust in comparison to Europeans. Adult height is a positive indicator of long-term health and good nourishment, and from the seventeenth through the nineteenth centuries the Plains Indians were among the world's tallest people. At first contact, American Indians also had one of the world's lowest rates of parasites.[19]

The number of Indigenous people living in what is now the United States in 1492 is unknown, but it was much higher than most people imagine. In 1966, a new estimate of this population was set at 9.8 to 12 million. Today, the majority of scholars working on this subject consider the number to be between 2 and 7 million. Whatever the actual number was, American Indians and their governments had sustained and supported themselves for centuries with economic activities of every possible means. And tribal governments were sophisticated and capable of building massive public works. Most tribes, Indian peoples, and their economic systems produced surplus foods and the items necessary to have a relatively comfortable life.[20]

The primary event that changed this centuries-long existence and began the slide of Indians and tribal governments into poverty was epidemic diseases. European diseases destroyed Indian life and prosperity and negatively impacted the governments and cultures that Indian peoples had created over thousands of years. Many tribal communities were hit by wave after wave of epidemics that each destroyed 30 to 50 percent or more of a tribe in the 1500s–1800s. Many tribal populations were reduced up to 80 to 90 percent in just a few decades, and Indian communities, homes, and fields were left vacant. The few survivors often had to regroup and reform their societies and tribal affiliations and start over in new locations. Just this fact alone helps to explain how Indians and tribal governments lost the ownership of many of their assets and how poverty and dependency ensued. It is nearly impossible today to imagine the kind of havoc that would be created if 80 to 90 percent of the U.S. population died in a relatively short time period.

## European and Indian Interactions

We will very briefly review the interactions and economic activities of Spain, France, and England with American Indians. We will then examine more closely the U.S. economic relations and policies with Indians and tribal governments.

### Spain

The first Spanish explorers encountered the most populous and complex societies north of central Mexico when they entered Florida in the early 1500s. The native peoples and their governments supported themselves by agricultural systems that regularly produced surpluses. The tribes had established trading networks that ran throughout the region and even to Cuba and the Bahamas. The Indian settlements were extensive and contained large temples and platform mounds. They also had established governing systems with distinct national capitals and chiefdoms.[21]

But Indian life changed dramatically and immediately when the Spanish entered Florida in 1513. In addition to the impact of looting and murder, the Spanish and their animals spread epidemic diseases that killed up to 80 percent of the native populations. The diseases spread farther as Spanish settlers moved into South Carolina in 1526 and western Florida in 1527. By 1539–1543, when Hernando de Soto's expedition also engaged in murder and pillage, the devastation from disease was already widespread. In many areas, native peoples had vanished and towns were completely deserted. Furthermore, de Soto and the animals he brought caused many new epidemics. One hundred years later French explorers found empty villages when they visited areas de Soto had crossed. One historian described the result: "Craft specialization diminished. Local societies could no longer produce abundant agricultural surpluses, and settlement patterns became more dispersed, while the authority of paramount chiefs decreased."[22] Obviously, these effects weakened governments, towns, and peoples, and decreased the food supply, all of which contributed to poverty and the breakdown of Indian societies.[23]

The Spanish reached New Mexico by 1533. The inevitable diseases accompanied them and the populations of the Pueblos plummeted. It is estimated that in 1500 perhaps 250,000 people lived in about 130 separate Pueblo settlements.

A 1678 survey, however, found only 17,000 Pueblo people living in only 46 communities. Obviously, the Spanish occupation greatly disrupted Pueblo life and societies.[24]

The Spanish also established short-lived missions in east Texas in 1690 and 1716. In addition, Spain established 21 missions in California from 1769 to 1823, from San Diego to San Francisco. The mission priests used forced native labor and severe corporal punishment, and, of course, there were serious population declines due to diseases, poor diet, and harsh working conditions.[25]

## France

The French explorations in North America began along the eastern seaboard of Canada and down the St. Lawrence River in the mid-1530s. Historians describe the French as being primarily interested in furs and trading with Indians. The Huron even became middlemen in the fur trade, and Huron chiefs enhanced their political authority by distributing the profits they received from trading to their citizens. But once again, epidemic diseases disrupted Indian life and economic activities. It is estimated that the Huron Nation and the Iroquois Confederacy lost more than 50 percent of their populations between 1630 and 1650.[26]

France also used international law to make bold claims of ownership to large areas of land in modern-day Canada and the United States. Due to the expeditions of Louis Joliet, Father Jacques Marquette, and Robert de LaSalle, the French claimed land on both sides of the Mississippi River. In the mid-1600s, Joliet and Marquette were the first Europeans to explore and map the northern portions of the Mississippi River and LaSalle explored much of the Great Lakes region and the entire Mississippi River, which he then claimed for France in 1682. He named the area "La Louisiane" in honor of King Louis XIV.

The French explorers also carried diseases to the Indians in these areas, and along with English slave hunters, they created epidemics and mayhem in the late seventeenth century in the lower Mississippi region. By 1700, French traders found virtually empty country with deserted, yet still standing, villages in the region.[27]

## England

England and its colonists had an enormously negative impact on American Indians and their cultures and economies. The English came to settle North America because colonists were lured by the promise of free land. But the first permanent English settlement of Jamestown in 1607 was very weak militarily and was even dependent on the Powhatan Confederacy for food. Needless to say, the Jamestown residents were friendly with the natives at that time. Land was abundant and initially conflicts were rare. With the apparent success of the colony, though, more and more settlers flocked to Virginia and raised the demand for land.[28]

The first epidemics hit the Powhatans in 1617 and 1619. In 1622, in retaliation for the diseases and because of other issues, the Indians attacked Jamestown and killed a quarter of its residents. The English counterattacked and burned Indian settlements and storehouses. As more settlers poured in, the English claimed more land, refused to recognize Indian land ownership, and raided native communities. These actions forced many Indians to move into the interior and the Powhatan became a minority in their own country. One historian notes that such "strategies rarely succeeded until a tribe had been decimated and stripped of its resources."[29] By 1646, the Powhatan Confederacy was no more.

English traders also penetrated the American Southeast around 1670 seeking trade and slaves. The Spanish had already transformed native life and economies in Florida, and now the English added to the devastation. Carolina natives were affected by the Spanish and the English, and their populations were soon reduced by epidemics. English traders from Virginia and Carolina even armed Indians to capture slaves. They raided deep into the interior and into Spanish Florida and helped to destroy some tribes and many of the Spanish missions by 1702–1704.[30]

In 1620, England began to expand its settlements in America and colonists began arriving in New England. The native peoples of the northeast coast, however, had already been trading with Europeans for perhaps a century. They had also become middlemen and traded European goods to tribes in the interior. Now European traders and settlers wanted furs, and some northeast Indians started hunting and trapping full time. A lively competition arose among the English, Dutch, and French traders for beaver pelts, and many Indians in the interior increased their beaver harvest while many coastal Indians worked as middlemen in this trade.[31]

As usual, European epidemics were a major part of colonization. In fact, widespread deaths had already occurred in New England from epidemics decades before English settlement even commenced. In 1616–1618, for example, smallpox reduced the native population of that region by 75 to 80 percent, and many villages and fields sat vacant. As mentioned above, King James I was clearly aware of these developments, and when he chartered the New England colony in 1620 he called smallpox "God's . . . wonderful Plague" because it was killing Indians and making room for English settlers.[32] The rapid depopulation fatally weakened many native cultures and governments. In this condition, they were plainly less able to resist English colonists who were pressuring Indians over land ownership. More and more settlers arrived and brought even more epidemics. Another big wave of smallpox hit the New England Indian communities in 1633. In addition, in 1637, Connecticut colonists unleashed a major military campaign against the Pequot Nation and nearly exterminated it. The survivors were sold into slavery or fled the area.[33]

In *Roots of Dependency*, Richard White argues that dependency on English trade and alcohol also helped to decimate the Choctaw Nation of the American

Southeast. It is instructive to look at his research and follow the general pattern that precipitated the decline of Indian populations, governments, and societies into poverty and dependency. White notes that at first the Choctaw were good shoppers and they bought moderately from French and English traders. The English, however, wanted to sell more goods, so they introduced credit and alcohol. By 1750, and certainly by 1763, White says the Choctaw needed European goods and had lost many of their traditional skills and pre-European technology. White states that the Choctaw's desire for trade goods exposed them to inevitable exploitation. (That statement is probably true for all peoples today.)[34]

Besides losing technological skills and trades, the Choctaw now put some of their food supply at risk. The deer herds that they had used as the backup food supply to their agricultural pursuits were now being overhunted to use deer hides to buy trade goods. Choctaw hunters began to hunt more often, and further from home, and to enter the hunting territories of other tribes. The increasing number of English hunters also added to the decline of game. White concludes that the rapid growth in deer hunting was a prelude to Choctaw dependence because once the deer became scarce the Choctaw would have only land to sell for goods. The magnitude of the deerskin trade is demonstrated by the fact that 22 percent of South Carolina's export value was deerskins as late as 1748. Over 100,000 deerskins a year were exported from that state for a decade.[35]

Alcohol added to the downward economic and cultural spiral. It was the perfect product for English traders. A trader could only sell the same person so many pots and blankets, but alcohol led to excessive demand and overuse. By 1770, one English company estimated that liquor made up 80 percent of its sales to the Choctaw. The sale of liquor certainly increased the volume of the deerskin trade, and the overuse of alcohol began to cause social chaos and facilitated the descent into crisis. According to White, this mixture of trade, alcohol, and later warfare corroded Choctaw society and created a dependency on European goods.[36]

Choctaws now began to go heavily into debt to buy goods and alcohol. English and American governments eagerly encouraged this debt, because tribal leaders would often sell land to pay their debts to trading companies. English and American treaties with tribal governments from this era often named specific traders and trading companies and arranged for treaty payments to be made directly to traders for debts Indians had incurred. We will see later that this was one of President Thomas Jefferson's favorite tactics to acquire Indian lands, and he used it several times against the Choctaw.[37]

This very brief overview of the economic, cultural, and social impacts that European trade and settlement had on many Indian nations is sufficient to demonstrate the pattern of Anglo-American settlement. This pattern no doubt explains General George Washington's 1783 advice to Congress that Indians and their governments would naturally disappear before the American advance. No wonder federal officials, federal Indian policies, and American citizens expected Indian peoples to become extinct.

# United States and Indian Interactions

The new U.S. federal and state governments and their citizens fully expected to acquire all the lands and assets of the native peoples and continued the same Indian policies they had pursued as English colonists. These policies were exemplified by George Washington's "Savage as the Wolf" idea. President Thomas Jefferson also pursued this aggressive principle, and he acquired Indian lands as quickly as possible, worked to move tribes west of the Mississippi River, and to "drive them along with the wild beasts" into the Rocky Mountains.[38] Historians state that "Jefferson appeared to embrace an enlightened notion of assimilation and agrarian acculturation while [he] in fact ruthlessly pursued a policy marked by war and concomitant treaties of land cession."[39]

The United States also took steps to control the trade with Indian nations and to manage their economic interests. In 1790, Congress began enacting laws at President Washington's request to prevent tribal governments and Indians from selling their lands to anyone but the United States, to stop private traders from entering Indian Country, to control the Indian trade, and to build federal trading posts along the frontier. Thereafter, the United States operated up to 28 Indian trading posts from 1795 to 1822. The specific purpose of these efforts was to control Indian trade, bring Indian tribes and peoples within the influence of the American economic sphere, and to cut European and private traders out of the market.[40]

The United States also signed hundreds of treaties with hundreds of tribes over many decades in which tribes put themselves under the sole protection of the United States and even allowed the federal government to control their trade. One has to wonder if these treaty provisions, written only in English of course, were fully explained to tribal leaders. Many tribes suffered from a lack of trade because of the federal attempts to operate and control this trade.[41]

After the War of 1812, in particular, historians note that the federal/Indian relationship changed dramatically in favor of the United States. The United States now began in earnest to pick off tribe after tribe and to acquire their lands and assets and force the tribes westward. One historian noted that "most American frontiersmen wanted the Indians removed west of the Mississippi so that their lands would be opened to white settlement."[42]

We cannot overlook one illuminating example that occurred during this time period. Many American presidents, in particular George Washington and Thomas Jefferson, often lamented in messages to Congress that the lawless element on the frontier was the Americans and that these "pioneers" would not obey federal law and stop invading Indian Country, settling, hunting, and taking Indian assets, and that these incursions often led the United States into conflicts with tribes. I wonder though if American leaders were sincere in these statements, because this takeover of Indian assets and lands was the exact result that Washington, Jefferson, and others had foretold and expressly desired. Washington's "Savage as the Wolf" policy and Jefferson's intentions to acquire

Indian lands was the American mantra. In fact, during the Washington and Jefferson administrations, the United States signed more than 50 treaties with tribes and bought millions of acres of Indian land at bargain prices. President Jefferson paid $0.05–$0.25 an acre for land he immediately sold to settlers and southern planters for $1.50–$2.00 an acre.[43]

President Jefferson is also probably the first federal official to put in writing the policy of Indian Removal, that all Indians were expected to move west of the Mississippi River to make room for American expansion. In 1803, he sent three private letters to Indiana territorial governor William Henry Harrison and two generals making this point. His administration also signed a compact with Georgia in 1802 promising to move the Cherokee Nation west as soon as possible even though the Cherokee had signed a treaty with the United States guaranteeing them their lands in Georgia forever.[44]

Jefferson also waged economic war against Indian tribes and peoples. He was not content just to get their lands when they were ready to sell or when a particular tribe had nearly died out. Instead, Jefferson's objective for the federal trading posts was to use trade to drive Indians into debt so that they would sell land to pay their debts. He wrote several times to federal officials that the goal was "[t]o establish among [the Indians] a factory or factories for furnishing them with all the necessaries and comforts . . . encouraging these and especially their leading men, to run in debt for these beyond their individual means of paying; and whenever in that situation, they will always cede lands to rid themselves of debt."[45] Jefferson's policy was successful because several tribes signed treaties which expressly stated that they were selling land to pay off debts and some treaty payments were even paid directly to trading companies.[46]

These kinds of pressures led several tribes and many Indians to voluntarily move west to escape American settlers. In addition, in 1830, Congress adopted the official federal policy of Indian removal when it enacted the Removal Act. The law stated that tribes would only be moved with their consent, but President Andrew Jackson put enormous pressure on tribes and used threats to obtain that "consent." The Cherokee, for example, were rounded up and imprisoned in 1838 before they "consented" to move west. Over 4,000 Cherokee people died on their Trail of Tears march to Oklahoma. Other tribes suffered similar trails of tears. Obviously, removal caused economic turmoil and losses. Indians were hastily taken from their homes and they lost the improvements and the knowledge of their ancestral lands that they had used for centuries to support themselves and they were forced to start over in new locations. In 1831, in response to threats of removal, the Cherokee Nation sued the state of Georgia in the U.S. Supreme Court, and in that setting the Court made the false statements pointed out earlier that the Cherokee were dependent on the United States for their daily food and clothing, and were in a guardian to ward relationship with the federal government.[47]

The idea of removing all tribes to the federally designated "Indian Territory" of modern-day Oklahoma did not last long. The United States and its citizens leapt across North America so rapidly with the discovery of gold in California, the opening of the Oregon Trail, and the conquests of the Mexican-American War that the removal of all tribes became impossible. So in 1849–1850, in Texas and California, a new policy developed of placing tribes on limited reservations. The economic effect of this policy opened vast reaches of tribal lands to U.S. citizens. Reservations became like prisons for Indians because they were not allowed to leave without a pass from the Bureau of Indian Affairs (BIA) agent and the BIA gained a stranglehold over reservation life. (The BIA is the federal agency charged with dealing with tribal governments. It was originally in the Department of War but was moved to the Department of the Interior in 1849.) For over one hundred years, BIA superintendents made most of the decisions for tribal governments and reservation Indians. Also, on most reservations, Indians did not have the tools or the arable land to support themselves, and they starved. The United States then returned to tribes time after time and Indians who were now starving were presented with new agreements to shrink their reservations further and the United States would pay for these land sales with food and clothing. As tribes and Indians lost their land base and their agricultural and hunting grounds, it is no wonder that poverty, dependency, and despair followed.[48]

By the late 1880s, George Washington's "Savage as the Wolf" idea reached its zenith. Under the disguise of helping Indian economic development, the federal government adopted the idea of breaking up and destroying reservations and tribal governments. In 1887, Congress enacted the Allotment Act in which reservations were to be divided up into small farming plots for individual Indians. The United States, though, would be the legal owner of the land and hold the title in trust for the Indian person who was called the beneficial owner. ("Trust lands" are lands that tribal governments or individual Indians own as the beneficial owner but the United States owns the legal title and is the legal owner.) Congress also provided that the "surplus lands"—that is, any lands on reservations that exceeded what was needed to divide up for the existing Indian population—were to be sold to non-Indians who were thus invited to live on reservations. Of course, since the "Savage as the Wolf" policy assumed that all Indian lands would one day belong to Americans, and since the express purpose of Allotment was to destroy tribes and break up reservations, no one assumed that tribal governments and reservations would still be around in 2012. Today, millions of acres of land located within reservation borders are owned by Indians and non-Indians in fee simple title. (Fee simple in Anglo-American property law describes the complete ownership of land.)

Indians who received allotted lands in restricted trust ownership were to receive the fee simple title in 25 years or earlier if they could demonstrate that they were competent. Many Indians who ultimately received fee simple titles lost their lands to voluntary sales or state tax foreclosures. During the Allotment Era, tribal governments lost the ownership of 90 million acres and were left with only 48 million acres of land by 1934. Even worse, about 20 million acres of the tribes' remaining lands were arid or semiarid. American citizens had acquired most of the best lands and assets on reservations. One historian notes: "by 1920 most federal officials [were] ... in favor of policies that would integrate Indian economic resources while keeping Native American communities marginalized from American society."[49] The U.S. Board of Indian Commissioners reported in 1921 that giving fee simple titles to Indians had been "a shortcut to the separation of the freed Indians from their land and cash."[50] Once again tribal economic potential and assets were greatly reduced. Moreover, the Allotment Era increased the need for more BIA employees and created more influence for the federal bureaucracy over tribal and Indian decision making. More dependency and poverty were the results of Allotment.

Conditions became so bad under Allotment that in 1934 Congress changed policies and enacted the Indian Reorganization Act. But Congress created yet another problem by freezing in place all allotments that had already been made. Tribal communities did not regain the surplus lands that had been sold to non-Indians, and any Indian person who still held an allotment in restricted trust ownership with the United States had that ownership status frozen in place. Today, in Indian Country, about 11 million acres of land are still held by individual Indians in trust, with the Indians as the beneficial owners, and the United States as the legal owner.

The United States continued its assault on Indian economic assets after World War II. The argument was made that the United States had to stop the "fascism" of tribal governments. So in 1953, Congress enacted a resolution that it would terminate the political relationship between tribal governments and the United States as rapidly as possible. The "Termination policy" ultimately led to the loss of another million acres of land from tribal ownership. Once again, while the argument was made that termination would be good for Indians, "the policy also was championed by western economic interests and politicians who wished to open the remaining reservation lands to economic development."[51] This federal policy ended fairly quickly in the early 1960s. Thereafter, President Lyndon Johnson's Great Society included Indians and tribal governments for the first time in federal poverty programs, and tribes could access federal training programs and use federal funds to hire employees. Moreover, in 1970 President Richard Nixon called for an end to BIA paternalism and the federal management of Indian life. He said that tribes and Indians should be allowed self-determination and should be allowed to tell the federal government how best to serve their needs.[52]

In conclusion, Professor White notes that Euro-American colonists and American officials always wondered why the people they conquered and colonized starved and fell into poverty. They thought it was because Indians had always starved. This idea literally became part of the rationale and justification for colonization itself. But, in contrast, as White notes, economies made up of a diverse mix of hunting, gathering, and horticultural systems were remarkably stable, and American Indian cultures had supported themselves for centuries before first contact. It was only when new diseases, new trade items, new relations with Euro-Americans, and the loss of the majority of their lands and assets altered native economies and subsistence systems that American Indians fell into dependency and poverty.[53]

## Corporate Interactions with Indian Nations

Large and multinational corporations are important parts of the global and American economies today, and they have also had significant impacts on economic conditions in Indian Country. Corporations have long been interested in benefiting from tribal resources. In the 1880s, Congress first opened Indian Country to American and corporate development. Congress began authorizing the granting of easements across reservations for telephone, telegraph, highways, pipelines, reservoirs, and more. In the modern day, corporations have the same interests in Indian Country. Corporations are designed, of course, to make profits for their shareholders, so their interest in reservations is based on profits and not necessarily on contributing to the economic and social needs of tribal communities. As a result, the primary role that major corporations have played in tribal economics has been to use Indian lands and assets. Often, tribes have seen very little benefit from these dealings and all that happened was that Indian Country experienced economic penetration and exploitation by outside interests.[54]

One key factor that cannot be overlooked is that due to the federal trust responsibility (a legal duty requires the United States to care for Indians and tribes), and the fact that the United States is the legal owner of most tribal assets, the federal government is heavily involved in most business dealings in Indian Country. Almost all of the work that corporations have done on reservations has been approved and overseen by federal employees who had little or no incentive to obtain the best deals possible for Indian nations. In fact, commentators have noted that the long-term leases tribes signed with corporations for oil, gas, and coal development had to be approved by the BIA and virtually gave away the resources. Tribes and the BIA did not have the technical skills and information and advantages needed to negotiate favorable long-term mineral leases. Even worse, tribes and Indian landowners have often had to rely on the BIA and even the corporations themselves to truthfully report and pay the royalty amounts due for timber, minerals, and oil extracted. There is ample evidence, however, that corporations have stolen resources from tribes and Indians by false reporting. Even when outright theft is not the problem, tribes are often stuck in long-term leases that the BIA forced on them at below-market rates. In 1981, the Navajo Nation was receiving $0.15–$0.38 cents a ton for coal when American suppliers were selling coal for $70 per ton. The Navajo and Hopi also sold water to Peabody Coal for mining purposes and received very little in return. Today, their aquifers are being depleted as precious water is used to slurry coal to processing plants. In 1977, the congressional Indian Policy Review Commission concluded that "the leases negotiated on behalf of Indians are among the poorest agreements ever made."[55]

This snapshot of the activities of corporations in Indian Country demonstrates that they have had many negative impacts on the economic conditions and assets of Indians and tribal governments. Tribes and Indians can benefit from working with corporations on economic development projects in the future, but they need to be aware of the possible pitfalls and rely on themselves and not the BIA to manage those relationships.

## FEDERAL POLICIES IMPACTING ECONOMIC ACTIVITIES IN INDIAN COUNTRY

Considering that the goal of most American settlers and politicians was to acquire the lands and assets of tribal communities, it should be no surprise that numerous federal policies and laws also contributed to the loss of these assets, and to poverty in Indian Country.

## Federal Relationship with Tribes

The United States has always dealt with Indian nations as political entities that govern their people and territories, and exercise sovereign powers as governments. The "government-to-government" political relationship between tribal governments and the federal government is an important part of federal Indian law. The way this relationship has played out in economic terms, however, has had unintended consequences. The practice of the federal government in dealing solely with tribal governments as regards economic issues in Indian Country has played a major role in developing economies on reservations that are primarily controlled and organized by tribal and federal governments.

The U.S. Constitution, in fact, places the exclusive federal authority over American economic dealings with tribes in the hands of Congress. Congress has used this authority to pass laws on every conceivable issue regarding Indians and tribes, including economic issues. Consequently, Congress's power over tribal governments and the political relationship between the United States and tribes has drawn the federal government into a major and active role in managing tribal life. This power has created a much greater role for the United States in Indian and tribal economic affairs than the federal government plays in the U.S. economy in general.[56]

Another important aspect of the federal/tribal relationship that impacts Indian economies is the trust responsibility the federal government owes to tribes and individual Indians. The trust duty has arisen from the all-encompassing power that Congress has over Indians and tribes due to the guardianship duties the United States voluntarily assumed on behalf of tribes and Indians under treaties, the political relationship between tribes and the United States, and the dependent relationship tribes have with the United States. The Supreme Court says the United States has "charged itself with moral obligations of the highest responsibility and trust."[57] This duty requires Congress and the executive branch to exercise the responsibilities of a guardian on behalf of Indians and tribes.[58]

These legal principles have had unintended and negative impacts on economic development in Indian Country. The trust doctrine has contributed to the development of centrally planned reservation economies because it has led the United States and the BIA into day-to-day involvement in the majority of reservation economic activities and decisions, and into a guardian's ownership responsibilities for many of the economic assets of tribes and Indians. This is so because the federal government is the legal owner of the majority of tribal lands and assets in Indian Country as the guardian and trustee for Indian tribes and peoples. As a consequence, the United States makes or approves most of the decisions regarding these assets and economic development in Indian Country. The United States has this role because when tribal and individual Indian properties are held in trust they are jointly owned by the United States, and tribes and Indian owners cannot sell, lease, develop, or mortgage such assets for loans without the express approval of the federal government. Needless to say, having the United States looking over the shoulders of tribal governments and requiring federal approvals of most economic decisions, and the time it takes to gain these bureaucratic approvals, adds enormous costs and inefficiencies to tribal and Indian economic endeavors. The inefficient and non-business-oriented federal bureaucracy creates serious obstacles for tribal governments and Indians in using trust assets for economic purposes, and for non-Indian companies who want to work in Indian Country.[59]

## The Trade and Intercourse Era

The history of federal Indian policy is divided into seven distinct eras. The first era received its name from the Trade and Intercourse laws that Congress enacted from 1790 to 1834 to control trade and economic interactions between Americans and Indians. Most of the principles contained in these laws are still federal law today. The congressional policies underlying the laws attempted to protect Indians from unscrupulous American traders and to bring Indians and tribes into the U.S. economic sphere of influence. By accident, these laws also removed tribal governments, Indian peoples, and their assets from the U.S. economic marketplace for almost one hundred years. If anyone considered this point, they must have thought that North America was so vast that the United States could wait a few generations before utilizing all the tribal assets.[60]

The federal government even entered the Indian trading business at this time, as already mentioned. In 1795, at President Washington's request, Congress created federal trading houses that were ultimately operated at 28 locations across the frontier from 1795 to 1822. This process served the Trade and Intercourse Era goals and made Indians dependent on the federal government as they bought their supplies at federal stores, brought Indians and tribes within the U.S. economic orbit, and increased the market for U.S. goods.[61]

But federal control and suppression of trade and economic activities in Indian Country inhibited the operation of many Indian and tribal economic activities and development. In essence, Congress preempted tribal economies and became, as Vine Deloria put it, the "surrogate for Indian decision making in . . . economic relations with the settlers."[62] The executive branch also participated in isolating Indian Country from the U.S. economy. Most of the 375 treaties tribes signed with the United States required that tribal governments and Indians limit their previous trading habits and trade only with the U.S. government. Many tribes later found that they suffered from a lack of trade.[63]

Clearly, federal policies limited tribal economic activities and development from 1790 forward. Congress refused to allow tribes and Indians to use their assets to participate in the U.S. economic life to whatever extent they might have wished. As a result, federally imposed and planned economies were forced on tribal governments.

## Removal Era

As George Washington and Thomas Jefferson predicted, the United States began working quickly to acquire tribal land and assets east of the Mississippi. Treaties negotiated by Washington, Jefferson, Madison, and other presidents greatly diminished tribal lands east of the Mississippi and began forcing tribal peoples west.

After decades of debate, Congress began adopting Removal-Era policies in the 1820s. This new era of federal Indian policy had extremely negative impacts on tribal economies and resources. The Removal policy attempted to force the tribes to move to the "Indian Territory" in what is now eastern Oklahoma and states northward. The "Savage as the Wolf" idea motivated this desire to remove the tribes so that Americans could own their lands and assets east of the Mississippi.

In 1830, Congress enacted the Removal Act. The act required that tribes had to consent to sell their lands east of the Mississippi and to remove to the west. Ultimately, some tribal peoples did move voluntarily to escape aggressive U.S. settlers, but many others were forced to move by being rounded up by the army and marched west. A forced "Trail of Tears" was the reality for many tribes, and thousands of Indians died on these marches, often a quarter or more of a tribe's population. We can only imagine the economic and cultural disruption and destruction caused by these forced removals from the farms and territories where these tribes and Indians had lived for centuries.

## Reservation Era

The policy of removing all Indian nations to the Indian Territory became impossible once the United States expanded rapidly in the 1840s. Starting in 1849–1850, the federal government adopted the new policy of forcing tribes onto small and remote reservations. The idea was to separate Indians from American settlers to minimize conflicts over assets and to acquire more tribal lands for Americans.

This policy severely restricted tribal farming, hunting, fishing, and gathering economies, and often moved Indians far from their traditional resources and the agriculture of their ancestral lands. Tribal economies were replaced, if at all, with nonfunctioning reservation economies and economic activities imposed by the United States. Instead of being able to feed themselves from their own lands, resources, and labors, tribal governments and Indian peoples were now promised treaty payments and annual rations if they surrendered most of their lands and resources to the United States. As a result, Indians and tribes became far more dependent on the U.S. government.

## Allotment Era

In 1887, Congress took another step towards acquiring all tribal assets for U.S. society. Now, the reservations that tribes and Indians had reserved for themselves forever, were to be opened to the U.S. economy. In one sense, the Allotment Act can seem to have been a major change from the policies of the Trade and Intercourse Era in which Indian Country's assets were cut off from the U.S. economy. But the Allotment Era was just another part of the evolution of transferring Indian assets and lands to the United States. When the continent was vast and the United States was still weak, it was prudent to agree in treaties with tribal governments that they could reserve enormous parts of the continent for themselves forever. In treaties with western tribes from the 1850s forward, the United States agreed to tribes retaining reservations that were composed of millions of acres. With the patience and policy of the "Savage as the Wolf" plan, though, U.S. politicians knew they would soon abrogate these treaties, sign new ones, and continue to acquire Indian lands and assets.[64]

Even as tribal reservations were methodically whittled down in size by later treaties, in 1887 Congress was ready to speed up the diminishment of reservations. Congress thought it was time to open Indian Country to the U.S. economy. Politicians and U.S. citizens justified the new policy by claiming it would benefit individual Indians. The leading theory on how to help Indians develop economically and to get out of poverty was to "civilize" and "Christianize" them and liberate them from the control and communal life of their tribal governments. The idea developed to bring Indians into the American "melting pot" by assimilating them into mainstream society and economic life. This era in federal Indian policy also had the explicit goals of breaking up tribal ownership of land, ending tribal existence, and, most importantly, opening reservation lands to non-Indian settlement. The primary motivation continued to be the desire of Americans to own reservation lands and to open tribal lands and assets to the mainstream economy.[65]

Under the General Allotment Act and the tribally specific allotment acts that followed, Congress divided the communally owned tribal lands into individual allotments that were to be owned by individual Indians and operated as farms and ranches. The tribally specific allotment acts from 1890 to 1910 generally divided or allotted reservations into 160- and 80-acre plots that were given to adult tribal citizens and 40-acre plots that were reserved for minors. To protect supposedly unsophisticated Indians, Congress mandated that the United States retain the legal ownership of the allotments and hold the lands in trust for 25 years during which the land could not be sold or subjected to state taxes. The idea was that Indians would learn business affairs and farming and could then handle the full ownership of their lands in fee simple status. Significantly, on those reservations where there was more land to be allotted than there were individual Indians to receive it (which was nearly all of the allotted reservations), any land beyond what was needed for Indians was defined as surplus and was sold to non-Indians. As a result of Allotment and surplus lands sales, some reservations today have much higher non-Indian populations than Indian populations.[66]

At first, it might appear that Congress used allotment to provide economic development for individual Indians by granting them private ownership of reservation lands. The stated goal for Allotment, after all, was to teach Indians the value of private property and private land ownership. But this argument was mostly used to justify Allotment and to put a patina of good will on what was nothing more than another land grab. The real goal of Allotment was to destroy tribal governments and to break up the reservation landmass for the use of the majority society. The Allotment Act did not create positive economic results in Indian Country. Instead, Allotment created long-term problems that have plagued economic development on reservations and have stifled individual Indian and tribal economic activities down to the present day.[67]

Subsequent events almost totally prevented the Allotment Act from creating the claimed private property benefits. Many Indians quickly sold their lands or lost them to state tax foreclosures once they received the fee simple titles. Moreover, these lands were no longer in communal tribal ownership to help tribal governments coordinate and maximize economic development. Another problem, which was not foreseen in 1887, is the "fractionation" of the ownership of the individual allotments that remain in Indian hands today. This resulted because the original allottees died without wills and their lands passed to ever-larger numbers of heirs. Federal law did not allow Indian allottees to pass on allotted trust lands by will for the first few decades after 1887. Many Indians did not begin using wills even after Congress allowed it. Consequently, many allotments on reservations today have hundreds and even thousands of individual owners. This causes a serious lack of coordinated ownership and decision making and a nightmare of record keeping and legal work for tribal and federal governments. Many Indians today have severe problems putting their trust lands to work and to operate viably sized pieces of land to make farming or other endeavors feasible. Congress recognizes the seriousness of the fractionation problem it caused by Allotment and has tried three times to enact laws to solve the issue. The Supreme Court struck down the first two attempts and might do the same with the third.[68]

In addition to fractionation, more than 11 million acres of land are still owned by Indians today in trust with the United States as the legal owner. The individual Indian is the beneficial owner of the property. This occurred when the United

States ended the Allotment policy in 1934 and froze in place all trust allotments that had not yet passed to the Indian owner in fee simple title. The fact that the United States retains the trusteeship and legal ownership of these lands makes them almost totally unavailable for borrowing money and for developing economic activities. As a result, while Allotment policies appear to have had the goal of promoting private economic development, they only created more dependency and reliance on the federal government and bureaucracy. Today, the leftover effects of Allotment continue to seriously impede attempts to develop reservation and individual Indian economies.

One example is sufficient to show how Allotment impeded tribal and Indian economic development. The facts show that Indian reservation farming was more vigorous, efficient, and on the increase in the mid-1880s, before the Allotment Era, than it was decades later in 1928. Allotment also resulted in tribal communities losing two-thirds of all tribally owned lands, with the majority of that land passing to non-Indians. Tribal governments went from owning 138 million acres of land in 1887 to only owning 48 million acres in 1934, and 20 million acres of the remaining lands were arid or semiarid. These facts, in conjunction with the limitations on trust allotments that are still held by Indians today, have created severe impediments to the coordinated and effective development of reservation economies.[69]

In the Allotment Era, Congress took other steps to open Indian Country and its assets to the mainstream U.S. economy in ways that had been prevented by the Trade and Intercourse policies since 1790. Now, Congress began allowing non-Indians to use minerals and timber from Indian Country and to lease reservation lands for grazing and farming. Congress also used Indian lands in other ways to benefit the U.S. economy, such as for telephone, telegraph, and railroad rights of ways. Reservation lands have also often been used for dam, reclamation, and irrigation projects that were designed to only benefit non-Indian communities and which even injured reservations. For example, 92 percent of the lands taken for the reservoirs formed by the Pick-Sloan Missouri River flood control projects were tribal lands. Clearly, the Allotment-Era policies continued the economic decimation of Indian Country.[70]

## Indian Reorganization Era

Federal Indian policies changed radically again in the 1930s and resulted in major impacts on Indian and tribal economic interests. The policies now encouraged the formation of tribally controlled and planned economies. The policies are still in effect today and continue to influence tribal and individual Indian economic activities.

The Indian Reorganization Era ran from the early 1930s to 1945 and was marked by the enactment of the Indian Reorganization Act (IRA) in 1934. Under the IRA, the United States completely reversed its policy of breaking up reservations and destroying tribal governments, and now the federal government strongly supported tribal governments politically and economically. By the 1930s, it was clear that Allotment had led to disaster. An influential study conducted in 1928 showed that reservation Indians were living under far worse economic, social, educational, and health conditions after four decades of Allotment than they had faced in 1887. The report demonstrated clearly that the Allotment Era had been an absolute disaster for Indians and tribes. Consequently, along with other goals, the IRA ended the allotment of tribal lands and placed a freeze on any trust allotments that had not yet been turned into privately owned property.[71]

The United States now encouraged and assisted tribes to organize governments by adopting constitutions and bylaws. The IRA also had the express goal of increasing tribal economic activities to try to ameliorate the extreme poverty in Indian Country. The IRA allowed tribes to create corporations under federal law to engage in economic development and business. This provision significantly encouraged the predominant role tribal governments play in modern-day reservation economies. According to various commentators, the goal of the IRA was to enable Indian tribes to develop economically and to help tribes operate their economies. Many tribes still have and use their IRA chartered corporations today to operate tribal businesses and economic activities.[72]

The tribal corporations were granted powers to manage tribal properties, to buy, sell, and manage other properties, and "such further powers as may be incidental to the conduct of corporate business. . . ."[73] Tribal corporations can also borrow money from a loan fund Congress authorized for economic development. The IRA arguably had a significant impact on the economic life on reservations and helped create federally and tribally planned economies. Tribal governments were encouraged to operate reservation businesses and guide economic development, and federal efforts to assist these economic activities focused exclusively on tribal governments.[74]

For this very reason, the IRA encountered strong opposition within and without Congress and even by Indians, because the IRA allegedly promoted "socialism" and "communism." Some of the opponents of the IRA thought that Indians would be inhibited in their private property and U.S. citizenship rights by being subjected to the control of tribal governments. Many different groups described the IRA and the desire to keep Indians segregated from U.S. society and living in communal tribal societies as promoting socialism.[75]

Notwithstanding these doubts, the IRA was enacted in 1934 and has helped establish many strong tribal governments in Indian Country that today have nearly total control over the economic life and economies on reservations. Commentators argue that the IRA imposed new tribal governments, tribally controlled economies, and artificial economies in Indian Country. The all-encompassing tribal business orientation is demonstrated by the fact that many of the governing bodies that were formed by tribes under the IRA are officially called the tribal "business committee" or "business council." This is not surprising, since the IRA encouraged tribes "to organize along the lines of modern business corporations" and demanded that economic development proceed with a "tribal approach."[76] Tribal governments and their role in creating and operating businesses and economic activities on reservations have become so intertwined that even the federal government, courts, and others have confused the activities and identities of tribal governments that were formed under IRA section 16 and the tribal corporations that were formed under IRA section 17.[77]

Other aspects of the IRA have also created problems for tribes and Indians in economic development because the law created pervasive federal bureaucratic control over tribal and Indian economic activities. In addition, extensive federal control of tribal economic activities had already been imposed from 1871 to 2000, when Congress required the secretary of the interior to approve all contracts that tribes signed "relative to their lands."[78] The 1871 act and the new tribal governments and businesses created under the IRA led to wide-ranging federal agency oversight and BIA direction of tribes in their political and business decisions. It is universally accepted, however, that federal bureaucratic review and approval of tribal economic activities is a death knell for effective and efficient business decision making. Faced with these obstacles, with tribally and federally managed economies, and federal control of tribal decisions and assets, it is no surprise that reservation economies and economic conditions did not improve much under the IRA.[79]

## Termination Era

After World War II, the federal government developed a new Indian policy that was another complete reversal of federal policy and was a return to the express goals to destroy tribal economies and open Indian and tribal assets to non-Indians. In the termination era, from 1945 to 1961, Congress adopted the express objective of ending the federal/tribal relationship and terminating the legal existence of tribes. Once again political doubletalk was used to justify the policy. Members of Congress claimed that they wanted to "free" Indians from the domination of tribal governments, end the communal ownership of tribal assets, and distribute the assets to individual tribal citizens. This sounds remarkably similar to the justifications for the Allotment-Era policies. But the actual goal was to get tribal assets out of communal ownership and into individual Indian ownership so that non-Indians and corporations could ultimately obtain them. Many tribes were terminated in Oregon, for example, because timber barons hoped to obtain tribal timber in that state.[80]

Under the specific termination acts, the BIA was directed to draft plans on how to distribute the communal assets to individual Indians. Just as in the Allotment Era, once these assets came into individual Indian ownership they were often lost to state tax foreclosures or sold to non-Indians. Ultimately, 109 tribes were terminated and they lost 1.3 million more acres of land. These terminations seriously injured the economies of those tribes and tribal citizens. In addition, during this time, the BIA adopted a "relocation program" and removed Indians from reservations by giving them one-way bus tickets to big cities. Between 1953 and 1972, more than 100,000 Indians were moved to big cities in the west.[81]

The Termination Era lived up to its name. Tribes and their citizens saw a further diminishment of their land base and assets and they were pushed further into poverty and despair. One author stated in 2005 that the Termination Era "marked the all-time low for tribal existence on this continent."[82]

# Self-Determination Era

The Self-Determination Era of federal Indian policy began in the early 1960s and is still federal policy today. The principal legislative effort of this era is the Indian Self-Determination and Education Assistance Act of 1975, which instituted a major philosophical change in federal Indian affairs by allowing tribes to contract with the U.S. government for the delivery of services to Indians. Tribes can now plan and administer federally funded programs. Congress's intent is to end the federal "domination" of Indian affairs. The economic impact of this era has been to put tribal governments even more in control of reservation economic development programs and projects.[83]

The federal government has also tried to focus on economic development and poverty in Indian Country. During the 1960s, general federal poverty programs invested millions into new tribal programs and infrastructure. In recent decades, the United States has also worked with tribal governments through tribally specific programs to try to increase economic activities. Congress has instituted a few loan and grant programs for tribes and Indians to fund start-up businesses, and job training programs have been provided to Indians. But while some federal programs helped individual Indians, it can still be fairly stated that the United States looks primarily to tribal governments to create and operate most of the businesses and economic activities in Indian Country.[84]

After 50 years of the Self-Determination Era, the United States, tribal governments, and residents of the reservation are still seeking the answer to successful reservation economic development. Federal funding remains the backbone of the Native American economy, and the United States continues to look to tribal governments to create and operate economic development activities in Indian Country. But economies operated and planned by the federal and tribal governments are not necessarily the best way nor are they the only way that business and economic activities can be created on reservations. We will spend the remainder of this book examining what tribes and individual Indians are doing in the economic arena today and what they can do to expand investment and private entrepreneurship on their reservations and to develop economies that will bring more benefits to reservation inhabitants in addition to federal and tribal programs.

In conclusion, it is clear that the Euro-American impacts on Indian and tribal economies and their lands and assets have been a disaster for Indians. As George Washington predicted, the majority of tribal assets are now in the hands of non-Indians, and Indian peoples are the poorest Americans.

# Chapter 4

# Current Economic Activity in Indian Country

*A*merican Indian nations are involved today in a wide array of economic activities. This range of activities is no doubt due to the widely divergent geographies and circumstances where tribes find themselves. American Indian tribes are located from Alaska to Florida, and Maine to California, and are culturally, economically, and governmentally diverse. The 565 federally recognized tribes include small, medium, and large communities, which are located on small, medium, and large reservations. Some reservations are far from any town or city and some are located in nearly urban settings. Reservations also have different types and amounts of natural resources and economic advantages that they can utilize. It is no surprise, then, that tribal governments and Indian communities are currently engaged in a wide array of business and economic activities.

Encouragingly, the 1990s saw a significant rise in average incomes for Indian families across the United States. This was not all due to tribal gaming endeavors. The rate of increase in Indian family incomes was actually higher for tribal areas *without* gaming, at 33 percent, than the increase was in areas with gaming, at 24 percent. These increases far surpassed the 4 percent growth rate in the median U.S. household income during the same time period. Notwithstanding this encouraging increase in Indian family incomes in the 1990s, as of 2008, American Indian household incomes were still fall far below the American average.[1]

In this chapter, we take a bird's-eye view of some of the major business enterprises tribes are currently undertaking, and then we focus on three tribes to examine how they are approaching economic development. Gaming is discussed in Chapter 5.

## TRIBAL ECONOMIC DEVELOPMENT

Many federally recognized tribal governments have succeeded spectacularly in business endeavors and some have had fair to moderate results, while other tribes have failed in some or nearly all of their efforts. Some tribes today are among the leading employers in their states, such as the Mississippi Choctaw, or in their regions, like the Confederated Tribes of the Warm Springs Reservation in central Oregon, and the Confederated Tribes of the Umatilla Indian Reservation in northeastern Oregon. Many tribes are now able to offer jobs to any tribal citizen who is able to work. That is an amazing turnaround in economic conditions for tribes and reservations.[2]

# Timber

The timber industry is important to many tribes because they own more than 6.3 million acres of commercial timberland. In 1978, the BIA reported that timber contributed 25 to 100 percent of tribal revenues for 57 different tribal governments. And from 2001 to 2004, Indian forestlands produced nearly $290 million a year for tribal nations and individual Indian landowners. Clearly, these are important sources of revenue for tribal governments and provide employment for Indians and tribal employees. Over 60 timber tribes and Alaska Native corporations work together through the Intertribal Timber Council to promote sound forest management, establish natural resource-based businesses, and train and develop Indian foresters. Today, tribes are taking over more responsibilities to manage their forests from the BIA. The number of tribes managing their forests instead of relying on the BIA rose from 64 in 1991 to 121 in 2001. Congress supports this trend and has created a broader role for tribes in managing their timber.[3]

The Menominee Tribal Enterprises, for example, operates a large and very successful program that employs 300 people and manages 220,000 acres. The Menominees have vast experience in forestry and in managing their timberlands and have done so successfully since the 1880s. Moreover, the Confederated Tribes of the Colville Reservation operate an award-winning program and harvest 78 million board feet of timber annually. The Colville Tribes also own two lumber mills and a facility that participates in a biomass power project. The Confederated Tribes of the Warm Springs Reservation, the Fort Bidwell Indian Community, and the Hoopa Valley Tribe had their forests certified by the Forest Stewardship Council. In addition, the Warm Springs Tribes provide employment for private logging companies owned by tribal citizens, and they operate their own mill. By its twentieth anniversary, the mill had bought $130 million in trees from the tribes, paid $38 million in wages and $70 million to loggers, and paid net profits of $24 million to the tribal government.[4] These tribes are making profits and creating economic development and jobs from their forests, and they are striving to preserve their ecosystems and sustainable growth for generations to come.

It is no surprise that tribal citizens and tribal managers would make better decisions in these activities than federal bureaucrats. One Yakama Nation forester said that when tribal citizens and managers are the decision makers "the people who make the decisions for the land are accountable."[5] Interestingly, tribes are also accomplishing these tasks without the full support of the federal government. Even though the United States owes trust and treaty responsibilities to assist tribes with economic development and reservation resources, a 2003 report showed that tribal forestry programs received only $2.58 an acre in federal funding while national forests received $9.51 per acre.[6]

## Minerals

About 40 tribes in the United States own extensive mineral resources. In general, tribes own in trust with the United States about 56 million acres of land in the lower 48 states, and Alaska Native corporations own 44 million acres in fee simple. These lands contain about 4 percent of U.S. oil and gas reserves, 40 percent of the uranium, and 30 percent of the coal. These resources have produced enormous amounts of money for these tribes. In 1999, oil and gas leases alone generated over $100 million for tribes and Indian landowners, and tribes received more than $185 million in mineral royalties in 2000. In 2004, Indian oil and gas generated over $254 million in royalties. As with timber, Congress is currently giving tribes more control over their mineral development decisions and lessening the federal bureaucratic role.[7]

A few tribes have made spectacular progress through mineral development. The Southern Ute Tribe of Colorado has shrewdly turned the profits from its natural gas assets into a $1.45 billion investment portfolio. The living standard for tribal citizens has increased dramatically since the 1950s when most were living without indoor plumbing and electricity. Now, all tribal citizens are millionaires on paper and receive annual cash disbursements. The Tribe is also the number one employer in its county. In addition, many Alaska Native corporations have become very successful with royalties from oil and have diversified and expanded their business interests into many new fields, including defense contracting. Some of these corporations have earned outstanding returns and are major employers in Alaska.[8]

## Land Leasing

Tribes and individual Indians who own trust lands with the United States lease hundreds of thousands of acres. They lease land for rights of way across reservations for oil, gas, and water pipelines, subsurface mining leases, and surface leases for farming, grazing, and logging. In 1996, the BIA reported that tribal and Indian agricultural leases alone produced more than $43 million. Tribes have even begun entering long-term water leases with cities.[9]

## Manufacturing

Increasingly, tribal governments are getting involved in major manufacturing ventures. The ongoing success of the Mississippi Choctaw Tribe is probably the best-known story, but other tribes like the Cherokee Nation of Oklahoma and the Salish and Kootenai Tribes in Montana are also involved in manufacturing businesses. Other tribes, like the Passamaquoddy and Penobscot Tribes of Maine, have made commercial and industrial investments.[10]

In the 1950s and 1960s, the Mississippi Choctaw people were desperately poor and suffered from 75 percent unemployment, far lower than average life expectancy rates, and the highest infant mortality rate in the United States. By the late 1990s, however, tribal citizens enjoyed full employment, a 20-year increase in life expectancy, and infant mortality rates that were now better than state and national averages. Their family incomes and educational levels soared, substandard housing was greatly reduced, and the Tribe was among the top 10 employers in the state. In 1989, in fact, the Tribe employed more than 8,000 people, and more than 65 percent of its workforce was non-Indian. The success of the Tribe has also greatly assisted the surrounding counties and caused an economic boom in central Mississippi. Unemployment is way down in these counties, state and county tax revenues are soaring, and they have enjoyed a population boom in contrast to the decreases suffered by other rural counties in that state. The Tribe created this success by entering the manufacturing world. This turnaround did not happen by accident, of course, but in part because the Tribe took advantage of federal programs to train workers and managers, and because the Choctaw leadership and people made it happen.[11]

In 1969, the tribally owned construction company undertook its first project to build federal/tribal housing on the reservation. The Tribe also upgraded an unused industrial plant it had built with federal funds and in 1978 began to offer itself as a minority contractor. It then signed contracts with GM Packard to make automotive wiring harnesses and went to Washington, D.C., for Economic Development Agency loans and BIA loan guarantees. The Choctaw also involved the local city and the state by leasing the land under its factory to the city and having the city ask the state to issue bonds to finance a deal to make cards for the American Greetings Card company. The Tribe was successful at both endeavors, and it led to more manufacturing contracts with Chevrolet, Ford, Navistar, Oxford Speaker Company, AT&T, and Xerox and to the Tribe owning manufacturing plants in Mexico for over a decade. Tribal citizens returned to the reservation by the hundreds to take these newly created jobs. According to all accounts, this economic improvement did not come at the expense of the tribe's culture.[12]

# Agriculture, Ranching, and Grazing

More than 44 million acres of Indian land is range and grazing land. Many tribes and Indians raise cattle, buffalo, and horses, and lease lands to non-Indians.

Tribes also operate farming concerns such as the Navajo Nation and its Agricultural Products, Inc., the Oneida Nation, and the Ak-Chin Community. In 1975, the BIA reported the annual value of agricultural products grown on Indian range and croplands as $394 million.[13]

## Government Administration

Tribal governments are usually the number one employer on reservations and regularly employ up to half of the people working on a reservation. Most tribes give hiring preferences to tribal citizens and other Indians, so many of these jobs are held by Indians. These jobs are very valuable for tribal economies because they provide Indians with employment and management experience that tribes can utilize later, and they help to keep tribal payrolls circulating within Indian Country. It is reported that all of the upper management of the Confederated Tribes of the Warm Springs Reservation in Oregon gained their business experience working at the Tribes' Kah-Nee-Ta resort and that 50 percent of the jobs on the reservation are in tribal administration. These Tribes also partner with Portland General Electric in operating Pelton Dam. Several other tribes—for instance, the Navajo Nation and the Salish and Kootenai Tribes—also operate their own utility departments. These efforts employ and train tribal employees and managers and at the same time keep the money reservation inhabitants would normally pay to off-reservation utility companies circulating within the reservation economy because the utility payments now fund tribal utility departments and pay tribal employees.[14]

Many tribes have also taken advantage of the federal Self-Determination and Education Assistance Act of 1975 and the Self-Governance Act of 1994 to contract programs away from the federal government. Almost all tribes operate, to some extent, various BIA and Indian Health Service programs. Thus, they hire and fire doctors and nurses and dentists and employ foresters and biologists and plan and manage these federal/tribal programs themselves. These laws give tribes access to the full federal funding and the right to retain any efficiencies in the program they can produce. This program has been a great boon to help tribes employ and train their citizens and expand tribal capabilities. Studies have shown that tribal departments and employees operate these programs more efficiently than the federal agencies.[15]

## Tourism

Many tribes are developing recreational resources and promoting tourism.[16] The Navajo Nation is currently developing a tribal park and the Mescalero Apache Tribe has long operated a ski resort. The Warm Springs Tribes have operated a resort in central Oregon since the 1960s. Other tribes issue hunting and fishing licenses and offer guided tours for trophy hunting. Many tribes have built museums and cultural centers that serve the dual purpose of attracting tourists and providing tribal communities with facilities to engage in culturally relevant research, cultural preservation, and ceremonies. Gaming activities have led many tribes to build hotels, golf courses, and convention centers.[17]

## Intertribal and International Business

Various tribes are working together on economic development projects, and others are looking at the international trade market. The Confederated Tribes of the Siletz Indians and the Confederated Tribes of the Grand Ronde Community in Oregon are co-developing a 15-acre property, and the Muckleshoot Tribe from Washington formed a joint venture to build an intertribal casino in Las Vegas. The Cowlitz Tribe, also of Washington, partnered with the Mohegan Tribe of Connecticut to develop and manage the Cowlitz casino, and several other tribes are working together on other gaming deals. In 2005, four tribes partnered with Marriott to build a $43 million upscale hotel in Washington, D.C. In 2007–2009, some Pacific Northwest tribes, and their intertribal organization the Affiliated Tribes of Northwest Indians, drafted an intertribal treaty in which, if the treaty becomes effective, tribal governments could engage in economic development together and across reservations.[18]

Some American Indian nations are engaging in international business. Several tribes have looked into selling Canadian drugs over the Internet, and the Penobscot Nation of Maine and the Mashantucket Pequot Nation of Connecticut already sell prescription drugs online. Further, as mentioned, the Mississippi Choctaw Tribe owned and operated automotive plants in Mexico for a decade and employed thousands of workers. Plus, the Navajo Nation exported more than 230 metric tons of beans to Cuba in 2007, and is working with Brazilian Indigenous nations to develop wireless networks. It has also partnered with the Observatory for Cultural and Audiovisual Communication to build a facility for long-distance education and communications with Indigenous nations around the world.[19] Furthermore, tribes have engaged in foreign financing, and several are looking to expand their international trade and commerce. For example, on August 1, 2007, 11 Indigenous Nations from the United States, Canada, Australia, and New Zealand signed an international economic development treaty. Since then, other American tribes and international Indigenous groups have signed the treaty.[20]

## Fishing

Fishing is an important economic activity for many tribes and Indians. Many tribal governments fought for decades to protect and develop their treaty fishing rights in the Pacific Northwest and the Great Lakes region, in particular. Tribes are now involved in hatchery operations and stream and salmon regeneration.

The Confederated Tribes of the Umatilla Indian Reservation even restored salmon runs in the Umatilla River that had been extinct for over 70 years. While one might usually think of fishing as being an individual economic activity, many tribes and tribal organizations like the Columbia River Inter-Tribal Fish Commission and the Northwest Indian Fisheries Commission are heavily involved in these activities.[21]

# Water

Many tribes have legal claims to enormous amounts of water. Most of these claims, however, are as yet unquantified or are currently being negotiated or litigated. Needless to say, water is very valuable. Today, tribes are the key actors in the control of water in the West.

Unfortunately, the United States did nothing to protect Indian water rights for many decades while federal agencies raced to develop the West and provide water for non-Indian users. Even worse, tribal lands unfairly bore the brunt of many negative effects of these projects while the benefits were directed at non-reservation lands. One historian stated that "Indian lands have often been perceived as 'national sacrifice areas' so that greater resource developments can be achieved for the public at large."[22]

In a 1963 case, the U.S. Supreme Court decided that tribes have claims to large amounts of water. Since then, litigation and negotiation have led to defining some tribes' rights but have also left significant questions about just how much water is owned by tribes in the West. Litigating water rights is prohibitively expensive, time-consuming, and fraught with peril for tribes and non-Indians. The Big Horn stream adjudication in Wyoming took over 30 years and cost over $30 million dollars. It is no wonder that negotiating water settlements between tribes, states, and the federal government has become the preferred method. As of 2001, 14 water settlements had been signed and 32 more were in negotiation. Many of these negotiated settlements, which Congress enacted into federal law, allowed tribes to lease water to off-reservation cities.[23]

# Housing

The housing industry is crucial to the economic health and development of the United States. Tribal governments are well aware of this fact and try to do as much as they can in this arena. Almost every federally recognized tribe has a housing department and works with the U.S. Department of Housing and Urban Development to provide housing. The need for additional and better housing in Indian Country is the greatest in the nation because adequate housing is in short supply on most reservations. Tribes realize that housing construction and a rising home equity and private housing market would be a boon to their economic development.

# Developing Economies

This subject is addressed in Chapter 8, so we will only note here that many tribes realize that developing functioning economies and attracting new businesses to their reservations will create more business, financial, and economic activity and help keep money circulating on their reservations between tribal and privately owned businesses. Chief Phillip Martin of the Mississippi Choctaw stated proudly that part of his Tribe's success was that "[w]e developed an economy."[24] Many tribes are also working towards this goal by encouraging tribal citizens to start their own businesses and by trying to make reservations attractive locations for non-Indian businesses. Several tribes now offer business start-up loans for tribal citizens, some as high as $100,000. Other tribes in Oregon and South Dakota created programs to train and assist individual Indians to start and operate their own businesses. In 1991, four Oregon tribes created a nonprofit organization, the Oregon Native American Business & Entrepreneurial Network, to provide individualized and culturally appropriate training programs for Indians to draft business plans and to start and operate private businesses. This organization has successfully helped tribes foster an entrepreneurial spirit among their citizens and assisted hundreds of Indians to start their own businesses.[25]

## SPECIFIC TRIBAL ECONOMIC DEVELOPMENT

We now examine three specific tribes and what they have accomplished in economic development and building economies and self-sustaining communities. These tribes are a microcosm of the diverse array of economic situations, issues, and circumstances that American Indian tribes encounter today.

The Confederated Tribes of the Umatilla Indian Reservation are located on a 172,000-acre reservation in rural northeastern Oregon five miles from the small city of Pendleton, which has a population of 16,830. Interstate Highway 84 and railroad lines run through the reservation. Hence, a well-developed economy and transportation system are adjacent to the reservation and provide many of the amenities that life requires. The tribes ship their wastewater and sewage to Pendleton for treatment and, in turn, the city's water lines cross the reservation. The Umatilla Reservation was heavily allotted due to federal policies, and today the Tribes own about 30 percent of the land within their reservation borders in trust with the United States. Thousands of acres, perhaps another 30 percent of the reservation, are owned by individual Umatilla citizens and other Indians in trust with the United States, and some own their land in fee simple titles. Thousands of acres more, perhaps 40 percent of the reservation, are owned by non-Indians in fee simple. This "checkerboarded" pattern of land ownership created on many reservations by the Allotment Act causes tribes serious jurisdictional, regulatory, economic, and governmental issues. About 1,200 Umatilla tribal citizens live on or near the reservation, another 300 Indians from other tribes live on the reservation, and about 1,500 non-Indians live there.[26]

By comparison, my tribe, the Eastern Shawnee Tribe, is located in northeastern Oklahoma immediately adjacent to the small town of Seneca, Missouri, which has a population of 2,135. The Tribe and its citizens utilize the existing and long-standing economies of Seneca, Missouri, the larger town of Miami, Oklahoma, 10 miles away, and the much larger city of Joplin, Missouri, located 16 miles away. The Tribe has owned a 58-acre parcel of land, held in trust by the United States, since about 1937. This land was the Tribe's only asset for many decades. In recent years, the Tribe has bought hundreds of acres of land in Ottawa County, Oklahoma, for development purposes, tribal housing, and tribal governmental buildings.

In contrast, the Hoopa Valley Tribe is located on the Hoopa Valley Indian Reservation in a remote part of northern California. The primary part of its reservation, called the Square, is about 96,000 acres. This reservation was only slightly impacted by Allotment, and the tribal government still owns 95 percent of the reservation in trust with the United States while 2 percent is owned by tribal citizens in fee simple and 3 percent is owned by non-Indians in fee simple. There is one small town on the reservation called, appropriately, Hoopa. The nearest cities are Arcata and Eureka, California, with populations of 17,000 and 25,000, and are each a 90-minute drive from the reservation. So infrastructure, shopping, state services, and so on are not located near the reservation.

We could have studied many other tribes and reservations that are far more remote from economic services and from cities and the jobs, stores, and infrastructure they provide. And we could have examined many other tribes that encounter different economic issues and challenges than these three. But these tribes provide a good overview of the disparate issues tribal governments, communities, and economies confront due to their locations and unique historical situations regarding land ownership, jurisdiction, poverty, education, financing, and more, and the different paths to successful development available to tribal communities.

## Confederated Tribes of the Umatilla Indian Reservation

The Cayuse, Umatilla, and Walla Walla Tribes make up the Confederated Tribes of the Umatilla Indian Reservation (CTUIR) in northeastern Oregon. In 1855, the Tribes signed a treaty with the United States and ceded about 6.4 million acres they had owned and used for millennia in exchange for a 510,000-acre reservation. The reservation boundaries were incorrectly surveyed, however, and the Tribes were forced to accept a 245,000-acre reservation. Furthermore, immediate pressure arose from non-Indian immigrants to open the reservation for settlement. In 1882, this desire led to 640 acres being taken from the reservation for the city of Pendleton, which had had its beginnings in the early 1860s. Over time, the reservation was reduced to 158,000 acres.

In 1885, the reservation was one of the first in the United States to be allotted, and tracts of land were given in restricted ownership to tribal citizens. Significant amounts of land were later lost from Indian ownership due to voluntary sales and state tax foreclosures. Moreover, allotment led to the direct sale of thousands of "surplus" acres within the reservation to non-Indians, and the United States gave other lands to the railroad. As a result, lands within the CTUIR reservation are owned today by many different entities and in multiple types of land ownership. As mentioned, the Tribes own about 30 percent of the reservation in trust, CTUIR citizens and other Indians own about 30 percent of the reservation, some in trust and some in fee simple, and non-Indians own about 40 percent of the reservation lands in fee simple.[27]

In 1939, the Tribes finally convinced Congress to return 14,000 acres, and today the Umatilla Reservation comprises 172,000 acres. They also began working to govern themselves and free themselves from BIA control. In 1947, a committee was appointed to research governance issues and in 1949 the Tribes enacted a constitution and bylaws and created a board of trustees to manage tribal affairs. In the 1950s, the Tribes filed lawsuits to protect their rights to hunt and fish on their reservation free of state law and to protect their off-reservation treaty rights. They also filed suit against the United States for the loss of fishing sites at the world famous Celilo Falls, which was drowned in 1957 by The Dalles Dam. Ultimately, the Tribes settled this case for $4.6 million, and later settled other suits against the United States for $2.45 million. The citizens voted, however, to pay almost all of these monies in per capita payments to tribal citizens and they were not retained to finance tribal development or programs. Life on the reservation remained difficult. Unemployment was near 60 percent and many problems, such as critical housing conditions, alcoholism, and a lack of fish in the Umatilla River negatively impacted tribal citizens.[28]

The Tribes were completely broke in 1968 and 1969, and by 1970 the tribal government had no staff and no operating budget. The Tribes slowly began to build, however. The board of trustees began working on projects that lay unfinished from 1967. In 1972, the Tribes joined with three other Northwest tribes to create the Columbia River Inter-Tribal Fish Commission to protect their treaty and economic rights in salmon. By 1973, federal poverty programs and various grants were taking hold in Indian Country and allowed the Tribes to hire employees, and tribal employment grew in one year from 7 to 100 employees. The federal Indian Self-Determination Act was then enacted in 1975 and the Tribes used that law to begin operating federal programs, hiring and training employees, managing their own affairs, and removing incompetent BIA management. In all their programs and business endeavors, then and now, the Tribes have tried to create management training positions for tribal citizens and to secure commitments from non-Indian managers that they will train their future replacements. During this time, the Tribes laid the groundwork and created the departments, policies, and structures that created the successes to come.[29]

In the 1980s and 1990s, self-determination and careful tribal planning continued to produce more beneficial growth. The Tribes had created a housing program in 1966, and in the 1980s, with HUD assistance, they increased tribal housing on the reservation from 125 to 245 units. The 1980s also saw the development of a wide range of programs, laws, and policies including a tribal language program, a Head Start program, a market, a rural fire district, and expansion of the Yellowhawk health clinic. The Tribes also started a construction company, but it was not a success. The Tribes mark the start of their economic development from 1985 and the construction of a tribally owned grain elevator. This project provided the government with its first discretionary funding. Another major success from this period, which the Tribes can be very proud of, was the restoration in 1988 of salmon runs in the Umatilla River that had been extinct for nearly 70 years.[30]

The Tribes also adopted 10 significant projects in 1988 that were their priorities throughout the 1990s. Six of these projects were components of what became the Tribes' successful Wildhorse Resort and Casino complex. Moreover, in 1989, General Council Chairman Antone Minthorn suggested that all tribal employees meet to discuss all the projects then under consideration so that tribal enterprises and partners could learn about and help prioritize tribal goals. This meeting led to the Tribes hosting the first Indian Land Consolidation Conference, which ultimately spawned the creation of the Indian Land Working Group and the Indian Land Tenure Foundation. The Tribes also made the difficult decision to get involved in planning a commemoration of the 150th anniversary of the Oregon Trail. Some questioned why the Tribes would be interested; but they became involved because they wanted to tell their own history. They also insisted on being allowed to build on the reservation and to own one of the four Oregon Trail centers that would be constructed. The building that was completed in 1998, and which is owned and operated by the Tribes, is the Tamástslikt Cultural Institute. The institute has had a major impact in helping the Tribes and their citizens research, preserve, and practice their histories and cultures. It is also a tourist attraction and provides valuable jobs on the reservation.[31]

During this time, the Tribes operated a weekly bingo game and were carefully investigating a major investment in gaming. Ultimately, the Tribes opened the temporary Wildhorse Casino in November 1994 (in modular structures that later became tribal offices). This casino employed about 100 workers, 98 percent of whom were tribal citizens. This experience turned out to be very valuable for the Tribes because many of these citizens became the middle and upper management of the permanent casino when it opened in March 1995. Many citizens also stated that working in the casino was the first job they ever had that "they could think of as a career."[32] As of 2006, almost 90 percent of the casino department heads and managers were tribal citizens.[33]

The Wildhorse Resort and Casino has been a major economic boost for the Tribes and the region, and it has helped fuel other economic projects and the expansion of tribal programs and self-investment. The casino also helps the Tribes invest in their human capital because it employs and trains tribal citizens. Any CTUIR citizen who can hold down a job will be trained and employed at the casino. The complex also includes a hotel, an RV park, and an 18-hole golf course. The casino is currently being remodeled for the third time and has tripled in size, and the hotel is currently being remodeled for the second time and is being expanded. As of December 2008, the casino had 571 employees, of which 68 percent were non-Indians, 22 percent were CTUIR citizens, and 11 percent were citizens of other tribes. The total number of Umatilla citizens employed has fluctuated over the years from 1995 to 2008 and has ranged from an annual average of 103 to 162. But the percentage of tribal citizens employed has dropped over this time period from 44 percent to 22 percent, and the employment of non-Indians as a percentage has risen from 32 percent to 68 percent. This is a reflection of having more jobs to fill than tribal citizens to fill them. In addition, in 2001, the Tribes established the Wildhorse Foundation and give away 3 percent of their gaming revenues. As of January 2006, the foundation had given away nearly $2 million to local counties and organizations. These charitable donations and the employment of so many people, including hundreds of non-Indians, help fuel the economy of Pendleton and northeastern Oregon.[34]

Including gaming, the Tribes employed 1,297 people as of October 2008, with government administration employing 506, the Yellowhawk Clinic employing 76, the Housing Authority employing 18, and Cayuse Technology employing 114. Of this total, 54 percent were non-Indians, 33 percent were CTUIR citizens, and 13 percent were citizens of other tribes. In fact, the Tribes are the second-largest employer in Umatilla County after the state of Oregon. They are currently engaged in many other economic and governmental activities that contribute to improving their reservation and their region. The Tribes' economy consists today of agriculture, timber, livestock, technology, recreation, hunting, fishing, and a tribally owned market, gas station/truck stop, trailer court, and grain elevator. Moreover, the Tribes impose a utility tax on electricity, railroads, and pipelines that brings in around $1 million a year to help fund tribal government.[35]

All of this activity has produced results. The reservation was a beehive of activity on April 14, 2009, when I visited. Highway construction, paving the newly rebuilt tribally owned Arrowhead truck stop, the operation for one month of the first franchised business on the reservation, and the construction of the first tribal administration building caused a traffic jam. Traffic jams rarely happen on reservations due to economic development projects![36]

Business on the reservation is only going to expand further, because the Tribes have completed the infrastructure for a 530-acre business park on Highway I-84 and are looking for tenants. And the three-year-old Cayuse Technologies business is beginning to develop. This is a very promising venture in which the Tribes have partnered with Accenture to manage this tribally owned business. It currently employs over 100 people and engages in call center and document processing activities. It also offers free eight-hour employment training classes for Indians.[37]

An important part of the Tribes' culture has guided them to work cooperatively with their neighbors. In 1974, the Tribes drafted a joint land use zoning ordinance for the reservation with Umatilla County. They also worked with local farmers and irrigation districts in the 1980s effort to restore salmon in the Umatilla River. The joint effort succeeded in restoring fish runs and did not cost local farmers any water. The Tribes have also partnered with the Port of Umatilla, Eugene Oregon Water and Electric Board, and Diamond Generating to build a proposed gas-fired energy plant, and they are now working with Walla Walla, Washington, basin irrigators to restore salmon runs there. The Tribes have sought to deal fairly with all, even when their neighbors have sometimes appeared to resent having Indians at the negotiating table or when bigotry reared its ugly head. Tribal leaders work to build relationships with the leaders of Pendleton and northeast Oregon, and they clearly lay out their plans so that everyone can see the Tribes' intentions, and hopefully support them.[38]

The tribal leadership and the vast majority of citizens agree that the focus of the modern-day tribal organization has been to use the principles of planning to guide organizational, business, and policy-making decisions. They have gotten where they are by developing the tribal government and sophisticated self-governance. They agree that they would not have attained successful economic development, reduced unemployment from 40 percent to 20 percent, restored their river and land, and built the successful Wildhorse Resort and Tamastslikt Cultural Institute without tribal government.[39]

This economic success has led to the beneficial growth of the reservation community and preservation of cultural practices. A most promising example is that the Tribes can now afford to buy land on the open market. They have purchased 2,400 acres in western Umatilla County and 8,700 acres in Washington State and are buying back parcels of land on the reservation when they become available. What greater cultural and community benefit could a tribe engage in? Moreover, the livable wage jobs the Tribes can now offer are bringing Indian families home. In fact, there is a serious lack of middle class housing on the reservation. Tribal citizenship enrollment is increasing. It was 2,300 in 2002 and 2,536 in 2006, and about 1,200 tribal citizens live on or near the reservation. The Tribes can also now afford, and have the personnel and time, to offer more cultural programs, and every year they are able to restore more of their traditional knowledge. In 1994, they began a tribal language program and in 2004 started the Nixyaawii Community High School on the reservation. They also plan on opening middle and grade schools. In 2007, the Tribes' Department of Natural Resources took over BIA functions for forestry and rangelands, and they operate these programs consistent with tribal goals and cultural values. In 2009, the Tribes announced they would operate their lands and programs to protect their traditional first foods and to provide access to hunting, digging, and gathering lands.[40]

One final example demonstrates where the Tribes have been and where they are going. Their operating budget, which was apparently zero when they were broke in 1968–1970, was $1 million in 1990, $7.5 million in 1992, $16.7 million in 1996, $43.2 million in 1997 after the Tribes began operating the Yellowhawk Clinic and the Wildhorse Resort, $97 million in 2003, and $126 million by January 2006. That is an amazing and phenomenal growth.[41]

The Tribes now even have time and resources to research and write about their history, culture, and future. In 2006, they co-published an important book entitled *wiyaxayxt * as days go by * wiyaakaa?awn, Our History, Our Land, and Our People: The Cayuse, Umatilla, and Walla Walla*. I think it is a crucial step for tribes and Indian peoples to tell their own stories and to research and record these important matters for themselves in the scholarly media.

In this book, Chairman of the Board of Trustees Antone Minthorn wrote:

The CTUIR lost a tremendous amount of resources and culture . . . we can never go backward to make things right. That is done. It is over. The only way we are going to recover what we have lost of our original reservation promise is to move forward using the sovereign powers we have retained. . . . With it, we could make and implement our own plans to shape our own destiny without the interference of the BIA and other outside influences. We know the difference between oppression and freedom. . . . Our history is our strength. Our traditional cultures define us. . . . The best way to protect our culture is to learn and practice the teachings of the Indian ways. . . . The Treaty sesquicentennial [in 2005] is a victory celebration of survival for the Cayuse, Umatilla, and Walla Walla Tribes.[42]

## Eastern Shawnee Tribe of Oklahoma

The Eastern Shawnee Tribe is one of three federally recognized Shawnee tribes. The Shawnee people lived over several centuries in various areas in what is today Ohio, Kentucky, Pennsylvania, Tennessee, and South Carolina. It is accepted, however, that by 1650–1670 they were living in large numbers in what is now southern Ohio and northern Kentucky. Once major contact with Europeans commenced, the usual sequence of events occurred and Anglo-American encroachments on Shawnee lands and resources led to armed conflicts, treaties, and pressure on the Shawnee to move. Not surprisingly, a majority of Shawnee villages supported the French in the French and Indian War of 1754–1763, and then the British in the U.S. Revolutionary War and War of 1812. Like the vast majority of tribes, the Shawnee enjoyed trade with Euro-Americans, but they strenuously resisted the takeover of their lands and assets by Euro-American settlers.[43]

The traditional economy of the Shawnee people combined hunting with extensive agriculture, salt making, trade, and some wild food gathering. Men and women engaged in long hunting trips from their winter quarters, and men fished and trapped small fur-bearing animals while women primarily prepared the fields and planted crops near the larger towns the Shawnees occupied in spring, summer, and fall. Female chiefs from the town governments organized various feasts and directed the plantings. Interestingly, while the women worked collectively and assisted each other in farming, "each individual owned her own crops" and the fields "were owned by individual households" who had the "absolute rights to [their] products."[44] While hunting, men could leave deer or game hanging in trees with a piece of their clothing or some sign of ownership attached, and it would not be molested by others. Moreover, very valuable honey bee trees were claimed and protected as private property by the finder putting a mark of ownership on the tree. The Shawnee also utilized slaves for economic and household activities, and captives were often distributed as slaves according to the economic needs of tribal families. Moreover, they were salt makers and traded the excess of their production. From the early 1700s forward, many Shawnee also became involved in the European deerskin trade.[45]

Long before the Removal Era of federal Indian policy became official in 1830, and President Andrew Jackson began forcing tribes west of the Mississippi, many Shawnees voluntarily moved west to avoid Americans. Some left the Ohio area from 1763 to 1790, and crossed the Mississippi to settle near what is now Cape Girardeau, Missouri, and received Spanish land grants. In 1825, the United States established a reservation in what is now Kansas and moved the majority of Shawnees from Missouri and Ohio to this reservation. The Eastern Shawnee Tribe, however, was part of a mixed band of Seneca and Shawnee Indians who lived on their Lewistown, Ohio, reservation until they signed a treaty with the United States in 1831 and agreed to remove to the Indian Territory. The Tribe experienced its trail of tears during this removal in September–December 1832, because nearly 25 to 30 percent of its citizens died during the march.[46]

The Eastern Shawnee settled on the 20,000-acre Neosho Reservation in what is now northeastern Oklahoma. But in an 1867 treaty with the United States, they sold some of their land to make room for other tribes. Then, as part of the Allotment Era of federal Indian policy in the 1890s, the reservation was allotted to individual Shawnees and was ultimately lost from Indian ownership. Around 1937, the United States purchased 58 acres for the Eastern Shawnee Tribe under the new Oklahoma Indian Welfare Act. This piece of land was the entire extent of Eastern Shawnee territory until the Tribe made land purchases on its own in the 1980s and thereafter. The Tribe then organized its current government in 1939–1940 under a constitution and bylaws and is today governed by a chief, as the executive branch, a tribal business committee, as the legislative branch, and it uses a BIA court as its judicial branch. The Tribe is currently contemplating creating its own court system.[47]

Organized tribal economic activity was almost nonexistent from 1832 until the 1970s. In addition, due to the loss of the tribal land base after allotment, and the absence of economic opportunities in northeast Oklahoma, many Eastern Shawnees scattered across the country. Even after creating a tribal government in 1940, the Tribe had almost no resources and engaged in no economic activities until the late 1970s. The 58 acres sat unused. One ex-chief remembers his mother being on the tribal committee in the 1950s when the annual budget was $50. Chief George Captain, who was first elected to the business committee in 1946, stated that the committee met at the chief's home but that the Tribe had no money or assets and had very little business to conduct. Once, he even wrote a grant for $50 for stamps and then had to write several letters to Washington, D.C., to justify the grant.[48]

In January 1978, the Tribe distributed the first edition of a newsletter.[49] It was one page long and primarily reported that the Tribe had received a grant to build an industrial building on its 58 acres. The chief later warned, though, that it might be difficult to get a tenant and to find one who would employ as many tribal citizens as possible. He wrote: "However, time is on our side, as we have waited over two hundred years for some type of economic progress."[50] The chief was correct, and the building sat empty for nearly six years until the Tribe attempted bingo. The experience of the Tribe was not unusual. The federal government financed the construction of many tribal industrial parks and buildings in this time period, hoping to attract businesses to reservations, and most of them also sat empty for years.

In newsletters from 1978, Chief Captain reported that under an Indian Health Service grant the Tribe had created and was administering its own health department and had hired a manager and tribal citizens to survey tribal needs. Eastern Shawnees were also now eligible for U.S. Department of Housing and Urban Development assistance through the Cherokee Nation Housing Authority. The Tribe also received a $60,000 HUD grant to develop recreational facilities on its 58 acres. Today, there are powwow, picnic, and sports facilities on this land, including many tribal administration buildings, and a casino.[51]

In January 1979, total tribal funds were $4,465.16. So it was great news in February when the Tribe received a BIA training and assistance contract for $12,000.[52]

By 1984, the Tribe's industrial building was still vacant. The tribal government was moving ahead slowly using miniscule funding from the BIA and government programs and grants. But in that year, the Tribe was approached by a non-Indian who had just been fired from another tribe's bingo hall. He offered to fund and operate bingo for the Tribe in its empty commercial building. Tribal leaders decided to take the "gamble." Ultimately, bingo became the anchor business of the Tribe and the economic engine the Eastern Shawnees had been awaiting. Gaming and other projects initiated by the tribal council produced positive results. In April and May 1985, the chief reported that the bingo hall, which seated 750 people, was now open four nights a week and was doing well. The Tribe also finished construction of its fourth building on tribal land, a senior citizen center. The BIA Housing Improvement Program was also now available for tribal citizens. And the Tribe distributed a financial statement showing available funds of more than $45,000 at the close of fiscal year 1985 from bingo and various grants and programs. That was a significant improvement over the $50 budgets of the 1950s.[53]

In 1986, the tribal citizens showed their confidence in their government and made what I think was a wise decision. Instead of voting to disperse bingo profits in what are called per capita payments to each tribal citizen each year, the Tribe's General Council (all citizens 18 years of age and older) voted against receiving individual payments and instead voted to keep the bingo profits in the hands of the tribal government. The voters apparently intended that these funds be used to develop the Tribe, to create economic activities and jobs, and to serve the needs of the citizens. In 1996, the General Council again voted against per capita payments.[54]

In 1987, the tribal government took over the management of Eastern Shawnee Bordertown Bingo after troubles arose and profits declined. In 1989, the Tribe hired a tribal citizen, Danny Captain, and he successfully managed the bingo hall until 2005. In 2000, the Tribe moved the bingo hall from the 1979 industrial building (which had been expanded three times) into a new 57,000-square-foot bingo and casino facility.[55]

It is surprising to me that the Tribe's bingo and gaming operation has been so successful, because there are nine tribal casinos in Ottawa County, Oklahoma, today and the county is fairly rural. The Eastern Shawnee bingo and casino operation continued doing well in the economic downturn of 2008–2010, began rebounding in 2011, and has fared well against its competition for the past 20 years. Many tribal officials give much of the credit to the decision to keep operating a large bingo hall to cater to the longtime loyal customers of Bordertown Bingo even when the Tribe expanded in 2000 to its larger casino operation. In contrast, most of the other tribal casinos in the area gave up bingo to devote more floor space to video and casino games.[56]

The bingo operation has been the driving force for the expansion of tribal government and services for tribal citizens. In March 1986, for example, the Tribe bought 112 acres about five miles from tribal headquarters. This land lay fallow for many years, but in 1999 the Tribe built a gas station and convenience store there that also offered gaming. In late 2008, the Tribe opened its second casino in a brand-new building at this location and, using $4.8 million in various HUD grants, built three new buildings here in 2008–2009 to house tribal administration and new operations. The Tribe also built its first housing project of 11 single-family homes on this property with HUD funds in 1998. The Tribe still has about 200 acres at this location to develop, and it has the potential to become a real community for Eastern Shawnees. In addition, the Tribe acquired more land and in 2011 began building its third casino and first hotel.[57]

After the bingo operation was on solid footing, economic and governmental success in every sense of the word continued from there. This does not mean that there were no missteps or problems, but the tribal government, operating cautiously and carefully, built new programs, received new and expanded federal grants, and provided more and more services for tribal citizens. In January 1987, the Tribe started a library with one or two shelves of books, and that program has expanded to its own building today that also contains the beginnings of a tribal museum collection. In 1986, the Tribe hired its own community health representative. In 1988, tribal elders were provided with one hot meal a day in the senior center, 29 tribal citizens received college assistance, and a vision clinic was opened to serve tribal citizens and the public. In 1990, college textbook reimbursements and funeral assistance amounts were increased, and the Tribe began a women and children's feeding program. In 1993, the Tribe announced a new health and social service program for citizens, including school clothes, and expanded assistance with vision, dental, and prescription services, and tribal health care was provided through the Wyandotte Tribe's Bearskin Health Center. By 1994, day care services for working parents and federal vocational training programs were available for those who lived within 50 miles of tribal head-quarters. In 1996, the General Council approved expanded scholarship funds, and in 1997, the tribe created a housing authority that dedicated in 1998 the housing project for low-income tribal citizens mentioned above. In 1998, the Tribe budgeted $312,000 for social service programs, which was almost triple the year before. Into the twenty-first century, the Tribe continues to expand the reach of its social welfare and educational programs. The Tribe now provides significant college and trade school tuition and book reimbursements for tribal citizens.[58]

The Tribe also used its increased funding to develop its governance abilities. In May 1994, the Tribe allowed absentee voting for the first time and amended its constitution to be able to participate in the new federal Self-Governance program. In 1996, the Tribe became eligible for self-governance, signed a compact with the United States, and has assumed the operation of more and more federal Indian programs and funding.[59]

In 1996, the Tribe was one of the first investors in a new bank in Seneca, Missouri. Today, the Tribe owns 57 percent of the shares. Very few tribes in the United States own banks, and the Eastern Shawnee are one of only two or three tribes that acquired bank ownership through stock purchases. The People's National Bank of Seneca, Missouri, was especially profitable in 2004–2007 and the Tribe's investment in the bank more than doubled in value.[60]

The Eastern Shawnee Tribe's development has also helped the non-Indian community because it is the largest employer in its area, with about 660 employees. Tribal citizens only make up 4 percent of the employees, and another 8 percent of the employees are citizens of other tribes. Thus, 88 percent of the tribal employees are non-Indians. As a result, many of the benefits of tribal economic and governmental activities spill over to the surrounding non-Indian communities and governments, as these employees pay federal, state, and local taxes, and spend their money and live in non-Indian communities.

The Tribe is trying to increase the number of tribal citizens it employs. It has long had a training program and a hiring preference for tribal citizens. In 1989, the bingo operation employed 27 people, 17 of whom were tribal citizens. The Tribe needs to employ more of its citizens because, even though this figure is quite out of date, according to a 1997 BIA report, the Eastern Shawnee Tribe had a 23 percent unemployment rate among the 553 citizens who lived near tribal headquarters.[61]

With such a small land base, and such a widely dispersed population, it is perhaps unfair or unreasonable to expect the Tribe to create an economy that can benefit from the spending and re-spending of tribal monies by tribal citizens. Interestingly, however, in 1987, the chief wrote about trying to control leakage, the loss of grant funds and profits from the Tribe, its citizens, and the local area. He wanted to keep these funds in tribal hands as much as possible by giving jobs and grant opportunities to tribal citizens. That is an admirable goal for all tribes. It seems difficult, though, for the Tribe to keep its money within the tribal community since it still has such a small land base and so few of its people own private businesses. As of 2009, there were apparently only two tribal citizens who owned businesses in the Tribe's vicinity.[62]

Even in this situation, the Eastern Shawnee provide a good example for all tribal governments on how to keep tribal funds circulating within their government and community. The Eastern Shawnee have done this in one small way through operating a print shop. The Tribe has long had a separate print department as part of its government. The print shop has gotten so busy doing work for pay for the tribal casino and other jobs that it recently expanded, bought new machinery, and now employs two full-time people. This operation saves the casino and the Tribe significant amounts of money because, for example, it prints forms for the casino, the tribal newsletter, and other documents at one-quarter the cost of using retail printers. The print shop is even beginning to market itself to other tribes and customers. In this way, the tribal casino and government save money, the print shop makes money to supplement its governmental budget, the Tribe pays its money to tribal citizens/employees, and the money stays and circulates within the tribal community. This is a win-win situation for the Tribe, the casino, tribal employees, tribal citizens, and the tribal economy, even on a reservation that until relatively recently was only 58 acres in size.[63]

The tribal leadership has also carefully managed its ever-increasing gaming profits. In March 1987, it reported to tribal citizens a $250,000 profit from bingo and grants in the prior fiscal year. By July 1994, the Tribe's investment portfolio had a balance of $2.4 million, and in fiscal year 1995, bingo had a net profit of over $1 million. As of 2009, the Tribe had over $100 million invested in stocks and bonds.[64]

In the past decade, the tribal government has continued to produce steady growth and profits from the bingo/casino operation and its programs. As all careful investors do, the leadership is attempting to diversify, grow, and protect its investments and at the same time to increase tribal citizen employment opportunities. In 2004, the Tribe bought a small cabinet company and employed nine people in a 22,000-square-foot facility. It has now sold that venture. In 2009, the Tribe purchased a large wholesale tire distributor that worked in six states and had warehouses in Kansas, Georgia, and Texas. The company had been in business about 50 years and employed 58 people. The Tribe continues to operate and grow that business.[65]

The successes that the Eastern Shawnee Tribe has created are phenomenal when you consider the tribal budget of $50 in the 1950s–1960s and the absence of any economic activity except for an empty industrial building from 1978–1984. This Tribe demonstrates what tribal governments can accomplish with careful, conservative planning, and by using the governmental and sovereign advantages available to tribal nations.

# Hoopa Valley Tribe

The Hoopa Tribe is one of California's oldest cultures. Tribal history states that the Hupa (Hoopa) came into existence where they are today, along the Trinity River in northern California. First contact with Americans began in 1828. Subsequently, in 1864 the Tribe signed a peace and friendship treaty with the United States, but it was never ratified by the Senate and thus never became effective. The unratified 1864 treaty required Hoopa people to obtain a pass from the BIA agent to be allowed to leave their reservation. They also would have been required to surrender their guns and ammunition, which they could only get back temporarily for hunting purposes. The "squaws" would have been taught how "to make their own clothing, take proper care of their children, and become generally efficient in household duties."[66]

In 1864, the California superintendent for Indian Affairs issued an order creating the Hoopa Valley Reserve under the authority of Congress and instructions from the Department of Interior. In 1876, President Grant issued an executive order describing the boundaries of the Hoopa Valley Indian Reservation as encompassing 89,572 acres of land and as "set apart for Indian purposes,"[67] and President Benjamin Harrison enlarged the reservation in 1891. But in 1896, the Department of the Interior began planning to allot the reservation and, in 1909, President Theodore Roosevelt issued a proclamation to do so. Only about 5 percent of the land was ultimately allotted, and today 2 percent of the reservation is owned by Hoopa Indians in fee simple and about 3 percent is owned in fee simple by non-Indians while the Tribe still owns 95 percent of the reservation in trust with the United States. Today, the reservation consists of 96,000 acres, about 50 percent of the aboriginal territory of the Hoopa.[68]

The traditional economic life of the Hoopa consisted of semiannual salmon runs, which still occur in the Trinity River on the reservation, and hunting and gathering of wild foods, particularly acorns. Both salmon and acorns are still very important for subsistence and as ceremonial foods. The Tribe uses these foods to practice world renewal ceremonies, such as the White Deer Skin Dance, which help to heal the world.

According to the 2000 census, 2,633 people lived on the reservation, which included 403 non-Indians. A 1997 BIA report stated that 1,893 Hoopa, 337 other Indians, and 400 non-Indians lived on the reservation. The statistics also show that there is an enormous need for economic activity and jobs at Hoopa. According to the BIA report, 40 percent of the Hoopas who lived on or near the reservation, who were available to work, were unemployed. Furthermore, the 2000 census showed that 40.5 percent of the families living on the reservation were below the poverty line.[69]

The reservation is very remote, and that raises many issues regarding attracting economic activities and jobs. As the chairman told me, it is a 75-mile drive to see a movie or get takeout food. Most families make monthly shopping trips to Eureka, an hour and a half away, to shop at the large discount stores. Thus, valuable economic activity and the "multiplier effect" of circulating dollars on the reservation that could occur at Hoopa is lost to non-Indian communities. It's lost, of course, because there are few businesses on the reservation where consumers can buy the variety of goods they need at the lowest prices.[70]

The Hoopa Tribe has done a great job in the past couple of decades of creating and building economic activity. As of 2009, the Tribe had a $75 million annual budget, which is double the budget of a decade ago. It is made up primarily of tribal businesses, and the Tribe contracting and operating all federal BIA and Indian Health Service (IHS) programs directed at Hoopa, and some Bureau of Reclamation programs. The Tribe has been very proactive in this regard, and it has led to beneficial effects for the reservation and its citizens.[71]

The tribal businesses and governmental agencies that are directly involved in economic development activities include a small casino that employs about 42 people, a motel with 20 rooms, a campground, a gas station/mini market, and Hoopa Forest Industries, which harvests roughly 12 million board feet annually and provides the Tribe with about $4 to $6 million in annual revenue. In addition, the tribal government mines gravel from its river to operate Hoopa Roads Aggregate and Ready Mix. That entity builds logging roads and maintains reservation roads with federal funding and sells gravel, asphalt, and cement to the county, other tribes, and private customers. This business made a $900,000 profit in 2008. The Tribe leases buildings to a medium-sized franchise grocery store, to the county for a courthouse and holding facility, and to the United States Post Office. In addition, the Tribe built a major modular home construction plant, Xontah Builders, and hopes to sell homes to its own housing department, other tribal housing departments, and private customers. The housing and credit crisis of 2008–2010 seriously impacted that enterprise.[72]

The reservation also has a small private business economy. There are three cafés, a laundromat, a credit union, fishing, farming, and office supply stores, a nursery, a salmon packing business, a computer store, and a smoke shop. There is also some private agriculture on the reservation including growing hay and grapes, and five families raise cattle. As in every community, there is also an informal private economy. There are mechanics who make house calls and many tribal artisans work from home and are promoted on the tribal webpage. All these activities help to create a small-scale economy and contribute towards creating a viable place where individuals and families can live and thrive.[73]

There is much to learn from this brief overview of the major economic activities that American Indian tribes are successfully pursuing today, and from our closer examination of the history and modern-day activities of three specific tribes. This review helps us see what is working for these tribes and their people in their specific situations, and how they have accomplished remarkable economic, community, and cultural development in the past three to five decades.

In my opinion, the Eastern Shawnee Tribe has created significant economic activities and community development and has begun to build a better life and future for its citizens. It appears that the Bordertown Bingo operation that commenced in 1984 was the catalyst for the amazing success and development that has occurred in the past 27 years and the phenomenal building and expansion program the Tribe is creating at this time in a relatively rural Oklahoma county.

The Confederated Tribes of the Umatilla Indian Reservation have also profited significantly from gaming. But they had been building towards success for over two decades before they launched casino gaming in 1994. The Tribes had drafted their own constitution and developed their governmental and bureaucratic systems through careful, cautious, and extensive planning. They created the groundwork and a workforce that could successfully launch a major casino project and other programs and initiatives the tribes have introduced in the past 30 years. The Tribes have succeeded in rural northeastern Oregon. Their successes, and their position as the number two employer in their county, demonstrate the importance of the Tribes' economic initiatives to themselves, their citizens, and all the people of their region.

The Hoopa Tribe has also had a great success in a very remote and rural county with a small population base. The Tribe could not use gaming as the primary driver of its economic development. It had to develop other projects and economic activities to create jobs on its reservation. As the tribal chairman stated, they do not have the "cash cow" of gaming to rely on. Thus, the Hoopa have taken advantage of the federal laws of 1975 and 1994 and been very aggressive in taking over every federal program and job they could. The Tribe's annual budget is now $75 million and has doubled in the past decade. Taking over federal programs has worked to a great extent for the Hoopa. It also appears that they have entered the private business world to a far greater extent than have Eastern Shawnee and Umatilla citizens. To my knowledge, this is not because entrepreneurship is more natural for Hoopas than it is for Eastern Shawnees and Umatillas, but it might instead be an accident of history and location and something that was nearly forced on the Hoopas. In contrast, the Eastern Shawnee lands are immediately adjacent to Missouri towns and in an Oklahoma county with several fair-sized towns. The Umatilla Reservation is just five miles from a city of 16,000. These different situations have led these tribes to approach economic development in different ways.

Notwithstanding the different histories, cultures, and situations of tribal governments and communities across the United States, there is one thing almost every single one of them needs. They need to bring beneficial economic development to their reservations and their people. They need to use whatever tools and advantages are at their disposal.

# CHAPTER 5

# *Tribal Gaming*

T he most successful economic endeavor in Indian Country in the modern day is tribal gaming. Gaming tribes earned gross receipts of $5.4 billion in 1995, $11 billion in 2000, $19.5 billion in 2004, and in 2008 Indian gaming took in $26.7 billion. With the economic downturn in 2009 Indian gaming revenues fell for the first time in history by almost 2 percent to $26.2 billion. It is worth noting that most of the money that tribes in general take in as gaming revenues is earned primarily by a small number of tribes who are located closest to major metropolitan areas. In addition, only about 225 out of 565 federally recognized tribes nationwide operated gaming facilities in 2007. Consequently, the enormous benefits earned from tribal gaming have primarily benefited a relatively few tribes and their citizens.[1]

In fact, a 1999 study showed that the 20 largest Indian gambling facilities accounted for 50.5 percent of the total tribal gaming income and that the next 85 largest tribal operations accounted for only 41.2 percent of the total income. That percentage probably still holds true in 2011–2012. In 1996, a federal study showed that just eight tribes took in more than 50 percent of the total income earned by Indian gaming nationwide.[2]

The benefits from Indian gaming also spill over to non-Indian communities and to federal and state tax revenues. In 2007, tribes directly employed more than 670,000 Americans in 28 different states in their gaming enterprises, 75 percent of whom were non-Indians. Data also shows that Indian gaming indirectly creates many thousands of other jobs and billions of dollars of economic benefits in the states they are located. One commentator estimated that in 2005 the total direct benefit to state and local governments from Indian gaming was $8 billion and that Indian gaming directly and indirectly contributed $60.1 billion in output for the

U.S. economy, $22.1 billion in wages, 591,000 jobs, and $6.9 billion in tax revenues to the national economy. Furthermore, studies in 2003 show that state and local governments received approximately $1.5 billion in tax revenues from Indian gaming. A 2001 study in Idaho showed that tribal gaming created approximately 4,500 jobs in that state, $84 million in wages, and $11 million in state property and sales tax revenues. In addition, reservation unemployment dropped from 70 percent to near zero for some of the Idaho tribes, and state payments for public welfare entitlements declined by over $6 million annually. The diversification of tribal gaming also created another 850 Idaho jobs, which resulted in another $2 million in state property and sales taxes. Moreover, a Harvard study of Indian gaming concluded that in 2000, just one particular type of gaming in Oklahoma had a regional impact of $329 million, created 8,100 jobs (25% of which were held by non-Indians), and added $14 million to the state treasury.[3]

Older statistics also demonstrate the benefits Indian gaming has created for non-Indians and non-Indian communities. In Oregon, the Grand Ronde Tribe's casino hired 1,200 employees in 1995, its first year of operation, 1,000 of whom were non-Indians. Of the tribe's new employees, 46 percent had been unemployed, 35 percent had been on welfare, and 42 percent had lacked health insurance. In Wisconsin, the gaming tribes also had a valuable impact on the state economy. Gaming employed 18,000 workers, half of whom had been unemployed and 20 percent of whom had been on welfare, added $1 billion to the state's gross domestic product, and increased per capita state income and sales taxes. These positive developments also created significant decreases in the level of state aid Wisconsin paid for child and unemployment programs, and decreases in crime levels. And in Minnesota, Indian gaming was the state's seventh-largest industry and created more than 10,000 jobs directly and another 20,000 jobs indirectly.[4]

Gaming has been even more financially valuable for Indian communities. The BIA regularly reports that the average unemployment rate on all reservations is 40 percent. Many reservations suffer from unbelievably high rates of unemployment, as much as 70 to 90 percent. The great news for tribes and Indian people is that unemployment on some reservations is now near 0 percent because of gaming jobs. In fact, gaming has had its most important impact on joblessness on reservations where unemployment has traditionally been the highest. In North and South Dakota, 80 percent of tribal gaming employees are Indians, and they are gaining employment experiences that have never been available on their reservations until now. These jobs and new economic activities have brought Indian families home to live on their reservations now that they can support their families there. This is a very positive result for Indian nations and their peoples and cultures. Consequently, these positive economic developments created by tribal nations have benefited their own people and via the spillover effect have also helped the often rural areas around reservations and states and the federal government as a whole.[5]

## HISTORY

American Indian societies engaged in gaming activities as traditional and cultural pursuits and for pleasure for hundreds of years and more. Before contact with Europeans, Native American peoples gamed to settle disputes, for entertainment, for profits, and in specific ceremonies. Traditional tribal gambling activities also had cultural roots in creation stories and myths, and these foundations provided sacred circumstances to the games and frequently taught moral lessons. In the modern day, Indians continue to engage in traditional social games of chance like hand and stick games and horse racing events, all of which are usually held at powwows on most reservations.[6]

## *EARLY ATTEMPTS AT TRIBAL GAMING*

In the mid-twentieth century, as economic conditions in Indian Country continued to be dismal, tribal governments became desperate to try anything to bring jobs and prosperity to their citizens. Some tribes attempted gaming at that time, but this was risky because under federal law gambling was illegal in Indian Country. Some federal criminal prosecutions ensued.

States also began to look to gaming for revenue, partially because, as has been noted, gambling is "as American as apple pie." New Hampshire apparently started the first state lottery in the modern era in 1964. In the 1960s and early 1970s, several tribes in Florida, New York, California, and Wisconsin also pursued this opportunity and opened high-stakes bingo parlors. The Seminole Tribe of Florida is recognized as the first tribe to successfully defeat efforts to close its bingo operation and to begin to earn significant amounts of money from bingo. As that endeavor boomed, and especially after a federal court approved the Seminole operation, other tribes also began offering high-stakes bingo.[7]

Federal officials also began to notice the potential for tribes to make substantial profits from gaming. This opportunity could serve several federal interests. The United States has for at least 80 years attempted to help tribes with economic activity and to help their citizens get out of poverty. The United States also supports tribal economic development to help strengthen tribal governments. Therefore, to serve these interests, and perhaps to lessen the federal burden to support tribes, between 1979 and the mid-1980s, the U.S. Department of the Interior and the BIA began funding tribal bingo facilities.[8]

In the 1970s and still today, almost all tribal governments lack a viable tax base and they struggle to find funding to operate governmental services and social welfare programs. It is no surprise that tribes and the federal government, just like the states, began to look at gaming as a resource. And the results turned out to be spectacular for some tribes. Indian gaming has grown since its humble beginnings around 1979 to 2005, for example, when 225 federally recognized Indian tribes conducted gaming operations at 366 locations in 30 states. The gross receipts have grown exponentially from $200 million in 1988 to more than $26 billion in 2009.[9]

## STATE RESPONSE

Many state officials looked askance at tribes conducting gaming. Tribal and state governments have a long relationship of mutual suspicion and often conflicting interests. States were offended, perhaps, by gaming activities being conducted within their borders without their permission or regulation, and they were primarily worried about tribal competition with state lotteries, racetracks, and other gaming endeavors designed to raise state revenues. States began to resist Indian gaming. Tribes looked to the federal courts and the federal government to protect their sovereign rights to offer gambling on reservations free from state control.

# Butterworth

As sovereign governments, tribes assumed that they had the political authority over their territories to operate gaming free of state control. State officials disagreed. In 1979, the sheriff of Broward County, Florida, took exception to the high-stakes bingo hall of the Seminole Tribe and threatened to make arrests on tribal lands for violations of state gambling laws. The Seminole Tribe filed suit, *Seminole Tribe of Florida v. Butterworth*, in federal court for a declaratory judgment that state law did not apply on its reservation.[10]

Sheriff Bob Butterworth argued that Congress had directed that state law applied on Indian reservations. He pointed to Public Law 280, enacted in 1953, in which Congress had extended some states' criminal and civil laws into Indian Country. He alleged that Florida's "criminal" gambling laws applied in Indian Country and prevented the Seminole Tribe from offering high-stakes bingo since that was illegal under Florida law.

It appears that if the state's gambling laws had truly been criminal laws that they would have applied on the Seminole Reservation because of Public Law 280. Consequently, in 1981, the federal Fifth Circuit Court of Appeals had to decide whether Florida's bingo statutes were criminal laws that prohibited all gaming in Florida or whether they were really just civil laws that only regulated bingo. This question had to be answered because the U.S. Supreme Court had already narrowly interpreted the Public Law 280 grant of state civil law authority in Indian Country in *Bryan v. Itasca County*. In *Bryan*, the Court held that the application of state civil law in Indian Country did not mean that all of a state's civil laws applied on reservations. Instead, the application of state civil laws only meant that individual Indians and non-Indians in a Public Law 280 state could use the state courts for lawsuits and could apply the general common law of the state, such as the law of torts and contracts, in their private lawsuits. Consequently, if Florida's gaming laws were only civil laws and only regulated but did not outlaw bingo, then they would not apply in Indian Country under the *Bryan* case.[11]

Sheriff Butterworth argued that the Florida statutes provided jail sentences for violations and that made them criminal laws and thus they applied in Indian Country under Public Law 280. But many state laws that no one would ever claim are criminal can lead to prison sentences if a person repeatedly violates them. The federal court did not accept the sheriff's argument and instead relied on a test developed by another federal court to determine whether a law is a "criminal" law or a "civil" law under Public Law 280. The Ninth Circuit Court of Appeals had defined a criminal law as one that completely prohibits certain conduct and a civil law as being a law that only regulates an activity while still allowing the conduct under certain circumstances. After applying this test, the Fifth Circuit held that since Florida's bingo laws allowed and only regulated that conduct they were not criminal laws, because they did not completely prohibit that conduct. Since Florida's bingo laws were only civil laws, they did not apply in Indian Country under Public Law 280 and the Supreme Court's *Bryan v. Itasca County* case. The Seminole bingo hall could continue to operate without state regulation or control.

Similar issues arose in other states as tribes across the country began to offer high-stakes bingo. States filed lawsuits and brought criminal prosecutions to oppose Indian gaming. The states won a few of these cases under their specific facts, but other federal courts agreed with the *Butterworth* analysis and did not let states like California and Wisconsin use Public Law 280 to enforce state bingo laws in Indian Country. As a result of these victories and federal policies supporting the sovereign authority of tribal governments to offer gaming, the activity and the controversies continued to grow.

## *California v. Cabazon Band of Mission Indians*

States continued to oppose tribal gaming because it competed with state lotteries and other gambling operations such as horse and dog tracks, and because states were envious of the independent tribal sovereigns operating gaming operations inside state borders. State governments also claimed to be worried about organized crime becoming involved in high-stakes tribal bingo. The issue finally reached the U.S. Supreme Court in 1987 in *California v. Cabazon Band of Mission Indians.*[12]

In *Cabazon*, the Supreme Court affirmed the Ninth Circuit Court of Appeals decision that California's gambling laws did not apply on the Cabazon and Morongo Reservations. The Court used three different lines of analysis. First, it adopted the test that the Ninth Circuit had devised to decide when state laws apply in Indian Country under Public Law 280. The Ninth Circuit, and now the U.S. Supreme Court, used a "criminal/prohibitory" and "civil/regulatory" analysis to determine when a state law is actually a criminal law and applies on a reservation under Public Law 280. In this case, the Ninth Circuit, as the Fifth Circuit had done in *Butterworth*, agreed that state laws that govern and control bingo but allow it to some degree are not laws that absolutely prohibit and criminalize bingo. Hence, they are not criminal laws and do not apply on reservations. Instead, laws like these are only regulatory, civil laws that do not apply on reservations according to the Supreme Court's 1976 *Bryan v. Itasca County* case. The U.S. Supreme Court in *Cabazon* agreed that California's laws only regulated bingo and thus they were civil laws that did not apply on reservations.

Second, the Court also looked at public policy issues and concluded that tribal bingo was not against the public policy of California since the state allowed bingo, hundreds of card rooms, a state lottery, and pari-mutuel horse and dog racing. Obviously, California could not claim with a straight face that its public policy did not allow gaming.

Third, the Court also seemed to engage in a balancing test, known as the pre-emption test in federal Indian law, to determine the comparative weight of the state's interests versus the federal and tribal interests to determine whether the application of state law in Indian Country was preempted in this instance. The Court noted that tribal economic development was an important federal and tribal interest and that creating jobs and economic activities on the Cabazon and Morongo Reservations was of the highest interest to the tribal and federal governments. The state interest, on the other hand, amounted to nothing more than an attempt to prevent competition for state gaming and a desire to tax Indian gaming. The Supreme Court concluded that the federal and tribal interests heavily outweighed the state's interest. In sum, this case was an enormous victory for Indian nations on every level. The Court held that states, even states where Public Law 280 applied, could not control or regulate Indian gaming because tribes are sovereign governments that have the exclusive right to authorize and regulate that activity in their territories.[13]

After the *Cabazon* decision, tribal gaming was apparently legal in all 50 states unless the gaming violated a state's public policy or was conducted in a Public Law 280 state whose criminal laws absolutely prohibited gaming. Tribes were delighted with this victory and its affirmation of tribal sovereignty. Most states, though, were dismayed at the prospect of an expansion of Indian gaming.

As the states feared, an enormous expansion is exactly what happened after the Seminole Tribe's victory in *Butterworth* in 1981 and the Cabazon and Morongo Tribes' victory in the Supreme Court in 1987. The Department of the Interior estimated in 1985 that about 80 tribes were then offering gaming on their reservations and that some tribes were grossing nearly $1 million a month. The growth of Indian gaming surged even more after *Cabazon*.[14]

## CONGRESSIONAL AND STATE ATTEMPTS TO CONTROL INDIAN GAMING

States were working diligently even before the *Cabazon* case to rein in Indian gaming. Several bills were introduced in Congress from 1983 forward to regulate tribal gambling, and congressional hearings were held. States urged Congress to control Indian gaming to protect state interests and to prevent organized crime from infiltrating Indian Country. Most tribes opposed any federal or state regulation of their gaming.[15]

While *Cabazon* was making its way through the courts, and especially while it was pending before the U.S. Supreme Court, many tribal advocates feared that the Court would rule for the state. Consequently, some tribes supported the idea of federal regulation of tribal gaming during this time instead of any form of state regulation. After the tribal victory, however, most tribes did not support even federal regulation of Indian gaming. In contrast, now that the states had lost *Cabazon*, they clamored for a congressional solution to what they said was a mistake by the Court. Congress listened to the states. In line with what Congress had already been considering, it enacted the Indian Gaming Regulatory Act (IGRA) on October 17, 1988. The IGRA represents Congress's attempt to compromise between tribal, state, and federal interests. In light of the tribal victory in *Cabazon*, though, IGRA looked like a defeat for tribal interests, a partial rollback of the *Cabazon* decision, and a compromise that favored states. As we will see, IGRA has definitely proved to be a victory for the states in the ensuing two decades.[16]

State power over federal legislators, state fear of competition from tribal gaming, and the absence of state jurisdiction over Indian gaming surely played a large role in the creation of IGRA. But Congress certainly did not state these factors as reasons for enacting IGRA. Instead, Congress noted the spread of Indian gaming, the federal government's ongoing involvement, and that federal law did not yet possess clear standards for tribes to conduct gaming. Congress also stated that a principal goal of federal Indian policy is to promote tribal economic development and self-sufficiency, and that tribes already possessed the authority to offer gaming on their lands if the activity was not specifically prohibited by federal law, and was conducted in a state that did not as a matter of criminal law or public policy prohibit the gaming activity.[17]

The IGRA is an extensive and detailed law. Importantly, it makes clear that only tribal governments can own and operate gaming activities and they can only be conducted in Indian Country. Congress also waived the application of several federal laws that previously prohibited gambling in Indian Country. Congress attempted to fine-tune a compromise between tribal, federal, and state interests and appears to have been pretty fair in balancing these interests. As discussed below, however, subsequent events have skewed IGRA in favor of the states. Today, state governments exercise a much stronger role over tribal gaming than Congress appears to have intended in the IGRA.[18]

## Class I Gaming

Congress divided Indian gaming into three classes. Class I gaming is defined as "social games solely for prizes of minimal value or traditional forms of Indian gaming."[19] This class covers gaming that was conducted in the past as ceremonial or traditional tribal activities, and games that are played for minimal prizes and stakes. The Senate report on IGRA noted that this would include traditional horse racing, and stick or bone games that are usually played at ceremonies and pow-wows. A treatise on Indian law written by the attorneys general of several western states suggests that Class I gaming could be almost any type of gambling as long as it is played for low stakes. Class I gaming is not subject to IGRA or state control. The games are regulated only by the tribal government where the gaming occurs. Class I gaming has raised almost no issues to date.[20]

# Class II Gaming

Class II gaming is defined as bingo and games such as pull tabs and tip jars, and includes non-banked card games that are conducted in compliance with state law. Non-banked card games are where the house just provides a dealer and a table and chairs but the players, in poker for example, only play against the other players at the table and not against the house.[21]

Under IGRA, Congress intended to give tribes maximum flexibility from state control in using Class II gaming to foster tribal and reservation economic development. But at the same time, IGRA provided for extensive federal regulation of Class II games. In fact, IGRA created the National Indian Gaming Commission (NIGC) to regulate this class of Indian gaming. The NIGC costs federal taxpayers nothing because it is funded by fees paid by all tribal Class II and Class III gaming operations. The NIGC's primary role is to oversee, monitor, and inspect tribal Class II operations. States are not supposed to have any role in Class II gaming because this activity is to be directly regulated only by the tribal and federal governments. But IGRA does limit tribes in Class II gaming somewhat because they are expressly limited in how they can spend the revenues generated, and they must provide outside annual audits, contract audits, and perform employee background checks. In contrast, Congress does not interfere, regulate, or control how states operate and use their lottery and gaming programs and revenues.[22]

There are two important conditions placed on tribal Class II gaming. Although there is supposed to be no direct state regulation, state law still controls whether a tribe can offer Class II gambling on its own reservation because it can only be "located within a state that permits such gaming for any purpose"[23] and the tribe's governing body has to have adopted a gaming ordinance that is approved by the chairman of the NIGC. Also pursuant to IGRA, a tribe must issue licenses for each class II gaming establishment and the NIGC monitors the gaming unless a tribe has been issued a certificate of self-regulation.[24]

Tribes do not, however, have to operate their Class II games in the exact same manner as the states where they are located. Most courts have held that if the state allows Class II gaming in any form, then tribes can offer Class II gaming through similar games and even in different formats. The western attorneys general *Indian Law Deskbook* interprets this provision liberally in favor of tribes and notes that all Class II games are permissible unless state law explicitly prohibits them. But it must be noted that IGRA does require that non-banked card games have to be "played in conformity with those laws and regulations (if any) of the State regarding hours or periods of operation of such card games or limitations on wagers or pot sizes in such card games."[25] And, as already mentioned, while states cannot regulate tribal Class II gaming, they do have the ultimate word on whether a tribe can offer Class II gaming. If a state does not allow any kind of Class II gaming, then tribes within that state cannot offer any type of Class II gaming either. Thus, in Utah and Hawaii, which are the only states to ban all forms of gambling, Indian tribes cannot offer Class II gaming. Consequently, state law does play a role even in Class II tribal gaming.[26]

Interestingly, in this computer age, Congress provided that Class II games can be conducted with technological aids. Many Class II machines and Class II tribal casinos today are difficult to distinguish from full-scale Class III casinos. Tribes and gaming machine manufacturers have pushed this issue by developing new machines that have sometimes been called in jest "Class II and a half" devices. Congress made this a very complicated issue by stating that Class II gaming can include electronic video or computer versions of Class II games and that they can be played with "electronic computer, or other technologic aids," but that they cannot be games that are "electronic or electromechanical facsimiles of any game of chance or slot machines of any kind."[27] Language like that is bound to lead to litigation, and this provision has done so. For example, one case held that computerized electronic pull tab machines were illegal because they were facsimiles of the regular pull tab game and were not just a technological aid to play the regular game. Thus, the machines were Class III machines. In ruling on some of these cases the federal courts appear to have forgotten that Congress wanted tribes to "have maximum flexibility to utilize games such as bingo and lotto" and that they should not be limited to "existing . . . technology."[28] Two commentators have noted that if an electronic device merely facilitates the ability of multiple players to play a game, with or against each other, then it is not a facsimile of a game and is not a Class III machine but it is just a technological aid for playing the regular game and is a Class II machine.[29]

The NIGC is heavily involved in overseeing and regulating Class II gaming. For example, the NIGC issued Class II minimum internal control standards in 1999, and amended them in 2002 and 2005. The NIGC chairman also has to review and approve all tribal Class II management contracts. Most tribes used management contracts when they were new to gaming and hired experienced companies to manage their bingo halls and gaming operations. Under IGRA, these contracts cannot normally exceed five years, but they can be granted for up to seven years if the NIGC chairman is satisfied that it is necessary. Also, the fees charged by management companies cannot normally exceed 30 percent of tribal gaming revenues, but they may go to 40 percent if the chairman approves.[30]

## Class III Gaming

IGRA also regulates full-scale Las Vegas-style casino gambling in Indian Country. Class III gaming is defined as "all forms of gaming that are not class I gaming or class II gaming."[31] Class III includes games like slot machines, roulette, craps, and house-banked card games like blackjack, and electronic machines that are facsimiles of these games. Class III gaming is usually where most of the action and the big money are found.

IGRA provides three conditions before a tribe can offer Class III gaming. The first condition is unremarkable; the gaming must be authorized under a tribal ordinance approved by the NIGC chairman. The second and third conditions, however, have led to extensive litigation and conflicts. The second condition requires that before a tribe can offer Class III gaming, the state where the tribal activity is located must permit "such gaming for any purpose."[32] And, third, the gaming must be conducted in accordance with procedures set out in a tribal-state compact approved by the secretary of the interior or be conducted under procedures imposed by the secretary following a state's refusal to negotiate a gaming compact in good faith with a tribe.[33]

IGRA also requires tribes to use their gaming revenues for only five purposes:

1. to fund tribal governmental operations or programs;
2. to provide for the general welfare of the tribe and its citizens;
3. to promote tribal economic development;
4. to donate to charitable organizations; and,
5. to fund the operations of local government agencies.

Under these provisions many tribes have very generously set up funds to distribute tribal gaming revenues to charitable programs and governments in their regions. The Confederated Tribes of the Grand Ronde Community in Oregon, for example, created the Spirit Mountain Community Fund in 1997 and have given away more than $54 million as of 2011 from casino revenues to local governments and nonprofit organizations.[34]

IGRA also allows tribes to pay out all or part of their gaming profits to tribal citizens on a per capita basis. This option is better known as "per cap payments." Only 25 percent of the 225 American Indian nations that operate Class II or Class III gaming operations currently make per cap payments of all or some of their gaming profits. The other 75 percent of gaming tribes do not make per cap payments. Instead, all of the gaming profits are retained by those tribal governments like taxes and are used to operate their governmental and social welfare programs, and to engage in long-term investment, economic diversification, and land repurchases. IGRA requires tribes considering per cap payments to prepare a plan that must be approved by the secretary of the interior before distributions can commence. The distributions to individual tribal citizens are taxed by the federal government and by states too in certain circumstances.[35]

## "Such Gaming"

IGRA requires that a state permit "such gaming" before a tribe can offer Class III games. There have been major battles over the definition of this phrase and the question of whether a tribe can offer a different type of Class III gaming when a state offers some Class III gaming in general but not the particular type of Class III game that a tribe wants to offer. The U.S. Courts of Appeals for the Eighth and Ninth Circuits have very narrowly defined the term "such gaming." The Ninth Circuit held that California only had to negotiate with tribes to allow the exact types of Class III games that the state allowed; it did not have to allow tribes to conduct all games that fell within the general category of Class III gaming. The Eighth Circuit reached this same decision. One Ninth Circuit judge dissented vigorously from this restrictive definition and to limiting tribes only to the specific type of Class III games that a state allows.[36] Tribes and states usually avoid this conflict today by expressly defining the kinds of games a tribe can offer in the tribal-state compacts mandated by IGRA for Class III gaming.

## Tribal-State Compacts

IGRA also requires tribes to enter compacts with states before they can conduct Class III gaming. Congress tried to balance state and tribal interests and provided for negotiated and shared state and tribal regulation and jurisdiction over Class III gambling, with a minimum of federal oversight. The Senate report on IGRA viewed the compact approach as the "best mechanism to assure that the interests of both sovereign entities are met with respect to the regulation of complex gaming enterprises."[37] In fact, a tribal-state Class III compact may include provisions on the application of state criminal and civil laws to the gaming; the allocation of criminal and civil jurisdiction between state and tribe; the assessment of state fees to defray its costs of regulating compact activities; remedies for breaches of contract; standards for operating the gaming and tribal facility; and any other subject directly related to the operation of Class III gaming.[38]

While IGRA gave states a major role in Class III tribal gaming, Congress also attempted to protect tribes in the compact negotiations from being held hostage by a state. Therefore, as part of Congress's attempt to balance tribal and state interests, IGRA requires that states negotiate Class III compacts in good faith. When a tribe requests a state to negotiate a compact, states are required to negotiate, and are required to negotiate in good faith, and if they do not then tribes were given the remedy to file a federal lawsuit against the state for failure to negotiate or to negotiate in good faith. IGRA even put the burden of proof on the state, who would be the defendant in these suits, to prove it had negotiated in good faith. This provision helped the Mashantucket Pequot Tribe in 1990 in its suit versus Connecticut to open Foxwoods, the largest casino in the world. State interests were also protected because they are allowed to sue tribes to enforce the terms of a compact.[39]

The process for a Class III compact begins with a tribal request to a state to negotiate. If the state does not negotiate or the tribe feels the state is negotiating in bad faith, the tribe is authorized to bring a lawsuit in federal district court against the state. If the court agrees that the state has not negotiated or has negotiated in bad faith, the court orders the parties to reach a compact within 60 days. If they do not, the court appoints a mediator and directs the parties to submit their last best offers for a compact to the mediator. The mediator then chooses the one that best comports with IGRA, with other federal laws, and with the court's orders, and sends it to the state, which has 60 days to accept it. If it is accepted, then this is the Class III tribal-state compact. If the state does not accept the mediator's decision, the mediator is to inform the secretary of the interior, who is then to "prescribe, in consultation with the Indian tribe, procedures . . . under which class III gaming may be conducted on the Indian lands."[40] All in all, IGRA looked to be a pretty fair balancing of state, tribal, and federal interests.

## Seminole Tribe v. Florida—The Balance Is Broken

In 1996, the U.S. Supreme Court upset this finely tuned congressional balance between state and tribal interests in *Seminole Tribe of Florida v. Florida*. In that case, Congress's attempt to provide tribes with a remedy to sue states that refused to negotiate Class III compacts or who negotiated in bad faith was ruled unconstitutional, because the Court held that Congress lacked the authority to waive state sovereign immunity to lawsuits in IGRA. Consequently, tribes cannot sue states as IGRA provided for failing to negotiate a compact or for negotiating in bad faith unless the state has agreed on its own to waive its immunity to the suit. States now have the best of both worlds under IGRA; they have a major role in deciding whether tribes can conduct Class II gaming at all, since state law has to permit similar gaming for tribes to be able to offer Class II, and a state can now completely prevent Class III tribal gaming, even if the state allows casino-style gaming, by just not negotiating a compact with a tribe. The enormous impact of *Seminole Tribe* on Indian gaming is demonstrated by the fact that there were no tribal-state Class III compacts concluded for over two years after the case was decided.[41]

## Secretarial Class III Procedures

One might think that the *Seminole Tribe* case should not have had a major impact on tribal gaming. After all, Congress was farsighted enough in 1988 to even include in IGRA a provision for the secretary of the interior to issue Class III regulations for a tribe to conduct Class III gaming if the lawsuit remedy did not work. In fact, when the Eleventh Circuit considered the *Seminole Tribe* case, before the Supreme Court heard it, the Circuit Court expressly mentioned the secretarial procedures as an alternative route for tribes to conduct Class III gaming without a state compact.[42]

The secretary of the interior finally promulgated regulations to allow tribes to conduct Class III casino gaming in the absence of state approval and a tribal-state compact in 1999. To my understanding, Congress had several times prevented the secretary prior to 1999 from drafting these procedures. But when the secretary finally attempted to use the regulations in 2005 to allow the Tiguas Tribe of Texas to conduct Class III gaming in the absence of state consent, the U.S. Fifth Circuit Court of Appeals rejected that effort and the U.S. Supreme Court refused to hear the tribe's appeal. So the Tribe has been stymied from using the secretarial procedures Congress provided as an alternative to state consent. This issue will no doubt appear before other federal courts again and might have to be heard by the Supreme Court some day.[43]

Plainly, the congressional compromise between state and tribal interests is broken and states now have the upper hand. States demanded a voice in Indian gaming and Congress gave them an important role under IGRA. Now, various court decisions have raised the level of state control and literally given states complete veto power over tribal Class III gaming. Although Congress expressly stated that IGRA was designed to benefit tribes and not states, and was intended to expand tribal self-determination, self-government, economic development, and political stability, states are reaping greater benefits from Indian gaming than Congress ever intended.

## *CURRENT ISSUES*

There are two current and very controversial issues regarding Indian gaming. First, many states are demanding revenue-sharing agreements so they can reap major benefits from tribal gaming. For example, California governor Arnold Schwarzenegger infamously stated in 2003 that "it's time for [tribes] to pay their fair share."[44] Tribes were outraged by this statement. Second, tribes have tried to increase their profits by locating gaming facilities off reservations and closer to major population centers.

## Revenue–Sharing Agreements

Many states have opposed Indian gaming from the beginning because they see it as competition with state gambling revenues, and for other state and private economic and noneconomic reasons. States and state officials have cast envious eyes on tribal gaming. As with most governments, states want a share of any economic activities occurring within their borders. Also, states are irritated that tribes can conduct gambling activities within state borders with very little state input or regulation.

As pointed out above, states worked through Congress to gain some control over tribal gaming to protect their interests, and they have litigated an amazing number of cases through the federal and state courts to gain even more control. States now have the upper hand in Class III gaming because they can refuse to negotiate the necessary compacts and tribes are then legally prevented from offering that kind of gaming. States have exercised that advantage. Tribes can now be held hostage by states under IGRA and the 1996 *Seminole Tribe* case.

In contrast, Congress stated clearly that tribal gaming is to benefit Indian tribes and peoples, and that states cannot tax or directly benefit from that gaming. States and tribes, however, have gotten around that obstacle by entering revenue-sharing agreements in which a state ostensibly grants a tribe some right other than just the right to offer Class III gaming in return for the tribe sharing gaming revenues with the state. California and Connecticut, in particular, have gained enormous amounts of revenue from tribal gaming. Connecticut receives more than $450 million annually from the Mashantucket Pequot Foxwoods Resort Casino and the Mohegan Tribe's Sun Resort. Those tribes agreed to pay the state 25 percent of their gross slot machine revenues for the exclusive right to offer slot machine gaming in the state. California is reportedly receiving $1 billion a year from tribal gaming. Tribes in Arizona, Louisiana, Michigan, and Washington have also agreed to fund local governmental services.[45]

The consideration for these agreements and for receiving payments directly from tribal gaming is that Connecticut and other states grant tribes the exclusive right to offer certain kinds of gaming in the state. The NIGC has approved these compacts and so far federal courts have agreed. One commentator among many, however, has noted that these agreements are of "questionable validity in the light of IGRA's prohibition on state taxation of Indian gaming revenues."[46] In fact, under IGRA, a state attempt to tax tribal gaming is evidence of bad faith negotiation of a Class III compact. In 2010, the U.S. Court of Appeals for the Ninth Circuit held that California could not demand 10 to 15 percent of the Rincon Band of Luiseno Mission Indians' gaming profits because this was actually an attempt to tax the Tribe, which IGRA does not allow.[47]

Revenue-sharing agreements are controversial. But so far tribes have been willing to sign them instead of foregoing the profits and benefits they can reap if they can operate Class III operations.

## Off-Reservation Casinos (Location, Location, Location)

Not surprisingly, the most successful tribal casinos in the United States are located near large population centers and interstate highways. The unbelievable success of casinos in Connecticut, Southern California, and Minnesota prove that point. The most profitable tribal casino in Oregon is the closest one to Portland. Most tribes, however, are located in rural areas with small populations. These casinos struggle to even make a profit. Many tribes in locations that are not good for gaming are interested in off-reservation sites.

IGRA sets out a strict process for tribes to locate casinos off reservation or for tribes to acquire new lands on which they can offer gaming. In fact, as of 2008, only three tribes have been allowed to open casinos off their reservations. Congress, the NIGC, and the BIA have considered this issue several times in recent years and the prevailing trend is very much against tribes "reservation shopping" and locating gaming facilities off reservations. Congress even considered enacting a law to prevent any off-reservation casinos. In 2006 and 2008, the BIA issued new guidelines on how it would approve off-reservation casinos that seemed to create tougher standards. But in 2011, the assistant secretary of Indian affairs seemed to retreat from that tough stand while also stating that the Obama administration would not be more lax in reviewing applications for off-reservation casinos. It is certain that this issue will continue to be raised as tribal governments seek better markets for their gaming operations so that they can better serve their citizens.[48]

Currently, there are several ongoing tribal efforts to locate Class III casinos off reservations. The Confederated Tribes of the Warm Springs Reservation from rural central Oregon is attempting to locate a casino only 40 miles from Portland. The ex-governor had approved the new casino but the BIA seemed to be dragging its heels on making a decision, partly because off-reservation gaming is so controversial. This particular decision is also fraught with problems because environmentalists are appalled at the idea of a casino in the Columbia River Gorge National Scenic Area and another Oregon tribe is resisting a competitor being located so close to the Portland market.[49]

## SECONDARY EFFECTS

Gambling is always controversial in the United States, yet it is also of great interest to Americans and seems to be riding a peak of popularity at the present time. It has been noted that gambling in the United States rides 70-year cycles of peaks and valleys of interest and legality. In 2011, we must certainly be at a peak of interest since about 40 states offer lotteries and other types of officially authorized gaming, and shows on poker proliferate on television. If the 70-year cycle of gambling holds true, maybe we will see a decline in interest and legality in the next few decades. Tribal governments are well aware that there is a saturation point where gaming will naturally recede and limit their markets, and that active resistance could develop as states and local governments perceive adverse impacts from all types of gaming. There is even speculation that under IGRA, if a state were to change its mind and make gaming illegal, that this might prevent a tribe from being able to continue offering Class II or III gaming. One state court has agreed with that statement. In addition, most Class III compacts between tribes and states are for a set number of years, and then they have to be renewed. If a state made Class III gaming illegal, or just decided to use its sovereign immunity defense to refuse to negotiate another Class III compact, it is possible that Indian gaming might have to cease. Tribes could be left holding very expensive investments and debts in now-empty gaming facilities.[50]

One question that impacts the public perception of gaming is the widespread speculation that gambling causes crime, pathological gambling, and other negative social effects. Let's be clear: the evidence proves that gambling establishments do *not* increase crime. But the majority of the public and politicians probably think they do.

In 1999, Congress created the National Gambling Impact Study Commission (NGISC) to study gambling in the United States. The NGISC noted that there is very little "impartial, objective research" on legalized gambling. Therefore, the NGISC authorized the University of Chicago to conduct a study. The study examined 100 communities across the United States, with and without casinos, over a 20-year period, and concluded that the presence of a casino in or near a community did not increase the crime rates. In fact, the study showed that, to the contrary, crime rates reduced slightly in communities with casinos over communities without casinos. That is the exact opposite of what most people might have guessed. The study further concluded that communities where casinos were located experienced consistent and substantial net benefits and few, if any, harms.[51]

The NGISC study did not include any tribal communities in its sample. Thus, to answer the same question whether casinos in Indian Country increased crime, the Harvard Project on American Indian Economic Development applied the NGISC findings to tribal communities. The Harvard study concluded, in line with the NGISC study, that tribal casinos may have actually reduced crime on reservations and not caused any increases. The study also found that tribes and reservations experienced far greater socioeconomic gains from new gaming developments than did the non-Indian communities with new casinos studied by the NGISC.[52]

These are very important facts that have to be considered in determining the costs and benefits of Indian gaming to Indian nations, reservation communities, and to non-Indian communities.

## Positive Effects

Any discussion of the secondary effects of gaming must also weigh the upside. Indian gaming has had an enormously positive economic, social, and cultural effect for tribes over the past three decades. Many tribal governments and citizens are experiencing for the first time beneficial economic activities located on their reservations. These operations have created significant economic improvements for Americans with the lowest economic, health, and education levels, and the highest poverty and substandard housing rates in the United States. Tribal casinos have produced amazing benefits for many tribes and for countless Indian people and their communities and for non-Indians and the non-Indian areas surrounding reservations. Unemployment on some reservations is now zero because every tribal citizen who wants a job can have one. And college scholarships, health clinics, and expanded governmental services are now available to tribal citizens. Housing is being improved on some reservations and the possibility of a future without poverty is opening up for many people who previously did not have such hopeful futures. Moreover, tribal families are moving home to their reservations because jobs that pay livable wages are now available. It is nearly impossible to quantify the value and the overall positive effects for tribal communities that arise from such changes.[53]

We must also note two remarkable examples of the positive effects that tribal gaming and economic development can produce. In 2003, Duke University Medical Center conducted a study of the Eastern Band Cherokee of North Carolina. The Tribe had already been operating a successful gaming operation for several years. The study showed that psychiatric disorders among Cherokee children had improved as the number of Cherokee families in poverty declined. The decline in Cherokee family poverty rates was due to tribal casino revenues and employment at the Tribe's casino. In addition, in the 1950s and 1960s the Mississippi Choctaw Tribe suffered from 75 percent unemployment, a lower than average life expectancy, and the highest infant mortality rate in the United States. By the late 1990s, due to tribal economic development, which only included gaming after 1994, tribal citizens enjoyed full employment, a 20-year increase in their life expectancy, and an infant mortality rate that was better than state and national averages. Family incomes and educational levels had soared, substandard housing was greatly reduced, and the Tribe was among the top 10 employers in the state. It is nearly impossible to overstate the significance and importance of these kinds of positive effects that came from tribal gaming and economic development.[54]

Other examples demonstrate what tribal governments are now able to do for themselves, their people, and for non-Indian communities. The median annual household income on the Barona Reservation in Southern California now exceeds $100,000, two and one-third times the national average. This positive change is due primarily to the Barona Casino. The Mashantucket Pequot's Foxwoods Casino enables the Tribe to send all its children to a private school that serves a sizeable non-Indian enrollment as well. Indeed, the Pequot saved the school from closing and helped all the students, Indian and non-Indian. Many tribes also make direct contributions to state and local governments from gaming profits via the revenue-sharing agreements mentioned above, and through payments to defray state Class III regulatory costs, and payments through tribal charitable funds. In fact, the percentage of gaming revenues that tribes have shared with states since 2005 has gone up faster than Indian gaming revenues themselves in that same time period. The 2005 report already mentioned concludes that when one factors in the indirect benefits states gain from Indian gaming, through taxes on casino employees, reduced social welfare payments, and ancillary business activities, the total fiscal benefit of Indian gaming to state and local governments was $8 billion in 2005 and included $22.1 billion in wages, 591,000 jobs, and $6.9 billion in tax revenues for the national economy.[55]

States and local non-Indian communities continue to benefit from tribal casinos in more recent times. In 2007, it was estimated that Indian gaming directly created more than 670,000 jobs and that 75 percent of them were held by non-Indians. These tribal employees pay federal, state, and local taxes. People with jobs are obviously better able to care for their families economically, and states and counties where Indian casinos are located have seen major decreases in welfare caseloads and social welfare costs. All of these governments and communities have benefited economically from Indian gaming. Many of these communities and the non-Indians working in tribal enterprises are avid supporters of tribal gaming.[56]

It bears repeating, though, that the majority of tribal governments offering gaming have only received modest revenues. The 20 most successful tribal facilities accounted for 50.5 percent of total tribal gaming revenues in 1999. Also, not all tribal facilities are successful. Some tribes have operated their casinos at a loss and a few have even been forced to close. But I am not downplaying the crucial role tribal gaming plays even for tribes that operate marginally profitable facilities. Those tribal governments and communities have also gained immense benefits. The North and South Dakota Tribes, for example, are now able to offer jobs, salaries, and health care. A few tribal citizens are now full-time permanent employees and are acquiring work and management experience. Families are coming home to live and work on their reservations. And money now has a chance to circulate on reservations to create more economic activities, and tourists are visiting, and Indian vendors and Indian-owned small businesses are being created in communities that have heretofore been without privately owned businesses and without real economies. These are concrete and exciting benefits for tribes, reservation communities, and Indian cultures. Tribal gaming has been and is a very beneficial activity for almost every tribal community that offers it.[57]

## Negative Effects

As with almost every human endeavor, legalized gambling has some negative effects. These have to be compared to and weighed against the undeniably positive benefits discussed above. The two potential negative effects from tribal gaming most often mentioned are the effects on Indian cultures and pathological gambling.

### Tribal Cultures

Some commentators argue that tribal cultures can be injured by gaming. There seems to be no question that new and prosperous economic activities in Indian Country will have impacts and create some changes. The question that tribal governments and reservation communities have to answer is whether jobs, income, and economic benefits are worth possible risks to tribal cultures? Every society faces a choice about how to deal with economic success and failure and every society and family has to adjust to such situations. The chairman and CEO of the Oneida Nation in New York stated the conundrum about his tribe's successful gaming operation in this perhaps satirical way: "We had tried poverty for 200 years, so we decided to try something else."[58]

Personally, I think it is better materially, culturally, and as a family and a nation to have to deal with having too much economic activity and benefits than it is to have to deal with too little. As pointed out in Chapter 2, Indian tribes and cultures have never purposely strived to live in poverty. In contrast, almost all tribal cultures honored individuals and families who could support themselves and who had enough material resources to help others and to support tribal ceremonies and traditions. Many tribal cultures also honored individuals who could amass a bounty of material possessions to participate in potlatches and giveaways, and many individuals worked hard to gain that status. I do not know of any tribal culture that demanded or that today demands that its people live in poverty.

In addition, a tribe and its citizens who enjoy a measure of economic success are no doubt better able to study, preserve, and participate in cultural activities than is a tribe where everyone is barely able to survive day to day. A reservation that has employment opportunities attracts Indian families to move back home, and that is undeniably an enormous benefit to the practice and preservation of tribal cultures and reservation and tribal life.

There are no doubt challenges that societies and cultures face from suddenly having new wealth. News reports in 2008 suggest that the Seminole Tribe of Florida is experiencing just such adjustment problems. Even though this Tribe is suddenly quite wealthy and tribal citizens receive an annual income of about $120,000 from tribal gaming revenues, the average age of death is dropping precipitously. Some are blaming the sudden wealth and the fact that people no longer need to work as being a cause of increased alcohol and drug use. One tribal citizen stated that "you don't have to work. Maybe the lifestyle on the reservation is too easy."[59] Now that's an ironic twist on the history and present-day conditions of most American Indians: life is too easy on a reservation?

In a 2008 book about the Seminoles and gaming, a professor opined that tribal gaming and the wealth some tribes have acquired has had the most dramatic economic impact on the lives of Indigenous peoples and economies since the massive land dispossessions and loss of Indian wealth to the United States and American settlers. She states that just as those land transfers and the loss of these assets caused enormous disruptions in the lives of American Indians, so too can we expect to see changes and adjustments as modern-day Indian communities reacquire some measure of wealth from the depths of poverty. But she also states that even though economics has altered Seminole households, they have reproduced their valued forms of cultural and political distinctiveness, and the tribal government is using money to provide free lifelong education and universal health insurance for tribal citizens, and to care for their elders. She suggests that indigenous sovereignty opens up new ways of understanding the nature of money and its material effects. She states that Seminoles wrestle less with alligators these days to earn tourist dollars than they do with how to spend money for cultural opportunities, to diversify their economy, to preserve their language, to teach their children the value of hard work in the absence of financial need, to know when enough money is enough, and to protect and expand tribal sovereignty. That is a lot to deal with for any family and any culture. The experience can change both families and tribal cultures. But it has to be up to the Seminole people and their government, and other tribal cultures and governments, to say when enough economic development and money is enough, and when and how they will stop or limit their money-making activities.[60]

Another issue appears to have created a negative impact on tribal cultures from gaming. In a few tribes, citizenship disputes have raised very serious issues over tribal enrollment. Some tribes have narrowed their requirements for citizenship/membership and some have taken the extraordinary and rare step of disenrolling some citizens and removing them from tribal rolls. Many people claim that these moves are occurring almost exclusively in gaming tribes and that they are disputes about dividing gaming profits and represent pure greed. Obviously, under a per capita distribution system every tribal citizen will receive more money if there are fewer enrolled citizens overall. Also obvious is the fact that these disputes can be very injurious to tribal cultures and harmony. Since these actions limit tribal citizenship, they also limit the resources and families that tribes need to rely on for future citizens and for preserving culture and languages, for example. I am unaware of anyone who has proved that disenrollments have been caused by a desire for larger casino payments. The tribal governments involved vigorously deny these charges. But these actions are troubling, to say the least, and they carry a major risk of damaging tribal cultures and governments.[61]

The possible negative effects of gambling on tribal cultures are issues that tribes and their citizens will have to consider if they are thinking of starting, expanding, or ending gaming.

## Problem and Pathological Gambling

A second potential negative effect from gaming is problem and pathological gambling. Pathological gambling is defined as "persistent and recurrent maladaptive gambling behavior" that meets five or more of ten specifically defined factors. A problem gambler is someone with maladaptive gambling behavior who meets four or less of the criteria.[62] It seems reasonable to assume that making gambling more widely accessible will exacerbate problems for tribal citizens and non-Indians with gambling problems. This issue cannot be overlooked in weighing the beneficial and negative effects of tribal gaming. States recognize these problems as regards their own gaming endeavors and offer various programs to treat problem gamblers.

Tribes are well aware of this problem and do not want to add problem gambling to the list of social issues they face. Tribal governments also want to be good neighbors and they do not want to add to the social problems of non-Indian communities. In light of these concerns, though, states and tribes have still decided to offer gaming. They have decided that the value of gaming and its economic benefits to society at large outweigh the social and economic costs of problem and pathological gambling.

The NGISC federal study mentioned above reports that as of 1998 between 1.2 to 1.5 percent of the U.S. population, or more than 3 million Americans, have been pathological gamblers at one point in their lives. Another 1.5 to 3.9 percent, or more than 3 to 7 million Americans, have been problem gamblers at some time. The problems that families and society face from problem gambling include debt accumulation, crime, substance abuse, domestic abuse, and suicidal tendencies. These are all very serious issues for individuals, families, and society. While casinos in general are not linked to an increase in crime, according to the NGISC study, there does appear to be a link between pathological and problem gamblers and crime. The study also estimates that all these problems cost the U.S. economy about $4 billion each year. But commentators have pointed out that this cost has to be weighed against other findings of the 1999 federal study that communities where gaming is started had a 12 percent drop in unemployment, a 13 percent decline in income paid by states for welfare programs, and a 17 percent decrease in payments for unemployment insurance. On a cost-benefit analysis to society, commentators argue that those gains far outweigh the costs of problem gambling.[63]

It is difficult to deal with this issue. Our society allows many activities that injure Americans, like alcohol, guns, smoking, and automobiles. Alcohol dependence, for example, impacts 13 percent of Americans, while the lifetime rate of pathological gaming in the United States impacts just over 1 percent of Americans. Gaming is of enormous economic and social benefit to many tribes and states, and is an important source of revenue for many governments. Forty or more states and several hundred tribal governments have decided that the benefits of gaming outweigh the costs, and this kind of gambling, as a source of governmental tax revenues for tribes and states, is now an accepted part of American life.[64]

## CONCLUSION

Indian gaming is now a major part of American life and, most importantly, it is now a crucial part of modern-day economic life on many reservations. Some people worry that tribal gaming is just another threat to Indian cultures. But no one questions that Indian people have to earn a living to be able to survive and to raise their families, and that tribal governments and communities have to support themselves if they are going to create sustainable reservations. Indian nations and Indian peoples are using gaming to survive. They are using gaming as one component of exercising their sovereign and human rights as governments and communities.

Some tribes have become fabulously successful at gaming. A few Indian families are now rich and do not even have to work anymore if they so choose. That "dilemma" is not faced by many American families. (In fact, most of us would probably like to deal with that "problem.") Some families of great wealth, like the Kennedys and Rockefellers, had members who used their wealth to go into public service and devoted their lives to politics and social causes. No doubt others in those same families were not able to cope with their wealth and did not live entirely productive lives. Certainly, we will see these same disparities occur in how some tribes and some Indians deal with financial success. Some tribal communities and some Indian families and individuals might not adjust well to sudden wealth, but the majority of Indian communities and peoples that have become really successful in gaming have so far used their new incomes and the wealth that they achieved to improve cultural, political, and community issues. Tribal gaming has been a major benefit for Indians and tribal governments when viewed in its entirety.

Many tribal governments that offer gaming now have a new and successful economic activity that provides jobs, income, insurance, education, health care, and training for Indians and helps tribes to address the myriad social and welfare issues they face. Tribal governments and Indians are also able to use an anchor business like a casino to help develop reservation economies and to create tribal and Indian-owned businesses to support that major economic activity.

Tribal gaming could end some day, or the demand for gambling may drop dramatically. But tribes and Indian communities have already benefited because of this new economic tool to train their people, to improve their financial, health, and educational levels, and to address cultural and social problems. They have also used gaming profits to diversify and develop their economies to build lasting economic benefits.

# CHAPTER 6

# *Attracting Investments*

$C$hapters 1 through 5 looked to the past and the present day to describe American Indian and tribal property rights, economic activities, and reservation economies. Chapters 6 through 8 look primarily to the future to examine and suggest factors and strategies that tribal governments and Indians might use to expand and diversify their economic activities, to create functioning economies, and to help remedy the poverty conditions found on most reservations. In this chapter, we consider some of the issues, challenges, and opportunities tribes and Indians face in attracting private and public investment. The importance of this issue is demonstrated by the fact that the U.S. Treasury Department estimates that there is a $44 billion gap between what is invested in all of Indian Country and what should be invested there in comparison to the U.S. economy in general.[1]

Attracting investment capital is about more than just borrowing money. Of course, one aspect of gaining investments in Indian Country entails tribal governments and Indians borrowing money and finding others who will invest money there. But attracting "investments" also includes getting non-Indian and Indian companies, individuals, and even other tribal governments to risk their human capital of time, expertise, and labor in opening and operating businesses on reservations. Therefore, tribal governments need to think about creating, to some extent, business-friendly environments where other tribes, Indian and non-Indian companies, and individuals will invest money and human capital in economic endeavors.

Tribal governments and Indians often encounter problems in raising money to start or expand businesses and in attracting investments for several reasons. First, the fact that most tribal governments and Indians are relatively poor and that most reservations are mired in poverty plays a big part. This might seem counter-intuitive, since a poor community with little economic development might sound like a place with great potential for development. But a country or a region's extreme poverty is one of the very reasons investors are reluctant to invest, because of the lack of financial and human capital. Investors can invest in many places, and locations that are already somewhat prosperous appear more promising than do reservations and poverty-stricken areas.[2]

Second, Indian people face major problems in securing private loans to start businesses because they have almost no access to the three primary means that Americans use to finance new businesses. Americans obtain the average start-up business loan in one of three ways: a mortgage on their home, accumulated family wealth, or an unsecured loan. Unsecured loans are also often called signature loans, because the only thing the borrower puts up to guarantee repayment of the loan is his or her signature. In essence, they are borrowing the money based on their promise to repay and the guarantee of their credit history.

But many Indians who own homes on reservations live on trust lands. In that situation, the United States is the legal owner of the land and individual Indians cannot give a mortgage on their land, and as a result the primary means Americans use to borrow start-up business funding is not available to most Indians in Indian Country. Moreover, since Indians are the poorest and most economically disadvantaged ethnic or racial group in the United States, it is no surprise that they have trouble using the second and third avenues for borrowing money for business purposes. Most Indian families simply do not have accumulated family wealth. Also, since Indian families and individuals are the poorest group in America, and jobs are very scarce on most reservations, most reservation-based Indians do not have the kind of employment and credit histories that would allow them to borrow thousands of dollars through unsecured signature loans to start businesses. Therefore, individual Indians face major obstacles in raising investment capital. This situation can only be remedied, it seems, through increased economic activity and prosperity on reservations over several decades.

The third perceived obstacle to attracting investments, however, raises issues that tribal governments can do something about. We will primarily discuss this subject for the remainder of this chapter. This "problem" is actually an opportunity in disguise; and it involves far more than just tribes and Indians borrowing money. When we say that tribes are seeking investments, yes, we are talking about getting institutions and individuals to loan money to tribal governments and Indians for business purposes, but we are also talking far more expansively. We are also talking about getting non-Indian individuals and companies to invest in building and starting businesses and manufacturing plants in Indian Country, and getting Indian individuals themselves to take the risk to invest their time, money, and labor in starting businesses and economic activities on reservations. This obstacle to acquiring investments in Indian Country is about more than just obtaining money for new enterprises on reservations. Overcoming this obstacle will require many tribes to literally change the rules of the game to successfully attract new economic endeavors.

The problem of attracting investments raises legal and institutional issues and involves ensuring the performance of contractual agreements, the repayment of loans, and assisting as much as possible the success of business ventures. Many businesses and investors have heard "bad things" about investing with tribal governments, businesses, and individual Indians, and about investing money or operating businesses in Indian Country. Many times these fears are misconceived and false. But such issues arise just often enough, and they get just enough publicity that investors have these fears. Even when these concerns are erroneous, however, that does not change the fact that some investors think they are true and will not even consider investing in Indian Country. Tribes need to be aware of these factors and the fears that the investment community might have and tribal governments need to address these issues if at all possible. As Professor David Haddock states, even though most tribes act reliably, many potential investors fear that they are unreliable.[3]

Before we commence a substantive discussion of the legal and political issues that can be obstacles to attracting investments to Indian Country, we need to note one point about the problems investors hear about dealing with tribal governments and Indians. To the non-Indian investor conditions can seem unusually risky on reservations because non-Indians usually only hear of the aberrational features of a few negative events from Indian Country. Most investors have little first-hand knowledge of reservation life. Perhaps, though, they have read or heard about some unusual business situation in which tribal courts applied tribal law differently than state law or about some bad experience that another business had in Indian Country. Newspapers rarely write about the ordinary events that happen on reservations and the thousands of non-Indians who do business in Indian Country without any remarkable or surprising incident. But newspapers, and especially the legal record, naturally report only the most sensational and extraordinary events, and they make it appear that doing business in Indian Country is risky.

Social and business arrangements that work as planned are rarely reported in the newspaper and are of course never litigated. Thus, the events that become public knowledge are only a tiny sample of the events that occur from working in Indian Country. Since litigation is very expensive, court cases come from an extreme set of the social and business arrangements that failed to work as planned. Consequently, newspaper reports and lawsuits from Indian Country business activities make these activities appear to be more risky and threatening than they actually are. One federal appeals court noted this fact in a 1991 case: "As is generally the rule in matters which come to this court's attention, the once-promising business relationship between the contracting parties soured."[4]

We now consider successful and unsuccessful tribal initiatives along with various ideas that can facilitate reservation economic development. But one very important point must be emphasized here and will be mentioned several times in this book. It is up to each tribal government, culture, and community to evaluate and select their own preferences when reacting to the following discussion and in deciding whether to make whatever systemic changes might be relevant to attract more investments. The policies that any particular tribal government chooses to follow might not satisfy all observers or all investors and might not reassure them about investing on that tribe's reservation. But the decision of how business-friendly a tribe and community wants to make its reservation is up to that specific tribal government and its citizens.

## ISSUES FOR INVESTORS

There are several unique issues that arise when investing with tribal governments and tribally owned businesses. Sovereign immunity is the power and right of a government to not be sued unless it has consented to the specific type of lawsuit and the specific court. The United States, all state governments, and all federally recognized tribal governments enjoy the right of sovereign immunity. Immunity protects the public treasury of governments from lawsuits that might bankrupt the government and injure all the citizens.

Tribal sovereign immunity is an important component of business investment in Indian Country and investors need to be aware of it. Tribal governments also need to understand how investors view this immunity when they are thinking of investing with a tribal government or when a tribe is hoping to get them to invest with the tribe or in a tribally owned business. Tribes need to know how to minimize immunity as an obstacle to acquiring the investments that a tribal community wants. It is important to note though that sovereign immunity has not been and need not be an impediment to acquiring investments. Federal, state, and tribal governments have waived and limited their immunities on thousands of occasions and in myriad ways. Businesses and tribes that use due diligence, planning, and careful negotiations can defuse sovereign immunity as a problem to investing in Indian Country.

Investors are aware of the issue of sovereign immunity. The federal and state governments regularly defend lawsuits on this basis. The U.S. Supreme Court has long recognized that tribal governments are protected to the same extent, whether a suit is filed in tribal, state, or federal court. Hence, tribes can only be sued if they have waived their immunity or if the U.S. Congress has waived it for them. Both types of waivers must be clearly and expressly stated.[5]

Sovereign immunity comes up in business activities and investments in Indian Country regularly because tribes are more often involved in business than state and federal governments. This is so because tribes own or control most of the businesses, land, and natural resources on the typical reservation. Due to fears of sovereign immunity, many businesses shy away from reservation opportunities due to the impression that tribal immunity is a major problem. Undoubtedly tribes lose economic opportunities from investors who never even approach them because of this uncertainty.

## Federal and State Waivers

Sovereign immunity should not be a surprise nor should it be a problem for investors. The federal and state governments possess this power but they and business investors have learned how to work around the issue. The United States did not fully waive its immunity to contracts lawsuits until 1887, and most state governments did not do so until much later; Oregon in 1959 and Pennsylvania in 1978, for example. The federal government only waived its immunity to torts lawsuits in 1946, and most states did so thereafter. Oregon did not waive its tort immunity until 1968. But most states still severely limit their exposure to torts suits and restrict their waivers to small amounts. For decades before 1989, for example, Oregon only allowed torts suits up to $100,000, and it only raised that amount in 2010. Nevada only allowed suits against it up to $25,000 as late as 1977.[6]

Furthermore, many of these tort waivers of immunity are only partial waivers. Federal and state governments still bar various procedures such as punitive damages, interest, and jury trials, and impose strict jurisdictional requirements. California retained its immunity for failure to provide fire protection, for example. These situations, though, almost never stop businesses from contracting and dealing with federal and state governments because they have learned how to successfully deal with this legal reality. Sovereign immunity is not a new aspect of dealing with governments and should not deter businesses and investors from dealing with tribes. It is a commonly understood aspect of working with governments and is dealt with by businesses every day.[7]

## Tribal Waivers

Tribal sovereign immunity is a well-understood legal principle that is easily managed by careful businesspersons. Tribes, businesses, and investors have successfully dealt with this issue for many decades. Almost all tribal governments have waived and will waive their immunity in specific situations and contracts to facilitate business deals. Tribes primarily do this on a case-by-case basis in contract provisions instead of by enacting laws that waive their immunity to all suits on a specific topic, for example. This prospective and individualized method of handling immunity waivers is about the only way to handle this subject for tribal property that is held in trust by the United States. This is so because specific BIA approval of contracts regarding trust property is necessary for the contract, and for any tribal waiver of immunity in the contract, to be valid, because the United States is the legal owner of trust property while the tribe or individual Indian is the beneficial owner. This is a major reason why waivers of tribal immunity are more effectively accomplished on an individual ad hoc basis.[8]

Many tribes have also enacted statutes that provide limited waivers and allow torts lawsuits to be filed against the tribal government in the same manner that federal and state governments have handled this issue. For example, the Grand

Ronde, Umatilla, Siletz, and Warm Springs Tribes in Oregon, the Grand Traverse Band of Ottawa and Chippewa Indians in Michigan, and the Mashantucket Pequot Tribal Nation in Connecticut have all adopted tort claims ordinances that waive their immunity to certain cases. This makes good business sense because these tribes operate casinos and commercial entities that invite the public to visit their reservations. These tribes, then, have made provisions to reassure the public of its ability to sue the tribe if they are injured. These tribes have exercised their sovereignty by making governmental decisions to enact limited immunity waivers and have opened their courts to litigants allegedly injured in tribal establishments.[9]

Businesses dealing with tribal governments, though, should exercise some sensitivity when dealing with tribes on the subject of immunity waivers. Respect for tribal sovereignty can even help facilitate business deals. Tribes expect to have their sovereign status and immunity powers taken seriously. Many aspects of federal and tribal law upholding tribal sovereignty have only been defined and enforced within the past few decades. Consequently, tribes are understandably concerned about being asked to waive these newly enforceable powers for every minor business deal. Potential tribal business partners can be sensitive to sovereignty and sovereign immunity by not seeking waivers in small deals, and/or by exploring the many viable alternatives to waivers of tribal immunity. Investors can often receive complete protection of their investments by partial waivers of immunity, waivers only to specific tribal assets, or by performance bonds, insurance, escrow accounts, arbitration dispute resolution methods, and other imaginative means to accomplish mutually beneficial business deals.

Moreover, there are literally thousands of examples of tribal governments voluntarily waiving their immunity in contracts and being amenable to lawsuits or arbitration procedures to settle business and contractual disputes. For instance, as of 2002, the Confederated Tribes of the Siletz Indian Reservation in Oregon had approximately 275 contracts with various business entities and 35 of them contained waivers of sovereign immunity. But examples of tribes allowing and then abiding by dispute resolution methods do not draw media attention. As mentioned above, it is only the extreme situations that draw press coverage and lead to "horror stories" about doing business in Indian Country. Inevitably, though, there have been instances in which some investors have not exercised due diligence and have not carefully protected themselves by obtaining adequate waivers of tribal sovereign immunity. This failure by the investors and by their legal advisors has worked to the detriment of some Indian and non-Indian investors. While this carelessness resulted in situations no different than when a party loses a case to the federal or state governments due to immunity, these kinds of cases frighten potential investors away from dealing with tribes and reservation businesses. We will look at a few examples to demonstrate the problems potential investors can encounter due to tribal sovereign immunity but also to demonstrate how simply these problems could have been avoided with proper planning, negotiation, and due diligence by the investors.[10]

In 1998, the U.S. Supreme Court gave businesses a lesson in dealing with tribal sovereign immunity. In *Kiowa Tribe of Oklahoma v. Manufacturing Technologies, Inc.,* the Tribe's chairman signed a promissory note for the Tribe agreeing to buy $285,000 in Manufacturing Technologies stock. The promissory note stated that it was signed on tribal trust lands. But according to the company, the Tribe signed and delivered the note to Manufacturing Technologies in Oklahoma City. The note required the Tribe to make its payments in Oklahoma City. The note did not, however, specify the law that would govern its interpretation, and instead of waiving tribal sovereign immunity the note did just the opposite: "Nothing in this Note subjects or limits the sovereign rights of the Kiowa Tribe of Oklahoma."[11] This business and its legal advisors were certainly mistaken if they thought the Tribe had expressly waived its immunity to suit under those terms.

The Tribe defaulted and the company sued in state court. The state courts held that tribes are not protected by sovereign immunity if a contract involves off-reservation commercial conduct. The U.S. Supreme Court disagreed. The Court held that Indian tribes have sovereign immunity from civil lawsuits on contracts, whether they involve governmental or commercial activities, and whether or not they are signed in Indian Country. Since Manufacturing Technologies failed to protect itself and did not use due diligence by negotiating and including an immunity waiver clause, it lost its chance of bringing a state lawsuit against the Tribe. This situation of course made big news and no doubt dissuaded some companies and investors from doing business with tribal governments. But clearly, this situation was the fault of Manufacturing Technologies and its failure to protect itself under the well-known and established legal procedures for waiving tribal sovereign immunity. This case should not frighten investors about dealing with tribes.

In contrast, in *C & L Enterprises, Inc. v. Citizen Band Potawatomi Indian Tribe of Oklahoma*, the U.S. Supreme Court held that a company did properly obtain the Tribe's waiver of its immunity and the non-Indian company had fully protected its rights. In this case, the Court held that the Potawatomi Tribe waived its sovereign immunity when it signed a standard form construction contract. The contract, which the Tribe provided, included an arbitration clause that any and all disputes under the contract would be arbitrated, that Oklahoma law would apply to any disputes, and that an arbitration award would be final and could be enforced in any court having jurisdiction. Here, the Tribe and C & L contracted to repair a tribal commercial building located on land owned in fee simple by the Tribe. Even though the contract did not mention the words "sovereign immunity" and even though it had no language expressly waiving the Tribe's immunity, a unanimous Supreme Court held that there was an express and clear waiver of sovereign immunity. This might sound strange since the contract did not mention "sovereign immunity" or "waiver." But the contract did provide that "[a]ll ... disputes ... shall be decided by arbitration. .... The award rendered by the arbitrator ... shall be final, and judgment may be entered upon it in accordance with applicable law in any court having jurisdiction thereof."[12]

Furthermore, it included a choice-of-law clause: "The contract shall be governed by the law of the place where the Project is located."[13] The Supreme Court concluded that these provisions, even though the contract did not mention sovereign immunity or waiver, constituted an express and clear waiver of tribal immunity to a state court suit because the language stated a waiver with the "requisite clarity."[14]

For the most part, arbitration clauses in contracts have been successful in waiving tribal sovereign immunity, but businesses do have to exercise care and due diligence in how they draft such clauses. The U.S. Court of Appeals for the Seventh Circuit held that contract language that provides for arbitration and states that the arbitration award is "specifically enforceable in accordance with applicable law in any court having jurisdiction" is an express waiver of a tribe's sovereign immunity.[15]

As pointed out in Chapter 5, tribal gaming in Indian Country has led to enormous numbers of non-Indian companies and investors working with tribes. Often, these businesses have been unfamiliar with dealing with governments, and tribal governments in particular, and issues of sovereign immunity. But this did not stop non-Indian investors from putting hundreds of millions of dollars to work building and operating tribal casinos. Tribes have had little problem raising capital for gaming pursuits. Once the industry was proven to be enormously lucrative by the Mashantucket Pequot casino in Connecticut, investors lined up to give tribes money. Tribal sovereign immunity has not been a stumbling block for those investors.

It is obvious that sovereign immunity is a crucial issue that businesses and investors have to investigate, negotiate, and settle with tribal governments before operating or investing in Indian Country. But it is important to emphasize that this issue is easily solved by knowledgeable investors and legal advisors who perform their due diligence. Furthermore, almost every tribal government will work with investors on this issue because they are interested in bringing new businesses and jobs to their reservations. Consequently, while sovereign immunity might be perceived as an obstacle for investors, it does not stand in the way of successful investing in Indian Country.

## Tribal Insurance and the Federal Tort Claims Act

Many tribal governments have contracted various Indian programs away from the United States and now operate the programs in lieu of federal agencies. In this situation, federal law treats tribal employees as if they are federal employees under the Federal Tort Claims Act. Consequently, anyone who claims to have been injured by a tribal employee working under these tribal/federal contracts can pursue an action against the U.S. government. In addition to this federal torts claims process, most tribes carry liability insurance policies to protect persons injured by the tribe or its employees and have often expressly waived sovereign immunity to allow lawsuits against their insurance carriers. These provisions protect investors and businesses and help to alleviate some concerns about working in Indian Country.[16]

# The Indian Civil Rights Act

Many investors might be concerned about working in Indian Country due to a lack of knowledge about what laws apply to protect their personal rights. In 1968, Congress enacted the Indian Civil Rights Act to clarify the answers to these questions. That law requires that "No Indian tribe in exercising powers of self-government shall . . . deny to any person within its jurisdiction the equal protection of its laws or deprive any person of liberty or property without due process of law. . . ."[17] This civil rights law requires tribal governments and courts to apply the well-known legal principles of equal protection and due process to all persons who come under tribal jurisdiction. This fact should also help to ease the concerns of non-Indian businesses and investors contemplating working in Indian Country.

## *POLITICAL INSTABILITY*

All governments encounter political problems at various times. In recent decades, the United States endured a hotly contested presidential election in 2000; President Clinton was impeached by the House of Representatives in 1998; and President Nixon and Vice President Agnew resigned from office in 1974 and 1973. Members of Congress have had to resign and some have even been convicted of crimes. State governments encounter similar problems. In 2003, California recalled its governor and economists predicted that the recall would hurt the California economy. The Illinois governor was impeached in 2009. Moreover, state and local politicians are often convicted of crimes. Tribal governments encounter these same types of situations.

In addition to issues of corruption, the change of governments and public opinions in federal and state elections often cause major changes in fiscal and political policies. The 2008 election of President Barack Obama, for example, led to calls for many changes in national policies. Similarly, in Indian Country, new elections and shifts in reservation opinions occasionally cause changes in tribal policies. Perhaps it is the nature of small reservation populations and tribal political entities that they appear to be heavily affected by turnover in the personnel operating the government and by shifting opinions of the electorates. Recall elections and wholesale changes in the makeup of tribal councils also occur. Sometimes such elections are deemed to be referenda on a past tribal council's policies and economic objectives, just as President Obama's election was considered to be a referendum on President George W. Bush's policies. In these situations, new federal governments and new tribal councils feel bound to change government policies.

In Indian Country, however, changes in tribal political and fiscal policies can sometimes have an immediate and significant effect on investors and businesses already operating on reservations. Occasionally, turnover in a tribal council has led to the rejection of existing contracts and business relationships. Obviously, it is anathema to those who have invested time and money in any jurisdiction to see the rules of the game change just because of a change in the political situation. When changes in tribal councils can lead to alterations of contracts and ongoing business activities, it chills the desire of investors to work in Indian Country. Tribal governments and reservation inhabitants have to be aware of this situation.[18]

Others have noted this issue and the effect it has on investors. One reporter stated that everyone in Indian Country knows of business projects that were cancelled after the latest election. And a law professor writes that tribes occasionally "intervene directly in and even legislatively terminate a particular [business] project. . . ."[19] In the same vein, a college professor noted that some tribal councils have changed the rules on investors and engaged in "opportunistic behavior" and that this "can go a long way toward discouraging Indians from investing their resources in their own businesses."[20] Clearly, this type of behavior is a serious concern to investors and businesses considering working in Indian Country and for tribal governments trying to attract investments.[21]

## Insecure Tribal Policies

The disparagement of contractual property rights by a few tribal councils in response to political changes is counterproductive to the goal of fostering an investor-friendly business climate. A solution to this problem, in essence a way to save tribal councils from political pressures to ignore contractual and investor rights, is not easy to suggest, since politicians are naturally inclined to try to please voters. Perhaps a solution for tribal governments is to adopt provisions similar to one in the U.S. Constitution called the obligation of contracts clause. The U.S. Constitution prevents states from passing any law that "impair[s] the Obligation of Contracts. . . ."[22] According to one professor's research published in 1990, the Salt River Pima-Maricopa Indian Community was the only tribe in the United States that had a constitutional provision barring the impairment of contracts. In its 2006 constitution, the Snoqualmie Tribe also included a ban on impairing the obligation of contracts. Similar provisions in tribal constitutions, or at least in the statutory laws of tribes, would prevent a new tribal council from altering contractual rights that an earlier tribal council had approved. This would go a long way to ensuring investors of their rights and the enforceability of those rights in tribal courts.[23]

A recent tribal initiative in the Pacific Northwest, briefly mentioned in Chapter 4, would also protect existing contractual rights. In 2007–2009, the Affiliated Tribes of Northwest Indians organization and tribal leaders convened a group to draft a treaty for tribal governments that would encourage economic development between tribes and encourage investments on reservations by tribes, Indians, and non-Indians. This group noted the problem that a few tribes have sometimes impaired the rights of existing contracts. The draft treaty this group produced would require tribal governments to adopt provisions to limit their ability to impair existing contractual obligations and rights. Even if this draft treaty is never finalized (the effort is being revived in 2012) or adopted by any tribe, this example still demonstrates that tribal governments and organizations are aware of this problem and are trying to address it.[24]

A few examples will highlight the seriousness of this issue for tribal governments and for investors. They demonstrate the problems that arise when tribal councils change their minds and work against the interests of the very investors that the council had earlier encouraged to invest on the reservation. We can only imagine the chilling effect these situations cause for potential investors. They create a perception of uncertainty and unfairness in dealing with some tribes and they raise the costs and risks of doing business with tribes that engage in this conduct; and even worse, they increase the general fear of working with any tribal government. A perception that this is a problem in all of Indian Country obviously harms the interests of all tribes. I repeat, though, that these cases are well known because they were well publicized and litigated as extreme examples of rare situations. They do not demonstrate the general rule.

In 1998, the Rosebud Sioux Tribe in South Dakota negotiated a lease with Sun Prairie, Inc. for the construction of hog farms on tribal lands. The BIA conducted an environmental assessment, instead of the more extensive environmental impact statement, and determined that the operation would not cause a significant impact to the environment. The BIA approved the Sun Prairie lease in September 1998. In November 1998, environmental groups filed a lawsuit to stop the development. In January 1999, the Assistant Secretary for the Bureau of Indian Affairs voided the lease, claiming that the environmental review performed by the BIA did not comply with the National Environmental Policy Act. The Tribe and Sun Prairie then sued the BIA and the court issued a permanent injunction preventing the BIA from interfering with the project. By February 1999, Sun Prairie and the Tribe had invested $5 million in the hog farms.[25]

After a new tribal election, the composition of the tribal council changed. In addition, the Tribe held a referendum on the hog project and 556 people voted against it and 451 voted in favor. The new tribal council members assumed they were elected with a mandate, and especially in light of the referendum, the new tribal council now voted against the hog project and to support the BIA's effort to void the Sun Prairie lease. The Tribe sought permission to change from being a co-plaintiff in the case, in which it supported Sun Prairie's lease, to becoming a co-defendant and supporting the BIA's decision to void the lease. The court granted the motion.[26]

Now that the Tribe had changed sides in the litigation, the federal court held that Sun Prairie alone did not have standing to continue the lawsuit, and its complaint was dismissed. Consequently, the shift of the Tribe to the BIA's side doomed Sun Prairie's chance to even litigate the issue. Furthermore, in 2003, the tribal council asked the BIA to shut down the 48 hog barns that Sun Prairie had built on the reservation, even though most of the employees working in the barns were tribal citizens. By then, Sun Prairie had invested $20 million. One person noted: "This fall another election will be held, which could change everything."[27] A federal judge asked how a new tribal council could simply void a contract that an earlier tribal government had signed, and he added: "It is important for tribes' economic well-being that contracts be enforced and not subject to elections."[28] In July 2005, the controversy and the lawsuits were still ongoing.[29]

Similarly, in 1970, the Tesuque Pueblo in New Mexico signed a lease with the Sangre de Cristo Development Company to develop part of the reservation into a residential community primarily for non-Indians. The secretary of the interior approved the lease. In 1971, neighbors and environmental groups sued to enjoin construction until the environmental impact statement was conducted. The federal government then worked on the study for four and a half years.[30]

In 1976, the Pueblo elected a new tribal council, who now asked the Department of the Interior to void the lease. Consequently, the Department of the Interior rescinded the lease due to environmental concerns and the Pueblo's new opposition. The new council could have agreed to an amended lease based on the completion of the proper environmental procedures, but this council did not want the development. Sangre then sued the federal government, but the court held that Sangre did not possess a property right in the lease because it was void since the department's initial approval had been in violation of federal environmental law.[31]

Our final example concerns leases United Nuclear Corporation signed with the Navajo Nation to mine uranium. The secretary of the interior approved the leases and the exploration plan and United spent more than $5 million looking for uranium. Under the leases, however, United had to receive secretarial approval of a mining plan before commencing actual mining. United's plan apparently met all the requirements, but the secretary refused to approve it without the Nation's approval. United then spent three years trying to secure tribal consent. Federal officials and the court believed that the Navajo Nation was using its veto power to force United to pay more money or was just stalling until the leases lapsed. When the leases expired because mining had not commenced, United sued the federal government for a Fifth Amendment taking and won, because the federal government had taken the company's vested property right in the lease by unreasonably refusing to approve the mining plan absent tribal approval.[32]

These examples demonstrate some of the situations that give investors concerns about working in Indian Country. Without question, tribes can point to a 400-year history and thousands of examples where they have been taken advantage of in treaties, and business, contract, and royalty arrangements, and in negotiations and court cases. But, as commentators have noted, it does not make economic sense today and it does not assist tribal economic development today to respond in kind. Examples such as the ones discussed above make Indian and non-Indian investors think twice about investing on reservations. Investors can invest wherever they wish, and they will go where their money is the safest and where the best return is reasonably assured. Tribal governments need to take the necessary steps to prevent the above-cited situations from occurring if they want to attract investors to Indian Country. For example, tribes should review their laws and rules regarding business investments and operations, ensure the separation of power in tribal governments, allow experienced boards of directors to operate tribal businesses instead of politicians, ensure tribal courts and judges are experienced and operated independently and impartially, and consider enacting constitutional or statutory provisions to prevent impairing the obligation of contracts. Such provisions would go a long way to ensure stable and fair tribal rules and policies and to attract investments to Indian Country.[33]

## Tribal Political Disputes

Two examples are sufficient to highlight how internal tribal political disputes can also interfere with business and investments on reservations. In March 2003, a political dispute over the governance of the Sac and Fox Tribe in Iowa led to the physical takeover of tribal offices and of the Tribe's casino by a group allegedly appointed by a traditional tribal leader. The group was not elected pursuant to constitutional requirements and the existing tribal government had not been legally removed from office. Therefore, the National Indian Gaming Commission (NIGC) gave the Tribe 30 days to put its elected government back into office or the NIGC would close the tribal casino. The government was not restored to power, so the casino was closed, putting 1,300 people out of work. Later, the federal government also froze federal funds that had been distributed to the Tribe, to keep the unofficial group from spending them. Obviously, this internal dispute interfered with tribal economic and governmental activities.[34]

In November 2008, a political dispute led to the Hopi Tribal Council suspending several tribal officials and its entire court of appeals. Reports alleged that these actions were taken due to decisions the officials made and rulings the judges made in an ongoing dispute between the tribal council and the tribal chairman. Any investor who considers working on the Hopi Reservation will not be very comfortable with this evidence of the tribal court's lack of independence.[35]

Changes in political policies and internal disputes occur in every government. However, tribal governments and their citizens must recognize that such changes can be very detrimental to current and future economic benefits. Plainly, the instances discussed above of political instability and occasional disregard of contractual rights makes investors very cautious about investing in Indian Country.

## TRIBAL COURTS

In 1987, the U.S. Supreme Court stated that "[c]ivil jurisdiction over [the activities of non-Indians on reservations] presumptively lies in the tribal courts ..."[36] Therefore, tribal courts are the primary forum for adjudicating civil disputes that arise in Indian Country. The Court has subsequently retreated somewhat from that broad statement but its spirit is still the law today. Investors and businesses who sign contracts with tribes, tribal entities, and reservation-based Indians, and who work on tribally and Indian-owned lands on reservations, will undoubtedly have any disputes that arise from these relationships litigated in tribal courts. Non-Indians probably assume that tribal courts are biased in favor of tribal or Indian litigants. This concern is completely false in the vast majority of tribal court cases, but it is a perception that is difficult to disprove to non-Indians.[37]

There has been tremendous growth in tribal court systems and tribal law in the past three decades. About 250 of the 565 federally recognized tribes in the United States have court systems. These vary in their complexity and workload, and range from the Navajo Nation's judicial system, which decides thousands of cases a year, to many tribes that have part-time judges who might hear only a few cases a year. But some tribes have yet to enact separation of power clauses to make their court systems fully independent from the legislative branch, the tribal council. Furthermore, in some tribes, the elected tribal council itself acts as the court or is the tribe's appellate court and hears appeals of decisions from the tribe's trial court. This structure would not be surprising to Europeans, because various countries allow different methods of legislative control over their judicial systems. Even in England, the legislative House of Lords long had review power over judicial matters. But in the U.S. political system, the legislative branch is not allowed to rule on judicial branch decisions.[38]

Businesses and investors contemplating Indian Country are well aware of tribal courts. Sophisticated investors analyze the specific court systems of the states, counties, regions, and, yes, the reservations they are considering for investments. A former tribal chairman from Montana addressed this issue when he stated that tribes must change their attitudes to attract business, they must stabilize their governments, clean up their courts, streamline their regulations, and use incentives to entice business. He also said that businesses need certainty and consistency from government. Tribal governments that want to attract businesses and investors must also critically examine their courts to see if they are set up and operated so as to establish legitimate and fair legal systems where the rule of law applies.[39]

Professors Joseph Kalt and Stephen Cornell have worked with the Harvard Project on American Indian Economic Development since 1989 and we will discuss their findings several times in this book. Their studies on tribal courts are very illuminating. They argue that tribal governments have to compete for jobs and investors along with states, counties, and cities. Thus, tribes must make their reservations attractive to investors and businesses by establishing the rule of law, by drafting and enforcing fair and sound business codes, and by establishing courts that are independent from politics. Kalt states that "without the building of an independent tribal court system, small business has virtually no chance."[40] The Harvard Project has conducted studies over 22 years that show the importance of this point, because it concludes that tribes with truly independent court systems have a 5 percent lower unemployment rate than tribes without independent courts. This statistic demonstrates graphically the importance to Indian Country economic development of tribes having independent and competent courts. The higher employment rate on reservations with independent courts demonstrates that businesses and investors do gravitate to localities where contractual and property interests are protected and the courts, for example, are free from political influence and control.[41]

Most tribal governments are aware of these issues and are developing their courts, increasing judicial competence, and granting their courts more independence. More and more tribes have adopted ordinances or constitutional amendments providing for separations of power between the executive, legislative, and judicial branches in order to increase the independence of their courts. For example, the Grand Ronde Tribe's constitution grants the tribal court authority "to review and overturn tribal legislative and executive actions for violation of the Constitution or the Indian Civil Rights Act of 1968."[42] Additionally, tribes have increased the expertise and competence of their courts by appointing legally trained and experienced judges. Tribes have also worked to ensure a systematic and fair judicial process by adopting rules of procedure for their courts. These rules are often patterned after the influential Federal Rules of Civil Procedure. Many tribal courts also utilize various case reporting methods and/or post their court opinions on the web to educate people about tribal courts and laws. All of these efforts help to lessen concerns about tribal courts.[43]

The vast majority of tribal court decisions are rendered after fair procedures and deliberations by a judge or jury, using standard rules and practices familiar to any attorney, and after granting all parties equal protection and due process. Notwithstanding this fact, as with all human endeavors, there have been a few tribal cases that hit the press and caused concerns for non-Indian and Indian investors. Foreign countries demonstrate what happens when investors fear the government, laws, and the courts, such as has happened in recent years in Russia and elsewhere. Foreign business investments in Russia dropped dramatically after 2002 due to concerns about the fairness of the court system. Such examples emphasize to tribal governments that they have to work to ensure their courts are impartial and fair, and to create governments that follow the rule of law and protect vested contract and property rights so investments can be made with confidence. Court systems that work in this fashion will help attract economic development to reservations, because no one, Indian or non-Indian, is going to invest their capital, time, and efforts building up businesses and property and contract rights where everything they have worked for can be taken away by an unfair or biased court. It is clearly in the best interests of reservation economic development for tribal governments to build fair court systems.[44]

## TRIBAL BUREAUCRACIES

Tribal bureaucracies and administrative agencies also play important roles in helping tribes attract economic development. It is axiomatic that business developers hate bureaucracies because bureaucrats can cause high business start-up costs, a difficult and slow start-up, and low productivity for existing businesses. It is also true that investors and businesses locate where they have the best opportunity to make the highest profits. Subsequently, an efficient tribal bureaucracy that assists investors and businesses to locate on reservations and operate is a major boost to attracting investments.

Like all governments, tribes have both good and bad bureaucracies. Varying levels of knowledge, experience, and helpfulness are encountered on reservations. If tribal governments are serious about providing business-friendly environments where investors will locate, this is another subject tribes must address. Studies by the Harvard Project demonstrate that efficient tribal bureaucracies and agencies are a significant factor in strengthening tribal sovereignty and economic development. This is so because efficient bureaucracies help investors work on reservations and are also helpful in operating tribal businesses. For example, a systematic Harvard study demonstrated that 49 tribes that had taken some control of their forestry programs from the BIA operated the programs more efficiently than the BIA. The tribal bureaucracies were significantly better at timber management and dramatically improved productivity by creating sharply higher prices and lowered costs over those produced by the federal bureaucracy. The conclusion of the study is that tribal institutions and tribal control are the keys to a more productive reservation timber industry. This is an example of efficient tribal bureaucracies that successfully assist tribes in developing economic activities.[45]

There are also examples of ineffective tribal bureaucracies that demonstrate that tribes, like all governments, have room to improve. In 2003, the BIA assumed operation of law enforcement duties on the Blackfeet Reservation after years of complaints about the performance of the tribal police. In addition, on the Pine Ridge Reservation in South Dakota, the head of the chamber of commerce stated that the difficulty in securing tribal business licenses stemmed from the fact that the tribal land committee rarely had any members experienced in business and that people who did receive licenses depended on family connections. He also noted that the Tribe only issues five-year leases and that few banks will make business loans based on such short leases. He alleged that there are many layers of tribal bureaucracy at Pine Ridge and that any of them can delay the business permitting process. Consequently, inefficient and unhelpful tribal bureaucracies inhibit starting and operating businesses on reservations.[46]

Tribes that create bureaucracies that assist investors instead of creating problems will be far more successful in attracting economic development. All tribes, as well as all governments, need to develop bureaucracies that fairly and competently create and enforce the necessary rules and facilitate economic activity as much as is prudent.

## TRIBAL TAXES AND REGULATION

Tribal governments possess the inherent sovereign authority to regulate and tax businesses operating on tribal lands. Tribes are becoming increasingly interested in this subject, as are all governments, because they desperately need funding and a tax base. Some businesses have been surprised to find that tribes possess the power to tax and regulate. As part of due diligence and proper planning, investors and businesses interested in Indian Country need to be aware of these tribal powers.

Tribes, though, should consider the impact that taxing and regulating businesses in the short term can cause. Some tribes have been locked in long-running battles with railroads, utility companies, and businesses over these subjects. After winning some of these cases in the early 1990s, tribes have more often been losing them under recent Supreme Court case law.

It is, of course, a political decision for tribal governments to make whether they will vigorously wield their taxation and regulatory powers or consider using incentives to entice businesses and investors to reservations. It is a difficult economic and political decision that all governments have to make. In 2001, the Navajo Nation approved a 25 percent business activity tax break for reservation-based coal companies. This is a tactic similar to what states and counties do to attract businesses to locate in their areas. Such strategies can also help attract investments to Indian Country.[47]

Many tribes also have extensive regulatory regimes that impact businesses, like those created by tribal employment rights ordinances (TERO). These laws require contractors working on reservations to make payments to the TERO office for each employee, for example, and a percentage of any contracts with the tribe. They also require all businesses on reservations to register with the TERO office, file reports, and give hiring preferences to tribal citizens and Indians. Such ordinances create paperwork and monetary burdens on businesses and increase the cost of doing business on reservation.[48]

Tribal taxes, regulation of business activities, and TERO ordinances are no different than many federal, state, and local governmental regulations. However, it is up to tribal governments to decide how aggressively to apply such taxes and regulations on businesses or whether they can be relaxed and used as incentives for investors to locate in Indian Country.

## UNITED STATES BUREAUCRACY

The federal government plays a major and nearly daily role in the majority of economic activities carried on in Indian Country. This stems from the trust and fiduciary responsibilities the United States owes tribes and individual Indians, and to its ownership as the trustee of much of tribal and individual Indian lands and assets. The United States holds the legal estate, the legal ownership of trust assets, while tribes, and individual Indians, are the beneficial owners of trust properties. Consequently, federal law requires that anyone seeking to buy or lease tribal or individual Indian-owned trust assets has to get the approval of the Indian owner and the United States. Moreover, tribes and individual Indians cannot pledge these assets as collateral for loans, or develop them, or sometimes even use their own assets without pursuing time-consuming federal bureaucratic approvals. Needless to say, this slows economic development and activity in Indian Country, increases the cost, and often completely stymies certain activities. For example, these federal approvals often require compliance with the National Environmental Policy Act, which can take years and can radically slow or completely stop projects.[49]

One example of how federal bureaucratic inefficiency hurts economic activity in Indian Country is the problem of the glacial pace of BIA title searches. These searches are needed to facilitate private mortgages on reservations, leases, and other business activities. The U.S. General Accounting Office reported in 2003 that the BIA had a 113-year staff backlog for completing title search requests. Indians have waited up to six years to get title search reports that other Americans can get in a few days! Obviously, this bureaucratic inefficiency seriously frustrates possible benefits that tribal economies could gain from the private home construction industry and other activities that require timely title reports. Further, the underfunded and understaffed BIA probate process is so far behind in its workload that it is near collapse. The unbelievable delay in probating Indian wills leaves questions of land ownership in Indian Country in limbo for years and seriously handicaps any economic development concerning these lands.[50]

Moreover, federal bureaucrats have to judge the potential and viability of various tribal economic development plans. These federal employees often do not have any particular business expertise; yet they can substitute their judgment for that of tribal governments and experts in deciding whether projects should proceed on trust lands. In the hog farm and housing cases discussed above, opponents of the projects argued that the secretary of the interior was required to tell the tribes the right thing to do as regards reservation economic development. In these instances, the federal bureaucracy stands as an obstacle to tribal economic development. Furthermore, from 1871 to 2000, Congress mandated that the secretary of the interior had to approve any contract with a tribe "relative to their lands." This statute, 25 U.S.C. § 81, caused enormous confusion and uncertainty about economic activities in Indian Country and led to countless federal lawsuits. Some of the most contentious situations regarding business activities on reservations have arisen around the issue of federal approvals. Congress and tribal governments were long aware of the problems that section 81 caused and that BIA involvement was an impediment to business development. Consequently, in

2000, Congress amended this law, and the law now only requires federal approvals of leases of tribal trust lands that encumber the lands and that last for seven years or longer. Tribes could and should continue to lobby Congress to lessen even more of the federal bureaucratic limitations on business development in Indian Country if tribal governments think that is in their benefit.[51]

Indian Country desperately needs more investors and investments of all types to help remedy poverty and economic development issues. Tribal governments should consider how best to encourage and incentivize Indian and non-Indian investments of financial capital, human capital, time, labor, and expertise in Indian Country. This aspect of economic development is crucial to creating reservation economies and tribal and Indian prosperity.

# CHAPTER 7

# *Indian Entrepreneurship*

$A$merican Indian cultures have always supported entrepreneurship; that is, the private operation of individual and family economic initiatives. Throughout history, Indians and their families pursued the economic activities that they desired and used the products and profits they created to support themselves. In fact, privately driven economic pursuits served and still serve well-known aspects of Indian cultures of individual freedom and community responsibilities. One tribally created entrepreneurial organization states that private business is an expression of native culture. This is true because Indian individuals and families are able to fulfill important tribal and family responsibilities by supporting themselves, their families, and their communities through their own efforts. Since most Indian tribes have been doing this for millennia, I suggest that Indians and tribal governments need to try entrepreneurship again in pursuit of economic development. Furthermore, as discussed in Chapter 8, private businesses play a crucial role in creating and growing Indian Country economies.[1]

Today, Indians own private businesses at the lowest rate per capita for any racial or ethnic group in the United States. This is exemplified by comments about the lack of privately owned businesses on the Pine Ridge and Rosebud Sioux reservations. Reports in 2000, stated that even though thousands of Indians lived on those two reservations, the private economy consisted of only a few convenience stores, gas stations, video stores, fast-food outlets, and a grocery store. This is a disastrous situation for Indians and tribal governments and their economies. First, this leads to more poverty and overall lower Indian family incomes. Second, since there are so few employers and jobs available in Indian Country, it leads to high unemployment rates. And, third, the absence of thriving economies, characterized by a sufficient number of privately and publicly owned businesses in Indian Country, adds to the impoverishment of Indians and their families. This is so because without an operating economy and a sufficient number of businesses located on reservations the money Indians and non-Indian reservation residents receive and spend leaks away to the surrounding non-Indian communities and businesses. Consequently, the money Indians spend does not circulate on their reservations between various public and private businesses and their owners and employees so as to create even more business opportunities and jobs. Clearly, if there are no businesses on reservations where residents can buy necessary and luxury goods, they will make those purchases off reservation. The lack, then, of small businesses on reservations leads to many negative economic impacts.[2]

The absolute necessity of having small and large privately owned businesses on reservations where consumers can shop is well demonstrated by the U.S. economy. As the recession of 2008–2009 showed, consumer spending is the engine that drives the U.S. economy. In fact, up to 70 percent of the U.S. economy comes from consumer spending. As the Harvard Project on American Indian Economic Development points out, new job creation is highly dependent on small businesses because "the vast majority of new jobs in the U.S. economy are created by small businesses."[3] The exact opposite economic model exists in Indian Country because there is almost no consumer spending occurring on most reservations. This is so because there are very few reservations that have more than a handful of privately owned businesses where consumers can spend money. The absence of a sufficient level of public and private businesses to keep money circulating on reservations and creating jobs and economic activities contributes mightily to the poverty in Indian Country.

Tribes are well aware of this issue. As mentioned briefly in Chapter 4, in 1991, four Oregon tribes created a nonprofit organization called the Oregon Native American Business and Entrepreneurial Network (ONABEN) to help them create private business sectors on their reservations. Other tribes have also created organizations and programs or worked with other entities to increase the number of Indian-owned businesses. We will highlight those initiatives and discuss what tribal governments and Indians can do to increase the number of Indian entrepreneurs and the number of privately owned reservation-based businesses. Creating more Indian entrepreneurs will help build functioning economies so that more jobs, economic activity, and money will be created and retained in Indian Country.

## UNIQUE CHALLENGES FOR AMERICAN INDIAN ENTREPRENEURS

Entrepreneurs in every jurisdiction and country face challenges in starting, operating, and building permanent economic enterprises. But American Indians face historical, financial, legal, cultural, and social challenges that are surely unique.

# Cultural and Social Issues

Many people believe that American Indian societies and Indians do not agree with or understand private property rights and entrepreneurial business principles. That is false, as was made clear in Chapter 2. But that does not mean that Indian entrepreneurs do not face important cultural and social issues when they are determining whether to start a business and whether to locate it on a reservation.

Questions such as these must be among the most unique of challenges faced by entrepreneurs anywhere. Are the tenets of any culture opposed to people starting their own business, making money to support their family, and becoming financially independent? Surely, the answer is no. After all, as a chairman of the Navajo Nation once stated: "Traditional Navajo values do not include poverty." In fact, Navajo culture requires that Navajo people work hard to support their families and to acquire enough material assets to be financially secure and to be able to participate in ceremonies and assist the needy.[4]

Plainly, though, Indian people do face diverse social and cultural issues in making business decisions. In addition to cultural issues, the history of economic activities on reservations and federal Indian policies have left many tribal communities leery of the businessperson and development schemes that are supposed to "save" the reservation. A long history of having their lands and assets exploited by the majority society has understandably made many tribal governments and Indians cautious about business and development. In fact, the very word "capitalism" causes visceral reactions in some Indian people. In these kinds of situations, Indian entrepreneurs do stand out.

Many commentators have noted these issues. One professor stated that for "many Indians development is the road to cultural ruin" and constitutes "a further walk down that non-Indian road that leads to assimilation and 'civilization.' "[5] He added that many Indians have "a profound ambivalence about the ethos of economic development that values only production and acquisition."[6] Another writer stated that Indian tribes were historically not oriented towards business and property ownership and that "the capitalistic principle of industry and commercial enterprise is arguably incongruous with Native American culture."[7] Moreover, at a tribal business conference in 2001 several speakers mentioned that the capitalist model does not fit Indian cultures and that business and who Indians "are" can cause conflicts.[8] As must be evident, Indian entrepreneurs face an important question at the very start of their decision-making process as to whether they should start their own businesses. Is business and economic development, is starting and owning your own business, a violation of Indian cultural mores? Will reservation inhabitants and tribal customs support the kind of business a person is considering developing?

I appreciate these concerns, but as I have argued, Indian culture and history are not anti-business or anti-private property rights. Instead, historic and modern-day Indian peoples and nations were not and are not opposed to economic activities, private property rights, and entrepreneurship. To the contrary, entrepreneurship and individual Indians and their families operating their own economic activities to support themselves and their communities have been a major part of native history, culture, and economic life. The very principles of operating a business at the free will and free choice of individuals and families and then having their societies and governments protect their private rights match up well with almost all tribal cultures, traditions, and histories.[9]

Many others agree with these conclusions. One of the leading programs to study tribal economic development, the Harvard Project on American Indian Economic Development, concludes that it is "not necessary to stop being tribal or 'traditional' to develop economically."[10] Professor Bill Yellowtail, from the Crow Nation and an ex-Montana legislator, states that "we must give Indians permission to pursue that age-old ... paradigm of entrepreneurial self-sufficiency."[11] And another native person who is both an academic and a tribal economic planner states that "developing reservation economies is vital to sustaining and developing Native American cultural identities."[12] He also states that sovereignty and self-determination goals are served by development and that a lack of economic resources "has an adverse influence on cultural activity."[13] He concludes that "developing reservation economies is vital to sustaining and developing Native American cultural identities ... [and that] economic development is a tool to achieve cultural integrity and self-determination with tribal sovereignty."[14] Plainly, according to these experts, business and economic activities are part of both tribal and Indian histories and futures. Without the ability of individuals to support themselves and their families and communities, Indian tribes cannot long survive as independent societies.

As already mentioned, poverty is not an Indian cultural trait. In fact, the opposite is true. Almost no culture demands that its people live in poverty. Instead, the historical proof shows clearly that many American Indians were well-fed, healthy, and fairly prosperous pre-Euro-American contact. Many tribal peoples actively sought and even openly displayed the accumulation of property and wealth. Tribal governments and laws protected the private rights that were created and Indians attained cultural and leadership status by pursuing individual and family economic activities. These activities were carried out as the right and the duty of individuals to support their families and nations.[15]

By no means am I downplaying the very serious and important concerns of preserving and perpetuating American Indian tribal cultures and traditions in the face of new economic activities. New types of businesses and significant expansions of development could lead tribes and Indians towards cultural homogenization. Many countries have also worried about this effect on their cultures from U.S. materialistic and economic thought.

But the decision whether to participate in a global economy or to support individual Indian entrepreneurship or specific types of businesses is for each tribal nation, community, and Indian individual to make. Careful considerations of possible tradeoffs between a reservation continuing in poverty and despair and what that does to culture and community have to be compared with the possible positive and negative aspects of economic development. It is an exercise in sovereignty and self-determination for tribal governments and communities to decide what kinds of businesses to allow on their reservations and what kinds of businesses and activities they will support. It is also the right of individual Indian entrepreneurs to pursue their own goals and their own self-sufficiency. If there is one economic factor that stands out in the history of America's Indigenous peoples, it is that individuals and families had the right to pursue the activities they thought necessary, and that what they produced and created was their property. That right should also be enforced for modern-day Indians.

Even if there are no major cultural issues preventing Indian entrepreneurs from starting private businesses, Indians do face issues that might be considered unique social challenges. One of the first decisions for any businessperson is where to locate their business. At first blush one might think that Indians would naturally open their businesses on reservations where they were raised or are related because they know the market, the client base, and the employment pool. Yet there are social and cultural challenges involved in making those decisions.

Some Indians have made the conscious decision to locate their businesses off reservations because of issues that can potentially affect the success of their business. They are worried that some types of businesses might not be supported or patronized by reservation residents for various reasons. Some Indian entrepreneurs have cited this concern and others that have led them to locate their businesses off reservation. They also mention cultural issues such as being expected to extend credit, employment, and assistance to relatives and tribal citizens. There are probably other cultures in the world where entrepreneurs face these same issues, but in the United States these appear to be unique to American Indians.[16]

Furthermore, commentators have pointed out that successful Indian business owners stand out on many reservations and sometimes encounter resistance for seeming to have pushed ahead of others. This phenomenon is called "social jealousy" and is well known in many cultures and communities, especially in poorer areas. This principle is known in Indian Country by the "crabs in the bucket" analogy, where a crab that tries to climb out is pulled back in by the others. This is a serious issue that Indian entrepreneurs have to understand, deal with, and factor into their business decisions. Will reservation residents support your business, work for you, and support you in the community, legal, and political issues you will face? Some entrepreneurs have asked these questions and then decided to locate their businesses off reservation. It is a discouraging sight when beneficial economic development is purposely located off reservations.[17]

Indian entrepreneurs face social and cultural issues when starting and operating businesses. The questions do not include, however, the issue of whether tribal cultures and histories support the idea of private business and wealth accumulation. But if the other issues discussed above are preventing beneficial economic development on reservations, then one necessary change, before entrepreneurs will be able to operate on certain reservations, will be for those tribal communities and governments to decide whether they want economic development. They will need to decide whether they will support businesses operated by their fellow citizens and relatives on reservations instead of only spending their money off reservation at non-Indian-owned businesses. It seems to me that the cultural trait of sharing and cooperation should lead Indians to help their friends, relatives, and communities by supporting reservation-based, Indian-owned private businesses. Spending money on your own reservation, after all, helps individuals and the tribal community by supporting Indian-owned businesses that benefit all reservation residents, employ reservation residents, and help create functioning economies, and keeps money circulating on reservation. Depending on the presence of these kinds of cultural and community issues, it appears that Indian entrepreneurs do face some unique cultural and social challenges in starting and operating their businesses.[18]

# Capital

Financial capital is the money and funding needed to start and operate a business. All entrepreneurs obviously need some level of financial capital to start a business. Human capital is the physical and mental tools and abilities needed to operate a business. Human capital includes an entrepreneur's own labor, education, experience, and abilities as a fundraiser, manager, operator, et cetera. The availability of human capital also asks whether there is a capable and available employee pool to assist in running a business.

## *Poverty*

As already mentioned, Indians and Indian Country are the poorest citizens and communities in the United States. This economic situation means that most Indian entrepreneurs have few resources to work with, and this poverty creates an extremely difficult challenge for starting businesses because of a lack of financial capital. This is so because American entrepreneurs generally find the capital to start businesses in three ways: accumulated family wealth; bank loans backed by home mortgages; and regular bank loans. The vast majority of American Indians, however, do not have access to any of these avenues to capitalize a business.[19]

Due to the long history of destitution, poverty, and lack of economic activities in Indian Country, very few Indians have access to accumulated family wealth. With the incredibly high unemployment rates in Indian Country and the incredibly high family poverty rates, this is no surprise.

Second, many of the homes owned by Indians in Indian Country are located on trust land and the United States is the legal owner. The Indian owner is only the beneficial owner. Due to the United States being the legal owner, Indians are unable to grant mortgages to bank on their homes. Thus, home equity, where it exists in Indian Country, can rarely be used to guarantee bank loans. This leaves many Indians unable to use their homes to help finance businesses.[20]

Finally, many Indian people have difficulties securing regular bank loans because of long-entrenched poverty. Also, due to the near absence of economic activity in Indian Country many tribal citizens do not have the consistent employment histories and the kinds of credit scores needed to acquire bank loans. The poverty of Indian Country and of many Indian people definitely presents a challenge to entrepreneurship and acquiring the financial capital needed to start businesses.[21]

## Education and Employment Experience

American Indians have among the lowest educational attainment rates of any ethnic or racial group in the United States. In addition, they often lack business and employment experience. As pointed out in Chapter 1, reservation and urban Indians suffer from unemployment rates that average 40 percent and reach as high as 70 to 90 percent on some reservations. That statistic helps to explain why many Indians lack general business education and employment skills. This is a serious challenge for Indian entrepreneurs. Additionally, because so few Indians own their own businesses, there are very few mentors to train others or to pass on information about owning your own business, and there is little work experience available on reservations or among urban Indian families due to a dearth of employment opportunities. These factors obviously impact entrepreneurship. Dealing with banks and federal, tribal, and state bureaucracies and legal, business, and accounting issues is surely more difficult for the relatively undereducated and inexperienced entrepreneur.[22]

Indian entrepreneurs face ancillary challenges due to the lack of economic activity in general and the horrendous unemployment rates on reservations and among urban Indians. These potential entrepreneurs and their potential employees usually lack long-term job histories, good credit ratings, and a variety of employment and management experiences in the business arena. Reservations that lack nearly any economic activities are also often devoid of business role models and job training opportunities for gaining the necessary experience for future employees and the human capital needed for entrepreneurship. Consequently, the workforce on most reservations is under-trained and inexperienced. This workforce is also oftentimes unmotivated, which is no surprise due to generations of underemployment, a lack of meaningful employment, and little opportunity to experience the benefits and pride that come from earning a living and supporting your family. These issues pose significant challenges for Indian entrepreneurs.[23]

## Health

An additional challenge for American Indians as business owners and as employees is that they suffer from the lowest life expectancy and the worst health issues as a group in the United States. Health care is at an abysmal level in Indian Country and has been for well over a century. The United States has woefully underfunded its treaty and trust responsibilities to Indian people in this regard. The U.S. Indian Health Service budget increases for decades have not even kept pace with inflation. Additionally, the United States spends far less on health care for American Indians, for whom it owes trust and treaty health care responsibilities, than it does for Americans in general and, specifically, for Medicare recipients and federal prisoners. And surprisingly, a new report out of Washington State shows that after making health gains in the 1970s to 1990s, Indian life expectancy and infant mortality rates in that state are getting worse in the twenty-first century. Health issues remain a challenge for Indian entrepreneurs and their employees.[24]

## Tribal Governments

Entrepreneurs contemplating financing or opening businesses in Indian Country face unique challenges in regard to tribal governments. In fact, there is a general idea that many tribal governments and reservations are not business friendly. This is not necessarily because they are considered anti-business but because they have often not yet enacted the laws and regulatory codes that are considered crucial for the success of business and for attracting new businesses and investments. Many tribes, for example, do not have incorporation, business standards, or uniform commercial codes. Some tribal court systems are also perceived as lacking the experience and expertise to decide complex business and contractual disputes. It is true that more than half of the 565 federally recognized tribes in the United States do not even have courts. Due to the relatively recent organization of many modern-day tribal court systems, there is an absence of written case law regarding business issues and the enforcement of contracts, property rights, and related rights and responsibilities. For these reasons and more, many Indian and non-Indian investors and businesses are uneasy about locating in Indian Country. This is no different than the concerns international businesses have about investing in countries around the world where open and fair systems for investing and impartial court systems might be new innovations.[25]

Crucially, many tribal constitutions do not contain prohibitions on ex post facto laws (laws enacted after the fact that change the legal consequences for an act), separation of powers provisions, or prohibitions on governmental impairment of the obligations of existing contracts. This is an ironic situation in that the United States originally handed out nearly identical constitutions for tribes to adopt in the 1930s and the boilerplate constitutions did not contain these important provisions. Entrepreneurs and investors are rightfully concerned about the authority and power of the government where they are thinking of operating. The absence of protections in Indian Country against the impairment of contracts and ex post facto laws, and the apparent lack of separation of powers principles, raise serious questions for private businesses and investors. Many tribes have been amending their constitutions and laws in the modern day, and some have adopted these well-known principles. In 1968, Congress also addressed this issue when it enacted a law that prevents tribal governments from imposing ex post facto laws on anyone.[26]

These issues are well known to businesses, investors, and tribal governments. For example, the attempt in the Pacific Northwest in 2007–2009 to draft an economic development treaty for tribes, already briefly mentioned in Chapters 4 and 6, would specifically require tribal governments to develop and maintain a list of business codes and to ban ex post facto laws and the impairment of existing contracts.[27]

Most tribal governments also have bureaucracies that can impose challenges and costs on entrepreneurs. It is a truism that businesses hate bureaucracies, "red tape," and the resulting costs and delays. "Time is money," and time spent dealing with bureaucracies is wasted time and money that could be used to develop and run a business. Entrepreneurs will encounter varying levels of bureaucratic knowledge, experience, and helpfulness on reservations. But one bureaucracy that businesses will encounter on almost all reservations is the tribal employee rights office (TERO). TERO ordinances usually require on-reservation businesses to register, file paperwork, give hiring preferences to Indians, and pay certain fees. These laws can be costly and can be an obstacle for business start-ups and ongoing operations.[28]

An additional challenge that new businesses and investors face on many reservations is finding a location to operate and obtaining tribal leases for these sites. One might think that the average reservation is all wide-open space, but in actuality many reservations have limited spaces where industrial and economic activities can take place or where they can take place profitably due to the remoteness of most reservations or the site under consideration, lack of infrastructure, social and cultural concerns over the potential use of the site, and checkerboarded land ownership issues arising from federal Indian policies. On many reservations it is also difficult to obtain site leases to operate a business. On the Navajo Reservation it is reported that it takes at least a year to get a business lease, and in past decades it took much longer and involved 20 separate steps. As of 2000, applicants had to provide bonds, certificates of deposit, letters of credit, or cash deposits equal to one year's rental. Few entrepreneurs can afford that kind of investment of their time and limited capital.[29]

Moreover, if the land under consideration is trust land, several different types of tribal and federal approvals must be obtained. And if the land is individually owned trust land, then all of the individual owners and the federal government have to approve a lease. Due to the lingering effects of the Allotment Era of federal Indian policy, many individually owned plots of reservation trust land now have hundreds and even thousands of owners. It can sometimes be impossible to get all the necessary approvals from individuals, the BIA, and tribal governments to secure business site leases.[30]

In addition to these regulatory and leasing issues, tribal governments possess the inherent sovereign powers of taxation, regulation, and jurisdictional authority in Indian Country over tribal citizens, tribally chartered businesses, and many non-Indians and businesses found on reservations. As with all governments, tribes are interested in taxing businesses, and tribes expect to regulate the activities occurring in their territories, including economic development. One township on the Navajo Reservation, for example, created a 2.5 percent sales tax and raised $670,000 in just 18 months. Tribal courts are also the presumptive venue for many lawsuits that arise in Indian Country. So entrepreneurs on reservations can expect to deal with tribal governments in many ways.[31]

In sum, it is clear that entrepreneurs need to study and know the reservation where they are planning on operating. They must also understand the tribal economic history and its enforcement of private property rights and laws. This is an important and unique challenge that entrepreneurs face when deciding to locate in Indian Country.

## Federal and State Governments

Federal and state governments also impose challenges for entrepreneurs and investors considering Indian Country. These challenges are quite different than what are faced by off-reservation entrepreneurs. These entities are eager to exercise taxation, regulatory, and jurisdictional authority on reservations. That is nothing unique for entrepreneurs, but businesses in Indian Country are faced with conflicting and even unsettled federal and state claims of taxation, regulation, and jurisdiction that might overlap tribal claims. Businesses can get caught in the middle of these disputes, and that uncertainty alone, one of the worst enemies of business and investment, is often sufficient to convince Indian and non-Indian entrepreneurs to avoid reservations.

Moreover, the federal government plays a major role in day-to-day economic activities in Indian Country. The United States assumed this role due to the Constitution; hundreds of treaties the United States signed with Indian nations; the fiduciary and trustee responsibilities it owes tribes and individual Indians; and its ownership as the trustee of about 56 million acres of tribal land and tribal assets and about 11 million acres of individually Indian-owned trust lands and assets. Since the United States holds the legal title to many of the assets of tribes and Indians, federal law requires that anyone seeking to buy or lease tribal or individual Indian trust assets has to secure the approval of the United States. In addition, tribes and individuals cannot pledge these assets as collateral for loans, develop, or sometimes even use the assets themselves without time-consuming federal bureaucratic approvals. Needless to say, this situation slows down and increases the cost of economic activities in Indian Country, interjects enormous uncertainty, and can even completely stymie activities.[32]

There are a few graphic examples that demonstrate the problems that federal control of tribal assets and federal bureaucratic red tape can cause Indian entrepreneurship. As mentioned in Chapter 6, in 2003 the BIA was reported as having a 113-year staff backlog for title search requests. These searches are needed for many reasons, including acquiring private mortgages and leases on reservations. It is impossible for a business, investor, or entrepreneur to operate under that kind of regulatory system.[33] Moreover, federal employees are often required to review tribal and individual economic plans for reservation and trust land developments and they pass judgment on whether federal approvals will be granted to projects. These federal employees often have no specific expertise in business, and some commentators have alleged that BIA employees are more dedicated to maintaining reservations than to developing them, and that they will even "stand[ ] in its path."[34] Yet the permission of these federal employees is often crucial to whether a project goes ahead. That is an intolerable obstacle for Indian entrepreneurs and investors.[35]

Furthermore, persons desiring to operate businesses on reservations need to check out very carefully the Indian traders' license requirement. Many entrepreneurs and businesses have overlooked or ignored these provisions in recent times. But the necessity of obtaining a federal license to sell goods on reservations has been a part of federal law for over two hundred years and is still the law today.[36]

State governments can also wreak havoc and business uncertainty on reservations. States are often interested in taxing and regulating non-Indian economic enterprises on reservations, and have even tried to intervene in the on-reservation activities of Indian entrepreneurs and tribal governments. Federal and state governments impose numerous obstacles, obligations, and uncertainties on Indian entrepreneurs and investors operating in Indian Country.

## Reservation Infrastructure

The infrastructure on most reservations also raises unique obstacles for Indian Country entrepreneurs and investors. First, most reservations are far from markets, cities, clients, employees, resources, et cetera. The physical remoteness of most reservations was purposely intended by the United States because it located tribes far from valuable resources and population centers. Many reservations remain very isolated today. This is an important factor that inhibits reservation economic activity. Concurrent with the remoteness of reservations, many are often poorly served, if at all, by railroads and highways. Many reservations are served only by two-lane highways and, as mentioned, up to 66 percent of reservation roads are unpaved. Reservations also suffer from other infrastructure issues such as a shortage of clean water, electricity, telephone, and Internet service. The average American entrepreneur is just not faced with these kinds of unique problems.[37]

The only reasonable conclusion is that Indian entrepreneurs face unique challenges in starting, locating, and operating businesses. It is no wonder, then, that individual Indians are underrepresented per capita in the ranks of private business ownership in the United States. This is not due to cultural prohibitions on pursuing economic activity, private initiative, private property rights, and wealth, but it is instead rooted in historic and systemic obstacles to business formation, entrepreneurship, profitability, and investment.

## UNLIMITED POTENTIAL

One encouraging factor about the near absence of privately owned businesses in Indian Country is that the upside for Indian entrepreneurship is enormous. A Harvard professor claims that there is an explosion waiting to happen in the private business sector on most reservations because of the absence of local stores and the distance people have to travel to shop. The reality in Indian Country today is a lack of private businesses, functioning economies, jobs, and prosperity.[38]

Surprisingly, though, the federal government released in both 1997 and 2002 some startling figures that made it look like a revolution had already occurred in Indian entrepreneurship. The U.S. Department of Commerce and the census reported a great increase in the number of American Indian- and Alaska Native-owned businesses; from 3,000 in 1969, to 197,300 in 1997, to 201,400 businesses in 2002. They claimed that these businesses had about 191,000 employees and $26.9 billion in revenues in 2002. I do not believe, though, that anyone thinks these numbers accurately reflect the reality of Indian entrepreneurship and reservation economies. Instead, these numbers are of dubious authenticity and do not reflect actual conditions.[39]

The 2002 census discounted its 1997 estimates because the 1997 estimate included tribally owned businesses, including Alaska Native corporations, and in addition its conclusions were based solely on samplings. Moreover, the 1997 estimate was based on a reporting system in which business owners were not even allowed to identify themselves as Indian or Alaska Native. It is unclear then how the census could even guess which businesses were allegedly owned by native peoples.[40]

The 2002 figures are equally suspect. They are again based on estimates taken from samplings. This time they apparently did not include tribally owned businesses, but they once again counted Alaska Native corporations. By no stretch of the imagination can those corporations be defined as individually owned Indian businesses. Those corporations, while owned by individual Alaska Native shareholders, were created in 1971 by Congress to benefit Alaska tribal governments and to manage extensive tribal landholdings and assets. Including Alaska Native corporations in a survey of individually owned Indian businesses dramatically skews the estimates of the 2002 report.

My optimism for the future of Indian entrepreneurship comes not from these inflated figures but from an awareness of the abilities and toughness of Indian people and communities, the growing tribal governmental emphasis on developing economies and helping individual Indians to start their own businesses, and the crying need for more businesses and jobs on reservations. Various commentators have also argued that Indians have the advantages of entrepreneurial skills, positive attitudes toward development, and available capital and financial assistance. American Indians and their governments have also survived hundreds of years of active political, social, and economic oppression, and even genocide. But they are still here and are growing in population and strength every day.

These facts show that the potential for Indian entrepreneurship and the improvement of Indian and tribal economic conditions is unlimited. This potential is also demonstrated by several items that we will address below; many of which help to counteract the challenges discussed above.

## Human and Financial Capital

The upside for Indian entrepreneurship is demonstrated by many positive developments that tribal governments and Indians are enacting to reduce the obstacles that individuals face in starting and operating private businesses.

### *Poverty*

Indian people still have a long, long way to go to catch up to the national economic averages. But very positive steps have already been taken to improve the financial status of American Indians. The facts demonstrate that individual Indian business ownership rates and family incomes are on the rise. This kind of progress can contribute to the momentum to grow even more businesses.[41]

In addition, as is discussed below, tribal and federal governments are working to overcome some of the obstacles that poverty causes for Indians in starting businesses. These governments have begun to devise ways for tribal citizens to borrow money for business start-ups and to overcome the fact that individually owned trust property cannot be mortgaged. Many tribal governments that have the resources are now making loans to tribal citizens to start new businesses, in amounts as high as $100,000. And some tribes have established banks or facilitated the opening of bank branches on reservations to provide services for tribal citizens. Other tribes are using their leverage and influence with local banks to ensure that their citizens have full access and even perhaps an inside track for bank loans to start businesses.[42]

In a few tribes with very successful casino operations, the financial improvements have been dramatic. About one-quarter of tribes with casinos pay out their net profits each year in per capita payments. This can be a substantial amount of money in a few tribes. A college education and jobs in tribal enterprises are guaranteed by several tribal governments to any citizen who desires.[43]

There is an added benefit for Indian entrepreneurs when their community poverty issues are lessened. As explained in a 2008 speech by Chairman Antone Minthorn of the Confederated Tribes of the Umatilla Indian Reservation, people who have savings and resources to fall back on as a safety net are more willing to take the chance of starting their own business. Consequently, tribal citizens who can reasonably rely on falling back on tribal jobs and accumulated resources if they do not succeed at their own private business will be more willing to take that risk.[44]

These kinds of factors help to lessen the poverty obstacle to starting private businesses in Indian Country and for urban Indians.

## Human Capital

Great strides have also been made in improving the educational level, overall health, and work skills of American Indians. Tribes and the United States have emphasized education in the past few decades, and a new generation of Indian leaders and businesspersons is emerging. At least 36 tribal colleges have been started in Indian Country, primarily in the past two decades. In 1968, the Navajo Nation started the first tribally operated college. Tribal colleges offer associate's degrees in many different subjects, and at least two of the colleges now grant bachelor's degrees.

Various studies have demonstrated the crucial educational and economic importance of tribal colleges to Indians and reservations. Indians who transfer from tribal colleges to four-year schools are four times more likely to succeed at the four-year school than Indian students who did not attend a tribal college. Also, tribal college graduates are far more likely to pursue further education and to be employed than tribal citizens who did not attend tribal schools. The potential of tribal and Indian benefits from tribal colleges is unlimited. Between 1997 and 2002, enrollment of American Indians in tribal colleges grew by 32 percent. Moreover, diversity efforts and scholarships are also helping Indians attend non-Indian colleges and postgraduate schools in never before seen numbers. In 1976, for example, 3,326 Indians received bachelor's degrees, but that number increased to 10,940 in 2006.[45]

Two examples demonstrate the progress and importance of improving the educational attainment levels of Indians and for far more emphasis on higher education. First, an informal survey in the late 1960s found that there were only two dozen Indians who were attorneys in the entire United States. There are now over 3,000 Indian attorneys. This is an amazing and encouraging change. At the same time there is still much room for improvement even in just this one professional field. That is because there would be about 5,000 more American Indian attorneys if Indians were lawyers at the same rate per capita as in the general U.S. population. Second, there is also a disproportionately low number of Indian dentists, because in 2004 it was reported that there were only about 140 to 150 American Indian dentists in the entire United States. Indians and Indian communities would certainly benefit from increases in the numbers of Indian doctors, lawyers, dentists, nurses, psychologists, and other professionals.[46]

Native peoples are also steadily improving their educational situations in other ways, and federal, tribal, and state programs are helping. Many tribes are creating financial literacy classes based on U.S. Small Business Administration materials and, as is discussed below, many tribal governments operate economic development departments that assist tribal citizens to learn about business and assist them to start their own businesses.

Moreover, as Indian employment rates rise, the human capital in Indian Country is improving. The work experience and skills that Indians learn in urban areas and as part of a reservation or tribal workforce are important factors in increasing the opportunities and potential for more entrepreneurs. In addition, critical management skills are learned when Indians operate tribal governmental programs and economic entities. Hence, as tribal governments expand their own governmental and economic activities, one positive external impact is the concomitant improvement of the tribal workforce.[47]

Health issues are still of very serious concern in Indian Country, and a troubling 2009 report out of Washington State says that Indian life expectancy and infant mortality rates in that state are actually getting worse. And diabetes is rapidly replacing alcohol as the leading Indian health issue. Increased tribal, federal, and state programs and personal efforts are needed to continue to address health concerns. The potential for improving Indian health is great, and reservation and urban Indian families will prosper in many ways as gains are made in this regard.[48]

## Tribal Governments

The potential for increasing Indian entrepreneurship is also improving due to factors under the control of tribal governments. Tribes are undertaking many positive developments and could do even more to help their economies and Indian entrepreneurs. They also realize that the issues entrepreneurs and investors face when considering working in Indian Country are similar to those confronting tribal governments. In a 1994 study, tribal leaders stated the five main issues they faced in bringing economic development to their reservations: 1) lack of capital; 2) lack of economic resources and an inability to obtain capital; 3) lack of natural resources; 4) lack of trained management; and 5) lack of trained personnel. We have identified most of these items as obstacles for Indian entrepreneurs too. So as tribal governments address these subjects for themselves, there should be collateral benefits for individual Indian businesses.[49]

Tribes are taking positive steps to address these developmental issues and coincidentally other issues that individual entrepreneurs face. As already mentioned, many tribes lack the basic laws and court systems that investors and businesspeople need. Tribal governments are slowly adopting these laws and systems. A few tribes long ago adopted parts of the Uniform Commercial Code (UCC), a set of standardized commercial laws that all 50 states have adopted. More tribes are adopting UCCs today. There is even a model UCC that was drafted specifically for tribes, and several tribal governments have adopted it. The Crow Nation in Montana, for example, enacted the tribal UCC in 2008 and is also using the Montana state bureaucracy for the filing of security interest notices for assets located on the Crow Reservation. Both of these moves look like positive steps for tribes. The benefit of using a state recording system for recording security interests is for the ease and comfort of investors and businesses and to help tribes avoid paying to duplicate preexisting state filing systems.[50]

Another effort under way in the Pacific Northwest (already mentioned several times and which remains a work-in-progress as of 2011) demonstrates that tribes are aware of the obstacles entrepreneurs and investors face in Indian Country and are attempting to address those issues. This treaty would expressly require tribes to enact a designated list of laws, including a UCC, business incorporation, licensing, and standards codes. This is a basic and yet major step for Indian Country and would greatly aid entrepreneurs and investors. This draft document also shows that tribes are aware of the problems businesses have in finding and leasing locations on reservations, because it would require tribes to designate at least one "trade zone" on their reservation where business activities could occur. This is an inspired idea, because defining and developing trade zones would make more certain where entrepreneurs and investors could get leases to locate their businesses on reservations and would greatly facilitate that process.[51]

This draft document also demonstrates that tribal governments realize they need to strengthen their court systems, because it addresses issues about tribal courts and the legal impediments that are perceived to exist for business, entrepreneurship, and investment on reservations. The document would provide for the creation of a court system that is experienced in business and contract law that tribes would utilize, or tribes could designate their own court systems if that is their decision. This demonstrates that tribal leaders are well aware of the importance of efficient, independent, and fair court systems in attracting Indian and non-Indian businesses, entrepreneurs, and investors to locate their businesses in Indian Country.[52]

Tribes are also addressing the lack of work and business management experience in their employee pool. One side benefit of the economic and governmental operations of tribes has been to train tribal citizens and employees in work skills and in management positions. Tribal forestry and natural resource departments, casinos, business ventures, and governmental bureaucracies have created a growing body of trained and experienced tribal citizens from which future entrepreneurs will be drawn. For instance, the Mississippi Choctaw Tribe is famous for successfully operating manufacturing businesses that most of Indian Country has not yet been able to replicate. The Tribe requires that each non-Indian manager train a Choctaw citizen to replace him or her when he or she retires, as does the Confederated Tribes of the Umatilla Indian Reservation in Oregon. In addition, the Warm Springs Tribe in Oregon has trained almost all of its administrators in the Tribe's luxury resort. These efforts will obviously increase the potential for more Choctaw, Umatilla, and Warm Springs entrepreneurs in the future.[53]

Furthermore, tribes have established programs to teach individual Indians to start privately owned businesses. As mentioned several times, four Oregon tribes started the Oregon Native American Business & Entrepreneurial Network (ONABEN) to help Indians on and off reservations develop new businesses. These tribal governments are focusing on creating a private business sector and trying to create functioning economies. ONABEN has developed innovative and culturally relevant training materials that are being used across the country and in many tribal colleges to teach Indians the basics of formulating a business idea, drafting a workable plan, and operating a business. The ONABEN model has been a success and has helped hundreds of individual Indians in Oregon, Washington, and Idaho to start new businesses and to attain an excellent survival rate for these businesses.[54]

In 1999, the Cheyenne River Sioux Tribe in South Dakota also created the Four Bands Community Fund to offer business training programs and assistance for reservation residents to secure start-up loans. The Mille Lacs Band of Chippewa Indians in turn created a small business development program that arranges loans and provides tribal entrepreneurs with training and technical assistance. Organizations across the country run other programs that range from classroom instruction, counseling, and technical assistance to help Indians develop and operate privately owned businesses and to find start-up loans and contract opportunities.[55]

Furthermore, tribes are also actively addressing financing issues for Indian entrepreneurs. Several tribes with the resources now provide large and small loans for business start-ups, offer business training, and have created banks or used their leverage with banks to acquire business loans for their citizens. The value of these types of efforts for both private entrepreneurs and reservation communities is graphically demonstrated by the successful privately operated Lakota Fund. The fund was created in 1987 on the Pine Ridge Reservation in South Dakota, which was the poorest reservation and county in the United States. The fund is a micro loan and business training initiative that was studied by four economists in 2009. Using the nearby Rosebud Sioux Reservation and the years of 1980 to 2006 to define a control group, the study demonstrates that the fund raised real per capita income at Pine Ridge significantly from 1987 to 2006 and that the number and diversity of business enterprises on the reservation rose from 2 to over 350 and that more than 750 new jobs were created. These results are nothing short of spectacular.[56]

Finally, and very importantly, tribes can help Indian entrepreneurs and investors and can increase exponentially the number of tribal entrepreneurs by working to create reservation economies. We discuss this subject in depth in Chapter 8. But one way for tribes to grow more entrepreneurs and businesses on reservations is for tribal governments to become the clients of Indian entrepreneurs and to purchase as many goods and services as possible from Indian-owned businesses. Tribal governments spend an enormous amount of money on their operations and economic activities. Many tribes now routinely have annual operating budgets of $75 to $100 million. But as is well recognized, tribes spend too little of this money on Indian- and reservation-based businesses. This is partially a "chicken and egg" issue. Admittedly, there are too few privately owned Indian businesses to provide a very large percentage of the goods and services tribes need. But there also seems to be a disconnect in getting tribal governments to patronize Indian-owned businesses. If even a fraction of tribal expenditures could be funneled to privately owned Indian businesses, it would go a long way to sustaining those businesses, enticing other entrepreneurs to start businesses, and helping to create reservation economies. Tribes need to seriously consider using their governmental expenditures and their "anchor" businesses, such as casinos and other major economic entities, to patronize Indian-owned businesses and to develop and support their reservation economies and Indian-owned businesses. Disappointingly, though, one commentator stated in 2010 that sales by Indian vendors to the multibillion-dollar Indian gaming industry comprised less than 5 percent of the total vendor sales.[57]

If tribal governments will direct their spending as much as possible at Indian-owned businesses, it will go farther than one might imagine in increasing the number of entrepreneurs on reservations. And increasing the number of businesses operating on reservations will then accelerate the process of creating and attracting even more businesses. This is so because as money stays and circulates on a reservation and is spent over and over between various publicly and privately owned businesses and their employees, it encourages even more people to risk becoming entrepreneurs. This increase then encourages other investors and entrepreneurs to create even more businesses on the reservations and that in turn increases the number of employed persons on reservations who are spending their money in the tribal economy too. Obviously, a reservation needs a critical mass of large and small businesses, public and private, to keep dollars circulating within its borders as long as possible. In this situation, more entrepreneurs will develop new businesses and innovate new ideas by playing off each other. Thus, two or three more entrepreneurs on a reservation will create a few more new businesses, which will then inspire a few more. Pretty soon, a reservation can have a functioning economy. The potential and the circularity of this process is endless.[58]

The lost opportunities from having so few privately owned businesses on reservations, and the need to motivate Indian entrepreneurs and to create functioning reservation economies is graphically demonstrated by a study conducted by the seven federally recognized tribes in Montana in 2000. The study showed that the seven tribes, their citizens, and the BIA payrolls equaled $200 million annually. Yet, nearly all of this money is spent off reservation in non-Indian communities and in non-Indian businesses and creates an economic benefit for Montana of $1 billion. The reason this happens is simple: there are very few privately owned businesses on these seven reservations where people can spend their money. Because the money is not spent on reservations, this enormous economic benefit goes to the state and not to the tribal communities, and reservation poverty is perpetuated.[59]

Tribal governments are well aware of the challenges they face in attracting businesses, economic development, and investors to their reservations. They have to compete for those investors and jobs with every other state and county government. Indian and non-Indian companies and even tribal citizens have to decide where to locate their businesses. Tribes thus have to make their reservations attractive to investors by establishing the rule of law and enacting sound business codes, and creating courts and agencies that are independent from politics because "without the building of an independent tribal court system, small business has virtually no chance."[60] Obviously, there is much tribal governments should do, can do, and already have done to increase the potential of Indian entrepreneurship. The tribal role in this process is to provide leadership, financing, and well-ordered societies with settled laws that are evenly enforced, and to become the clients of Indian entrepreneurs. In the long run, these efforts will help create economies on reservations that will benefit everyone—tribal governments, tribal communities and cultures, and individual Indian entrepreneurs and their families.

## Federal and State Governments

The state and federal governments also play important roles in nurturing Indian entrepreneurship. Indians are state and federal citizens, so these governments have responsibilities to assist them in improving their economic situations. State and federal governments can and do provide some economic, educational, and contracting opportunities for Indian entrepreneurs. They could do far more in that regard.[61]

State, tribal, and federal governments could also try to cooperate better on many issues, including economic development. States and the federal government could stop opposing tribal governments over every taxation, regulatory, and jurisdictional issue. States and tribes have in recent years settled some longstanding and intractable problems about jurisdiction and resources with intergovernmental compacts that help these governments work together and reduce the time and money spent on litigation and conflict. Tribes and states have made good progress on water rights agreements and cross-deputization agreements to control criminal issues, for example. Tribes and states and especially rural areas near reservations could work together on economic issues. Maybe by working together they could get increased assistance from the federal government.[62]

The federal government in particular has a trust and treaty responsibility for Indians and tribes, and it has the legal authority in Indian Country that allows and requires it to do beneficial things to improve economic conditions. Congress has sometimes used its authority to try to address problems impacting Indian economic development. Congress and the federal government could do a lot more to assist economic development on reservations.

The federal government has tried various efforts to ameliorate Indian economic conditions. In the 1960s, federal poverty programs invested millions in tribal programs that trained Indians and addressed some infrastructure issues. In recent decades, the government has worked to some extent with individual Indians by providing loan and grant programs for tribes and Indians for business start-ups. Job training and experience has been provided to Indians through several federal programs. The Small Business Administration has also focused somewhat on individual Indians, and the SBA section 8(a) program has benefited many tribes and some Indian entrepreneurs by allowing them to contract with the federal government to provide goods and services.[63]

One important step the federal government should emphasize that would have an immediate beneficial impact for Indian entrepreneurs would be to get serious about the Buy Indian Act Congress enacted in 1910 to encourage the BIA and the federal government to buy products from Indian and tribal businesses. "In fiscal 2009, the U.S. government expended $18.7 billion dollars through the General Services Administration alone to acquire materials, services, and office space from private vendors. If even 1 percent of these items and services were obtained from Indian entrepreneurs, it could jump-start Indian businesses on and off reservations across the country."[64]

Some state governments have also undertaken a few efforts to help Indian entrepreneurs. They could do more to help their own citizens and to address poverty in Indian Country. It is truly a win-win situation for state governments when they help all their citizens to improve their economic lives. Helping to alleviate poverty on reservations will also have a beneficial effect on states due to the spillover of improved economic conditions on reservations into non-Indian areas.

Plainly, all Americans will benefit as a society as Indians start to reach their economic potential as entrepreneurs. Studies conducted for ONABEN demonstrated that the financial assistance states and the federal government gave ONABEN to assist Indian entrepreneurs was repaid to those governments many times over in increased tax revenues alone. Thus, notwithstanding the duty of these governments to assist their own citizens, these governments also benefited on the dollar and cents side from helping Indian entrepreneurs. It is then both economically reasonable and humane for state and federal governments to assist Indian economic development.[65]

## CONCLUSION

Tribal governments need to build functioning economies on their reservations. This is the only way to keep money circulating on reservations and to capture the maximum economic value from the money that tribes and Indians possess. The only way to enjoy the multiplier effect, the re-spending of money in Indian Country, is to create more privately owned businesses on reservations and functioning economies. And the only way to do that is to encourage and support Indian entrepreneurs.

A mix of large and small, private and public businesses operating on reservations will encourage residents and visitors to spend money and to support reservation economic development and employment. Moreover, this effect will grow exponentially as additional reservation businesses and employment opportunities are created. The benefits that come from creating more entrepreneurs, more role models, more jobs, and more places to spend money on reservations will then become evident. An economy clearly needs the presence of numerous individually owned businesses, tribally owned businesses, and a wide variety of goods and services for sale. Consequently, increasing the number and variety of Indian- and non-Indian-owned businesses on reservations is a logical, reasonable, and important goal that tribal governments should pursue.[66]

There is no question that tribes and Indian entrepreneurs face some unique and even daunting challenges in increasing their rate of private business ownership. But these are not impossible obstacles. Many Indians already operate their own businesses and many others are learning job and management skills by working for tribal governments. The potential for Indian entrepreneurship is nearly unlimited. There are positive signs that the creation of functioning economies on reservations, raising the rates of Indian private business ownership on and off reservations, and moving Indian families out of poverty are achievable goals.

It also bears repeating that culture is not an obstacle to Indian entrepreneurship. In fact, the opposite is true. The histories and traditions of all American tribal cultures support the individual right and obligation of Indians to support themselves and their families. Increasing entrepreneurship and economic development on reservations in a careful and respectful manner will support tribal cultures, not injure them. After all, as one tribal economic planner stated, "economic development is a tool to achieve cultural integrity and self-determination with tribal sovereignty."[67]

In addition, cultural interests will be better served if poverty and its accompanying social ills are reduced and Indian families can choose to return to live on their reservations because jobs are available. This situation will be an enormous benefit to tribal cultures and governments as tribal youth could attend reservation schools, learn from elders, study tribal languages, and participate in ceremonies. Many concrete results already point out the positive effects on tribal cultures from increasing economic activities on reservations and as tribal citizens move home because jobs and economic activities are available. Moreover, as tribal governments, Indian families, and reservation economies acquire more assets, they can use their money, resources, and leisure time to invest in their tribes and cultures and to support programs and activities to study tribal histories and to perpetuate and renew tribal traditions. As an example, in 2009, the Suquamish Tribe used its new financial resources to open a 13,000-square-foot community center called "House of Awakened Culture" to hold ceremonies and celebrations.[68]

Improved economic situations can also help improve the general health, education, and other important aspects of reservation life. It is clear that many health and social problems that Indians encounter arise from poverty and despair. These issues have created very negative impacts for Indian and their families. Certainly, these problems can be better addressed and ameliorated if Indian families and communities have more financial assets and can increase their standards of living and improve their health care, and enjoy the positive affirmations that come from supporting one's own family. As one Umatilla tribal citizen said about her tribe's economic improvements: "My kids are going to have it better than I did. We have every right to feel good about ourselves."[69]

I agree with Chairman Antone Minthorn of the Umatilla Indian Reservation when he stated at an Indian business conference in 2008 that tribes and cultures need entrepreneurs and economic prosperity: "We need to make it acceptable in Indian Country to be in business; it's not about rejecting culture, it builds sovereignty."[70] Consequently, Indian culture is not an obstacle for Indian entrepreneurs. Instead, tribal histories demonstrate that operating individual economic enterprises to support families and communities is very much in line with who Indian peoples are and with their cultures and traditions. As Bill Yellowtail stated, "contemporary American Indian sovereignty depends directly upon a successful rekindling of [Indian] entrepreneurial spirit."[71]

# CHAPTER 8

# *Creating Reservation Economies*

**T**ribal governments and reservation communities desperately need to create functioning economies in Indian Country to increase economic activities and improve living conditions. The present-day development and the long-term existence and success of reservations and Indian communities and cultures are dependent on these factors. This is not an overstatement. If Indian families cannot find adequate housing and living wage jobs on or near their reservations, how are they going to support themselves and the development and continuation of their governments, homelands, and cultures?

Building an economy is not easy. It can be especially difficult in Indian Country, because reservations are often located in remote areas and are faced with the same problems as the rest of rural America such as declining populations, infrastructure and remoteness issues, and a dearth of viable economic options. There are many reasons why up to 65 percent of American Indians do not live on reservations, but the necessity of finding permanent employment to support a family and adequate housing certainly rank high among the reasons. We will examine some of the options and strategies that tribal, federal, and state governments and native peoples can pursue to help create viable economies and to improve living conditions in Indian Country.

In addition to providing more goods, services, businesses, and jobs in Indian Country, one of the key advantages of creating a functioning economy on a reservation is demonstrated by what economists call the multiplier effect. When people receive money they spend a predictable and set amount on the necessities and luxuries of life. The goal of any city, county, or state is to keep that spending and those dollars in the local economy as long as possible. When that happens, every dollar that a person spends on video rentals, food, clothes, and dining, for example, ends up as salaries, profits, and spending money in the pockets of other people in the local community who then also spend a predictable amount on goods and services and, hopefully, all that spending occurs in the local economy. In this way, one dollar circulates and recirculates throughout a local economy and community many times before it is spent elsewhere. Economists call it leakage when money is spent outside the local economy.

The multiplier effect and the re-spending of the same dollar in the local community can only occur if there are a sufficient number of businesses and services available locally where money can be spent on the necessities and luxuries of life. The multiplier effect demonstrates the importance of reservations having businesses and economies so that the money residents and visitors have can stay in the local community as long as possible. The multiplier effect also fosters the creation of new businesses and new jobs as the recirculation of money in a community creates the opportunity for even more economic activity in the local area.[1]

Generally, it is considered optimal for money to circulate five to seven times in a local economy before it spins out or leaks away from the community. But in Indian Country money does not circulate at all because there are so few places where money can be spent. In fact, the money that Indians and tribal governments possess is not even spent once on the vast majority of reservations, because very few tribes have economies in which residents can be employed, cash their checks, and spend their money for the goods and services they need. On the vast majority of the 300 reservations in the United States, the money Indians receive is immediately spent in off-reservation, non-Indian towns. This leakage, this loss of reservation-based income and economic potential, occurs because of the absence of a variety of small and large, publicly and privately owned businesses. Most reservations do not have movie theaters, motels, video stores, larger grocery stores, clothing stores, restaurants, or even bank branches where people can cash their checks and engage in business and shopping.[2]

Tribal governments and scholars have long been aware of the leakage problem. In 1994, a Navajo Nation official stated that eighty cents of every dollar reservation residents received left the reservation immediately. A 1973 study of the Zuni Pueblo demonstrated that 84 percent of all individual income was spent off reservation. A former commissioner of Indian affairs noted that a million dollars invested in most communities generates approximately $10 million in cash flow because of the multiplier effect, "[b]ut in Indian communities, one million dollars generates just one million dollars of cash flow."[3] Another observer also noted that money paid to Indians is immediately spent off reservations, and a Navajo Nation chairman in 1979 and the Nation's 1978 Annual Report stated: "The border towns, where there is a better delivery of goods and services, absorb a majority of incomes earned on the reservation. . . . Navajo government officials know that wealth is flowing off the reservation."[4]

The seven federally recognized tribes in Montana conducted a study in 2000 that demonstrates this problem. Even as poor as these reservations are, collectively their citizens receive and spend a large amount of money every year. In 1999, the citizens of those tribes spent $48 million dollars off their reservations. The study also demonstrated that the tribal, reservation, and BIA salaries combined equaled $200 million annually and created an economic benefit for the state of Montana of $1 billion. The study calculated that amount by assuming the funds were spent and re-spent in the Montana economy five times before the money leaked away. Sadly, the $1 billion benefit of this money, created by the multiplier effect, could have been felt in Indian Country if reservations had full-fledged, functioning economies.[5]

This leakage of the money reservation residents receive causes Indian Country to lose an enormous number of economic activities, benefits, and jobs. This factor significantly dilutes the value of the income that reservation residents receive to stimulate more economic activity in their communities. This predicament is a disaster for the economic situation and the standard of living in Indian Country. The loss of these dollars to off-reservation businesses prevents the development of tribal economies and promising economic opportunities. The simple solution seems to be that tribal governments and communities have to work intelligently and purposely to create and operate a diverse array of businesses in Indian Country to develop their economies, increase economic activities and new jobs, and to retain at least some of the consumer spending of residents and visitors on their reservations.[6]

The importance of consumer spending is well demonstrated by the U.S. economy and the recession of 2008–2009. As mentioned, perhaps 70 percent of the U.S. gross domestic product is created by consumer spending. When consumers reduced their spending in the fall of 2008 it contributed significantly to weakening the U.S. economy. This helps drive home the point of the absolute importance and value of building economies on reservations so that consumer spending can occur in Indian Country. Consequently, if tribes can create more privately and tribally owned companies in Indian Country that will help to capture and keep some consumer spending on reservations, the multiplier effect will then create further increases in economic activities and create new businesses, new jobs, and help to develop functioning economies.[7]

## THE TRIBAL ROLE

Tribal governments and political and community leaders probably play the most important role in creating reservation economies. The leadership, funding, legal climate, promotion of on-reservation investments and more come almost exclusively from tribal governments. I am not advocating centrally planned economies that are managed and operated by tribal governments, but the reality of political and economic life on the vast majority of reservations is that their economies are heavily impacted and oftentimes directed by tribal leadership. Tribal leaders should focus on building economies that consist of a mix of privately and publicly owned and large and small businesses.

## Tribal Businesses

A fact of life on reservations is that tribal governments and businesses dominate reservation economic activities and economies. When you add tribal government jobs to the federal government jobs, federal grant programs, and significant federal control of reservation economic activities, you have centrally planned and operated economies. Many scholars and economists have noted the phenomenon that federal and tribal governments are the primary employers on most reservations. At various times approximately two-thirds of all people employed on the Zuni Reservation worked for government agencies; 45 percent of the jobs at the Hualapai Nation were government jobs, as were 75 percent of the jobs on the Fort Mohave Reservation, and 69 percent of the jobs on the Northern Cheyenne reservation. In the 1980s, nearly 50 percent of all American Indian income in the United States came from federal and tribal employment. Since most of the economic resources in Indian Country are directed at federal and tribal jobs, this has resulted in an absence of diversity in tribal economies, very few privately owned businesses, and very little re-spending and multiplier effect occurring on reservations. Many commentators have noted that tribes have been the prime actors in operating businesses in Indian Country although federal, state, and local governments rarely do so. "Tribal governments directly control or participate in commercial activities more frequently than other governments," and in many instances "direct government participation is the only way economic enterprises are brought to the reservation."[8] In the United States, governmentally planned economies are not considered to be the ideal form of economy and instead private, free market, entrepreneurial capitalism is generally the goal. But in the recession of 2008–2009, the various financial stimulus plans implemented by the Bush and Obama administrations, and the extensive federal involvement in the economy, made many argue that the United States was turning away from capitalism.[9]

It needs to be pointed out, however, that in Indian Country it is natural for tribal governments to be far more involved in economic activities than are state and federal governments. The reason is that tribal governments own most of the land, resources, and assets on most reservations. It is no surprise, then, that tribes are very involved in planning, authorizing, and even operating on-reservation economic activities. I believe that the majority of tribal citizens accept that situation and might even insist on that process. Many Indians probably feel more comfortable with their tribal and community leaders making business decisions that could impact cultural and community issues than having private parties make those decisions when they are driven primarily by the profit motive.

There are also certain situations in which tribally owned businesses make very good sense. The Small Business Administration operates what is known as the section 8(a) program. This program allows certain minority-owned businesses to have preferences for providing goods and services to the federal government. Many tribes and especially some Alaska Native regional corporations have formed joint ventures with major corporations to provide goods and services for the federal government and have been very successful with the 8(a) program. Tribes and minority-owned businesses also have opportunities to work with the U.S. Department of Defense. Operating their own businesses helps tribes take advantage of these kinds of opportunities and programs to bring new employment and profits to Indian Country.

## Keeping Politics Out of Business

The primary problem with tribal governments starting and operating the bulk of the major business and economic enterprises on most reservations is that governments are not very good at that task. Some tribal enterprises have been successful, but the majority have not been, and many have failed. As many commentators point out, these businesses have not succeeded either because tribal, state, and federal politics and business do not make a good mix or because the tribal governmental operation of businesses creates inappropriate institutions that cannot efficiently operate businesses for profit. Even under the best of circumstances, commentators state that tribal operation of business is the least efficient method.[10]

The fact that tribal governments are heavily involved as owners and regulators of many reservation businesses and assets does not mean, however, that the tribal council, the legislative body of most tribes, has to be or should be actively involved in the day-to-day operations of businesses. In fact, most tribal governments and leaders are well aware that they and tribally owned businesses are better served if political leaders and political issues stay out of daily business affairs. (The tribal officials that I interviewed agree.) But tribal leaders are often pulled into disputes and into management decisions due to the politics of various situations, the tribe's ownership of the assets and businesses, the crucial importance of the business or the asset to the reservation community, and oftentimes due to the desires of tribal citizens.[11]

## Developing Business Expertise and Mentors

One major benefit that results when tribes operate their own businesses and governmental programs is that they develop their workforce and increase their overall management expertise and the potential for entrepreneurial activities among tribal citizens. Many studies have pointed out that the absence of this "human capital," the employment abilities and experiences of Indian people, is partly to blame for the limited number of Indian-owned private businesses. To the extent that tribal governments work to improve the expertise, experience, and potential of their workforces, they are also increasing the potential for businesses to be created and located in Indian Country and the development of reservation economies.

Another bonus from tribes operating governmental programs and business entities is that tribal citizens gain employment, jobs, and wages. We have already pointed out the unbelievably bad employment figures for reservation and urban Indians and the very low rate of Indian private business ownership. As a consequence, Indian people are relatively inexperienced in work habits, management, and business expertise. Also, young reservation residents rarely have mentors and private business owners that they can learn from, and where they can get their first jobs to begin learning about work and the business world. This is a serious issue for Indians on reservations. The absence of these kinds of jobs, mentors, and work experience leads to an untrained and inexperienced workforce. These problems are also an important concern for businesses and industries that are considering locating in Indian Country.

Consequently, when tribes operate casinos and other businesses and governmental programs such as court systems, law enforcement, social welfare programs, and more, tribal citizens are employed and learn sophisticated employment and managerial skills. This is a valuable externality that arises from tribes operating their own programs and businesses and hiring their own citizens. Furthermore, tribes can exercise other important opportunities that are available to them under federal laws such as the 1975 Indian Self-Determination and Education Assistance Act and the 1994 Indian Self-Governance Act. Under these laws, tribal governments can take over federal programs and use federal funding to operate medical and dental clinics, law enforcement, and a myriad of other federal programs. It is obvious that if tribes assume these kinds of functions that tribal citizens and managers will develop experience and tribal employees will acquire new skills. In addition, tribal citizens can experience the positive results that come from satisfying work, making your own income, and being self-sufficient, as Indian cultures have always been. Young people who see the adults in their families succeed will be encouraged to emulate them and will have mentors to learn from. As a Umatilla tribal employee stated about her successful tribal work experience: "My kids are going to have it better than I did. We have every right to feel good about ourselves."[12]

These positive externalities result from tribes operating businesses and governmental programs. Experienced tribal employees who succeed in these businesses and programs are far more likely to become successful private entrepreneurs and create and operate their own businesses than they would have been without the experiences they gain from tribal employment.

## *The Keys to Tribal Economic Success*

The Harvard Project on American Indian Economic Development has focused its 22 years of research on tribal governments and businesses. Its conclusions are very interesting and are closely followed in Indian Country. The project has addressed the proper role of tribal governments in creating reservation economic development, and in setting up and operating businesses. After studying more than one hundred tribes, the project concluded that there are three keys to creating successful tribal economic development.

First, tribal governments have to exercise their sovereignty. "Sovereignty matters." What professors Stephen Cornell, Joseph Kalt, and their associates mean by this is that tribal governments have to be in control and make their own decisions about what businesses to create and operate on reservations, how tribal natural resources, for example, will be developed, and how businesses will be structured and what their missions will be. Moreover, tribal leaders and citizens have to make these decisions, and they are in fact the best decision makers, because they are the ones most directly affected by the potential success or failure of such endeavors. The Harvard Project also states that tribal leaders know their own communities better than do federal officials and employees and that they can judge, and are charged with judging as elected leaders, what their communities will support and what kinds of businesses are culturally and traditionally proper for their tribes.

One Harvard study demonstrates this point exactly. This study examined 75 tribes with forestry resources, of which 49 tribes had taken over some of the federal aspects of managing their forests. The study demonstrated that the tribes that assumed these duties created efficiencies in both forest health and protection, and in the financial return the tribes received from their timber assets. In addition, an ongoing Harvard study in 2009 on tribal management of health services reemphasizes the value of tribal management. The study's preliminary findings show that tribes have significantly improved their citizens' access to health services. These studies graphically prove that when tribal governments and citizens make the decisions and operate the programs they will often make better decisions than do federal bureaucrats in Washington, D.C., who might have no personal investment or stake in the outcome of their decisions.[13]

But as discussed above, the Harvard Project agrees that once tribal governments make the basic strategic business decisions, they need to get out of the daily operation of businesses and allow experts and management who are not controlled by tribal politics to manage these concerns. To succeed, business entities need to be operated under sound business and economic principles, and not for political expediency. It does not work when political leaders are hiring and firing and making business decisions about products and profitability.[14]

The second key to successful reservation economic development according to the Harvard research is that tribal governments need to develop strong institutions to assist and regulate business development. Tribes need efficient and experienced bureaucracies that assist businesses to get established and to operate. And, as mentioned in Chapters 6 and 7, tribes need to address bureaucratic issues such as the timeliness of agency decisions and the difficulty of getting business site leases.[15]

Tribal governments also need to ensure the rule of law in Indian Country. This phrase sounds like it comes from Anglo-American law, but this is a very well-established idea in Indian cultures and laws. "Due process" and "equal protection" are not new ideas to Indian peoples. In my own experience working for years for tribal housing departments, tribal governments give people more procedural protections than do other governments. But, as commentators point out, tribes do need to carefully nurture their institutions and court systems to protect the private rights and assets that individuals and businesses develop on reservations. Without fair and balanced protection of these rights, what person will ever risk their human capital, financial capital, and physical resources trying to create a business in Indian Country?[16]

The third key to successful reservation economic development is that cultural issues are very important. The Harvard Project agrees that tribal cultures do not stand in the way of nor do they oppose economic development. But one cannot generalize, because tribal cultures are significantly different across the United States, and tribal governments and businesspeople need to understand the specific culture of the reservation where they are investing. Few tribal cultures and reservation populations, just as very few states or counties, will support businesses that are antithetical to their core beliefs and institutions. Consequently, there has to be some sort of match or compatibility between planned economic activities and tribal cultures.[17]

## Tribal Institutions and Laws

As discussed in Chapter 6, the generalized perception is that tribal governments and reservations are not business friendly. Indian and non-Indian investors considering Indian Country are very concerned about the specific tribal laws and institutions that will control their destinies. This applies equally whether investors are thinking of investing cash or the human capital of their time and expertise. No one, tribal citizen or not, is going to invest their life savings and their time and efforts in locations where the government might unreasonably take it from them. This risk and fears about the laws and institutions of a country are among the primary reasons some countries have problems attracting investments and building economies and wealth.

If tribal governments want to fix this mistaken perception about reservations and increase investments and develop economies, they have to review their laws and policies, and consider creating institutions, bureaucracies, and laws that help make reservations more business friendly. Studies conducted by the Harvard Project, for example, demonstrate graphically the importance of independent and fair court systems. Harvard studied 89 tribes for nearly 22 years and concluded that reservations that have independent and impartial courts have a 5 percent higher employment rate than tribes whose courts are not considered to be impartial. In addition, tribal governments that have true separation of powers provisions and independent courts had a 15 percent higher employment rate than tribes without such aspects. These are stunning but not surprising statistics. If tribal courts and governments are perceived as favoring the government or politically connected litigants, no investor is going to risk their time and money in such a jurisdiction.[18]

So how does a tribe create an experienced, knowledgeable, and fair court that protects property rights, investors, and consumers? There are many paths, of course, to that destination, but keeping the hiring and firing of tribal judges out of tribal politics is one primary way to do that. Sadly, in 2008–2009, the Hopi Tribe of Arizona was not able to do that. According to the news, the Hopi Tribal Council suspended its entire appellate court for decisions they rendered. Firing judges over judicial decisions is not a good way to show the world that a tribal government has an independent court system. Instead, hiring experienced, knowledgeable, impartial judges who serve under contracts for a set period of time and can only be fired for serious improprieties will reassure most investors.[19]

Tribes also need to consider adopting laws that businesses need and that will help attract businesses to reservations. The Uniform Commercial Code (UCC), adopted by all 50 states, is one example. Several tribes adopted parts of the UCC long ago and recently some tribes are adopting a newly drafted model tribal UCC. But the majority of tribes have not adopted such laws. Consequently, businesspeople who are comfortable working in different states, because they understand uniform state laws like the UCC, pause when they consider Indian Country. I am aware of one tribal council that took about three years to adopt portions of the UCC that a local bank insisted upon before it would open a branch on the reservation. Once the tribal council adopted the UCC provisions, the bank opened the branch and now employs several tribal citizens and provides banking services on the reservation for the first time in that tribe's history. That is one example of the importance of tribal governments adopting business-friendly laws that also serve their community's needs.

Tribal governments also have to fight the perception that they will confiscate private property rights and infringe on the obligation of contracts. We discussed this point in Chapter 6. As also pointed out there, almost no tribal constitutions have provisions analogous to the U.S. Constitution that prevent governments from violating the obligations of contracts. Enacting such provisions in tribal constitutions or laws would help reassure many Indian and non-Indian investors. Such a provision would even help tribal leaders politically, because then tribal law would prevent them from doing something their constituents might demand—for example, to oppose a currently unpopular business activity that was approved by an earlier tribal council.

Tribes can also use their laws and policies to attract businesses. All states, counties, and cities try to attract large business developments by giving tax credits or other assistance. Tribes have many opportunities to do the same. Since most state laws do not apply on reservations, tribes can offer investors locations where state laws might not apply. Tribes can also offer tax and regulatory relief and compete with states and counties for new businesses. A tribal government has to move very carefully here because such contracts and arrangements will possibly be in effect for decades and can have major impacts on reservations; but that is no reason not to consider such arrangements. The possibilities are endless as to how tribes can use their sovereignty, laws, and institutions to attract investors and businesses to reservations. In contrast, is also clear that if tribal governments do not institute and enforce the rule of law, their most educated and skilled people will leave and non-Indian investors will never even consider working on their reservations.

## Building Infrastructure

Infrastructure comprises the basic facilities, services, and installations that communities and societies need to function, such as transportation and communications systems, water and power, and public institutions including schools, post offices, and prisons. Most tribes face serious infrastructure issues and are also located in remote areas not well served by rail, car, or air services. In addition, many Indian homes on reservations do not have electricity, phone service, or Internet access. Infrastructure deficiencies such as these inhibit economic development.

On the other hand, improving and building infrastructure on reservations can play an enormous role in creating economies. Just as states and the federal government looked to spend public money on updating U.S. infrastructure in the recession of 2008–2009, so can tribal and federal governments address the needs of Indian Country and stimulate tribal economies at the same time by building and improving reservation infrastructures. In conjunction with the U.S. Buy Indian Act, federal and tribal dollars for infrastructure could be used to hire Indian labor and to help develop and support Indian-owned and reservation-based businesses.

One problem for tribal governments is the magnitude of the issues and the lack of resources tribes possess. Tribes rarely have tax revenues due to the absence of reservation economies. Tribes also rarely have extra governmental funds. They end up relying on and looking to the federal government for assistance in the crucial areas of health, education, roads, et cetera. As with so many issues we have discussed, though, tribal governments will probably have to address these problems themselves, with as much federal and state assistance as they can gain.

A few tribes have seen opportunities in infrastructure issues. Some tribal governments have learned how to provide jobs and training for tribal employees by providing utility services, for example. The Navajo Nation has operated its own utility system since 1959 and at least nine other tribes operate public utilities. The Confederated Tribes of the Umatilla Indian Reservation and the St. Regis Mohawk Tribe have investigated building their own power plants, and many other tribes are looking into building and licensing wind power operations and alternative energy systems. These kinds of innovative solutions and tribal involvement, along with federal, state, and private assistance, can help rectify to some extent the infrastructure deficiencies that most reservations suffer.[20]

## Tribes Should "Buy Indian"

The United States enacted the Buy Indian Act in 1910. This law provides the possibility of the federal government buying whatever goods and services it needs to serve and deal with Indians and tribes from Indians and Indian-owned businesses.

In 1974, Congress expanded this Indian preference policy. But the act is only used at the discretion of the secretary of the interior and regrettably has had a miniscule impact on tribal and Indian labor and business. A few lawsuits have been filed over the years claiming the United States does not use the act as it should.[21]

Congress has at least, however, thought of the importance of using local Indian labor and tribal and Indian-owned companies to carry out federal construction projects and to provide services directed at reservations and Indians. This is a laudable effort even though it has produced minimal results. One excuse for the United States, however, is that due to the near absence of Indian-owned businesses on and off reservations, the United States has not had a lot of Indian businesses and entrepreneurs to utilize.

The federal law is relevant here because tribal governments should also enact buy Indian laws and force themselves to support local, Indian-owned businesses. Tribal economic activities have brought major new spending and business activities to many reservations. Just think of all the money tribes spend now on janitorial, construction, maintenance services, et cetera, at their casinos and various business endeavors. This money and these new economic activities should be used as avenues to hire more Indians and to employ private companies owned by Indians. But are tribal governments giving this business to on-reservation companies owned by tribal citizens and other Indians? Are tribes using these opportunities to encourage the growth and expansion of Indian-owned private businesses and reservation economies to keep the multiplier effect working in Indian Country? Tribal governments should be doing this so that they can encourage their citizens and others to start and operate businesses on reservations. If tribal governments are not doing this, then a wonderful opportunity to kick-start their economies is being lost.

Sadly, the accusation is often made that tribes do not patronize individual Indian-owned businesses and that it is difficult for Indian entrepreneurs to sell their goods and services even to their own tribes and even on their own reservations. One obvious reason, perhaps, that tribes are not doing more is that there are so few private, Indian-owned businesses in existence. One tribal casino chief operating officer told me in 2004 and 2009 that while the casino and tribe spent $60 million on annual payroll and vendor payments only a fraction of the vendor benefits went to tribal citizens because so few Indians own businesses. Consequently, just as with the United States and the federal Buy Indian Act, tribal governments sometimes have a hard time finding Indian businesses to use and they cannot acquire the goods and services they need from Indian-owned businesses. But as with the chicken and the egg analogy, tribes have to provide the leadership and the seed money to help create new Indian-owned businesses, and then they need to become the clients of these businesses to help them become established and sustainable.[22]

The potential value of tribes "buying Indian" demonstrates again the circularity of the economic process and the multiplier effect. Tribes and tribal casinos and businesses need Indian-owned businesses to work with, but there will never be very many of them until tribal governments help create them and start using them. As soon as tribes start keeping more of their own money circulating within their own reservation economies by hiring Indian-owned businesses, then that will promote the creation of ever more privately owned businesses by providing more opportunities, and then that will also allow tribal governments to spend even more of their funds on the new Indian-owned businesses cropping up on their reservations. As that occurs, old and new Indian-owned businesses will hire and train more and more Indian employees, and when these new employees and business owners circulate their earnings on their reservations that will help create further opportunities for entrepreneurs to start even more new businesses. Pretty soon, a reservation community might just have a functioning economy.

## Potential Strategies

The points discussed in this section will hopefully give tribal governments, economic planners, and Indians some ideas and strategies to use to help create economies.

### *Housing*

The construction of new housing in the United States is one of the major indicators of and contributors to American economic health. In contrast, there is an absence of a private Indian-owned housing market on the vast majority of reservations. On most reservations there are few Indian-owned private homes located on privately owned land, and there is very little home construction occurring. There is also an almost complete absence of an escalating housing market where Indian families can build wealth and equity in their homes as most Americans do. Considering that the average American who starts a business does so by borrowing money by taking out a loan on his or her home, you can begin to see the importance of the lack of a private reservation housing market. This absence also inhibits the development of new businesses and economies in Indian Country because reservations fail to benefit from the home construction industry and the employment and sales of goods associated with that industry.[23]

This situation has arisen due to U.S. history, federal Indian policies, reservation poverty, and the types of titles that tribal governments and Indians hold to the more than 67 million acres of land they own in Indian Country. Due to the fact that most Indians and tribes do not own the complete title to their land, tribal governments and Indian families cannot borrow money from banks through the mortgage process to create economic activity and to build houses. The extreme poverty that has existed on reservations also helps to explain the absence of sufficient private housing and family wealth. Indian Country has long suffered a critical shortage of adequate housing.[24]

In 1962, the United States took a socially responsible step to address this housing crisis. In that year, the U.S. Department of Housing and Urban Development

began to assist tribal governments to create housing authorities to build and operate rental and for-sale housing on reservations. The United States has appropriated hundreds of millions of dollars almost every year since then to build and
maintain reservation housing through Housing and Urban Development, BIA,
and Department of Agriculture programs. These programs have helped alleviate
the shortage somewhat. These programs also helped to some extent to bring the
economic benefits of housing construction to reservation economies, although
very few Indian-owned companies ever participated in building reservation housing. Tribal housing departments do employ a significant number of people to
maintain their housing stocks.[25]

But these very beneficial federal/tribal programs might have had an unintended
consequence of inhibiting the growth of a private housing market in Indian
Country. As mentioned, and as is universally accepted as true, a private housing
market is an extremely crucial component of the U.S. economy, and it should also
serve that role on reservations. Instead of a private housing market in Indian
Country, though, tribal governments and the United States are mainly responsible for providing housing. This fact and the trust status of much reservation
land and the poverty of most Indian people have severely limited the development of a private housing market and a robust private home construction industry in Indian Country. Furthermore, federal funding and federal and tribal
housing construction and maintenance have even created a disincentive for the
development of a private market on many reservations. This is so because the
federal/tribal rental and for-sale housing programs on reservations provide housing at below-market subsidized rates and make private competition almost
impossible. I am not blaming the U.S. housing program or criticizing the U.S.
or tribal governments for this outcome, nor am I arguing that these housing programs should be ended. The current housing needs and poverty levels on reservations are still just too great. But I am pointing out that governmental involvement
has perhaps had the unintended consequence of inhibiting and skewing the
private housing market in Indian Country.

Other commentators have also noted this problem, and pointed out the disin-
centives that HUD programs and requirements have created for the development
of a reservation private housing market and even for being employed and earning
income. One study of the Lakota people on the Pine Ridge and Rosebud Sioux
reservations stated: "Housing is extremely limited on both reservations because
of the almost nonexistent private housing market."[26] This study also mentioned
that federal housing has not fixed the shortage on those reservations, as each tribe
has extensive waiting lists and enormous overcrowding problems. It also notes:
"Federal housing programs have distorted the development of market-priced
housing, creating contradictory incentives for reservation residents."[27] The contradictory incentive is that Indian families qualify for federal/tribal housing and
for lower and lower payments for their rental and purchased housing based on
their low incomes. In fact, these programs even allow for "negative rent," where
tribal housing department money is used to pay a family's rent and utilities if their

income is low enough. These kinds of (dis)incentives certainly do not encourage being employed and making wages.[28]

In 1996, in recognition of some of these issues, Congress enacted a new Indian housing law that attempts to bring private investment to Indian Country and to encourage tribal governments and Indian individuals to address their housing shortages by nonfederal means. Congress also recognized that Indian tribes and individuals cannot get bank mortgages on trust land. Under the 1996 act, several federal agencies have been working on proposals to allow mortgages on trust lands, and some private bank loans have now been made for the construction and financing of privately owned homes on reservation trust lands.[29]

Tribal governments can create major economic improvements on reservations if they can help tribal citizens to fund, build, and maintain private housing. The federal trust ownership of most reservation lands is a major problem, and Indian families need help to access private mortgages and bank financing. Tribal citizens will also need jobs, income, and savings to do that. Only then will a private housing market be created by both supply and demand; and only then will rising equity in private homes on reservations help create even more wealth in Indian Country.

If tribes can think outside the "federal box" and create innovative ways to develop a private housing market, they will go a long way towards building economies and increasing reservation populations. As one HUD official recommended: "don't forget the contribution housing can make. . . . It's really building that capacity toward an improved economy."[30]

## Banking

There are very few bank branches or even automated teller machines on reservations. As recently as 2001, one-third of all Indians living on reservations had to travel at least 30 miles to reach an ATM or a bank, and one-sixth had to travel up to 100 miles, and 86 percent of native communities did not have a bank or financial institution within their borders. Consequently, many Indians have never had a bank or checking account and most reservation residents have to travel to non-Indian towns to access banking services. This is a serious situation for developing reservation economies because it causes almost all residents to bank off reservation and cash their checks off reservation, and that naturally leads to shopping and spending money off reservation. If tribal governments can address this issue it will help develop their economies, stop the leakage of money from reservations, and create more business activity in Indian Country.[31]

In 2008, according to the Federal Deposit Insurance Corporation, only 21 banks were owned by tribes. It is believed that the first individually Indian-owned bank on a reservation was opened on the Turtle Mountain reservation in North Dakota in December 2007. Three of the four owners are tribal citizens. One stated: "A bank is the backbone to economic growth in any community. . . . But people wanting to do banking had to go at least 10 to 20 miles off the reservation to get to a bank."[32] Another owner added: "Most of the shopping and support has been going to towns around Belcourt [the main town on the reservation] because of the lack of commerce in town, including a bank. ... With the bank, you'll probably see more businesses pop up on the reservation."[33] Another owner stated that millions of dollars circulated on the Turtle Mountain Reservation each month but little of it stayed on the reservation because of the lack of a bank. "We were lucky to have that money here for one day. ... There was no time for it to circulate in our community."[34] After discussing re-spending and the multiplier effect, we can see the obvious economic value of having banks on reservations.

The Denver-based Native American Bank is owned by 26 tribes, Alaska Native corporations, and tribal organizations, and operates branches in Montana and Alaska. The president of this bank stated that tribal banks help American Indians learn about finances, and boost home and business ownership. This statement about tribal banks helping to increase business ownership is proved by the fact that the Blackfeet Nation Bank was estimated to have helped create 200 businesses on that tribe's reservation.[35]

In sum, tribal governments need to do everything they can to get bank branches opened on their reservations. Banks are an important part of keeping money circulating in a community and creating more businesses and jobs and increasing the rate of loans granted on reservations for home and business ownership.

## *Rural Partnerships*

Most Indian reservations are located in rural areas. This impacts business development in many ways due to a very limited consumer and employee pool, poor infrastructure, transportation issues, and more. Tribes also often find themselves in competition with local rural cities and counties for services, political power, and economic development.

But an innovative approach could be for tribes and rural towns and counties to work cooperatively instead of as rivals who obstruct each others' progress. Some tribes are already pursuing this option. The Confederated Tribes of the Umatilla Indian Reservation, located just five miles from Pendleton, Oregon, seem to work well with the local county and city. The Tribes have signed several memoranda of understanding on a variety of governance topics with local cities. The Tribes pay Pendleton to handle the reservation's waste treatment and the city's water line runs through the reservation. The city also honors several aspects of the Tribes' jurisdiction. It no doubt helps that the Tribes are the second-largest employer in the county and it is obviously in the city and county's interests to work with the Tribes.

All tribes and local counties and towns could cooperate to jointly pursue a multitude of federal programs and grants for rural areas. In fact recent research shows that tribes are not applying for very many of the available grants. It seems that tribal governments and rural towns and counties, who are all struggling with population loss and poor economic conditions, should partner and pursue joint economic activities and grants. These kinds of coalitions and cooperative efforts would produce more political and economic power and influence for tribes and counties and would save a lot of money if local governments and tribes worked together instead of opposing each other.[36]

## Intertribal Businesses and Investments

Throughout history, tribal governments cooperated and worked together on economic issues. Similarly, modern-day tribal governments could replicate these mutually beneficial arrangements to address economic development issues by working with their natural partners, other Indian communities.

Some tribes are already working together on gaming ventures. This is a natural because many tribes are now very experienced and successful at operating these endeavors and have ample expertise to share with other tribes who are just starting or who are struggling. Tribes have also worked together on other business ventures. In 2005 and 2007, tribes partnered with Marriott to build upscale hotels in Washington, D.C., and Sacramento, California. Working with other tribal peoples would seem to address some of the cultural issues that are raised when tribes do business with non-Indians, and even better, this situation helps keep "Indian money" circulating within the national Indian community. This is a great way for tribes to help each other and to keep the benefits of their economic activities within their communities.[37]

We have already mentioned several times the 2007–2009 effort in the Pacific Northwest to draft a treaty to help tribal governments work with each other across reservation boundaries. This effort demonstrates again that tribal governments are aware of the great variety of development strategies at hand and that they are attempting to use any avenue that might assist their citizens to benefit from increased prosperity.[38]

## Small Business Administration and Department of Defense

Tribal ventures and individual Indian businesses can seek certification under the Small Business Administration's section 8(a) program. Businesses and tribal joint ventures that are at least 51 percent tribally or individually Indian-owned can qualify for 8(a) preferences and contract with the federal government to provide services and supplies to the United States. The 8(a) program has enormous potential for assisting tribal and Indian businesses to grow if they can tap into contracting with the federal government. Alaska Native corporations have been very successful in recent years using 8(a) contracting.[39]

Tribes and individual Indian business owners can also use a U.S. Department of Defense program for minority contractors. Several tribes and Alaska Native corporations are already manufacturing products for the Defense Department, and there is ample room for tribes to expand their economic activities in this arena.[40]

## Encouraging Entrepreneurship

As discussed at length in Chapter 7, tribal governments can do themselves and their reservation economies a big favor by assisting Indian entrepreneurship. Tribes need to help their citizens learn how to start and operate businesses and to help finance the creation of new businesses in Indian Country. Every new business on a reservation goes a long ways to helping create functioning economies, because they help to keep dollars and consumerism on the reservation, and that helps new businesses and new jobs to be created. Small privately owned businesses are the mainstay of the U.S. economy, and they should also serve that same role in Indian Country.

Tribal governments should also help to teach tribal citizens how to become business owners. We have already discussed the successful effort that four Oregon tribes—the Klamath, the Grand Ronde, the Siletz, and the Warm Springs—established when they created an innovative program to teach individual Indians to start privately owned businesses. The sole purpose of this nonprofit corporation, the Oregon Native American Business & Entrepreneurial Network (ONABEN), is to help Indian individuals develop business plans, launch new businesses, and improve their business skills. These tribes realized that building their private business sectors and increasing the number of Indian-owned businesses are absolutely crucial to their futures and worthy of their attention and resources. Other tribes and organizations have also started their own programs to accomplish these goals and provide loans for business start-ups, classroom instruction, counseling, and technical assistance to help Indians develop privately owned businesses. The costs incurred by tribal efforts to create private businesses on reservations will return to Indian communities many, many times over as families start and operate their own businesses and as new money begins to circulate on reservations and helps create new jobs, businesses, and functioning economies.[41]

## THE ROLE OF INDIVIDUAL INDIANS

The importance and potential of American Indian entrepreneurship has already been covered in detail in Chapter 7. I raise it again here to reemphasize and even overemphasize the important role that privately owned businesses play in creating economies in Indian Country. Tribal governments need to understand that the only way to build true economies is by utilizing the skills and efforts of private entrepreneurs. Tribal governments just do not have the capacity to operate all the small businesses and to offer the wide variety of consumer goods and services that are needed to create reservation economies. A wide variety of businesses and service offerings is exactly what is needed to keep money circulating in local economies from consumers to businesses to employees and owners who then also become consumers and spend their money in the local economy.

A geographic region needs a widely diverse economy made up of large and small, publicly and privately owned businesses if it is going to attract, capture, and circulate the money of the inhabitants and visitors of that region. The only way to stop the leakage of money from a community is to have a wide variety of places where consumers can spend their money. The only way a tribal government can build a diverse economy is to enlist the assistance of tribal citizens, other reservation inhabitants, and outside investors.[42]

Once a reservation contains a sufficient number of public and private businesses, the local community will benefit from the multiplier effect and this re-spending will create more businesses by other entrepreneurs who take advantage of the new economic activities and, of course, even more jobs will arise from those new businesses. Then, even more re-spending and circulation of money and the multiplier effect will create another wave of innovation and the creation of new businesses and jobs in the tribal economy. This is exactly how economies are created and grow.[43]

Very few tribal economies will ever replicate the size and diversity of big city economies. Reservation inhabitants will still travel to cities to buy certain goods and services. But tribal economies can compete to keep some of the local money from leaking away immediately, and if money can circulate even one or two times on reservations, that will encourage the creation of more businesses. Tribal governments, officials, economic planners, and Indian individuals need to work together to renew and grow the entrepreneurial spirit that Indian people and families displayed over centuries. Building sustainable and lasting reservation economies and communities will go a long way towards sustaining and preserving tribal governments, tribal sovereignty, and tribal cultures.

In addition, there is another aspect that plays an important role in developing reservation economies. Indian families need to become consumers in their own communities. This issue is no doubt shared by all rural communities. The problem is that shopping in reservation border towns or even further away can be fun. The weekend or monthly shopping trip for many reservation inhabitants has become an outing that takes people away from their small local communities to places where they have more privacy and shopping opportunities. I saw this phenomenon in the mid-1990s when I worked for a Montana tribe and people would travel over one hundred miles to cash their checks, spend their money, and go to movies, department stores, and access other services that were not available on the reservation. Similarly, a study of the Navajo Reservation concluded that due to the absence of on-reservation businesses "going to town . . . has become a social affair among the Navajos" and trips to Gallup, New Mexico, became weekend getaways.[44] It will be difficult for tribal economies to overcome these issues. However, if similar goods and services are made available on a reservation, even if the price might be a little higher, inhabitants will shop more in the local economy because savings of gasoline and time could make it cheaper to shop on reservation than off.[45]

But more disturbing is another trend that several commentators have pointed out. They claim that some Indians will purposely not shop at reservation businesses and instead will shop at non-Indian, off-reservation businesses so as not to support their own relatives, fellow tribal citizens, and reservation economies. I hope this is not true. But if it is, then such people need to realize that by spending their money off reservation they are hurting themselves, their families, and their communities. As much as possible, Indian families need to engage in consumerism on their own reservations. That conduct will benefit themselves and their communities in the long run. But to capture this spending and the multiplier effect, tribal governments and individual Indians first have to start and operate on-reservation consumer-oriented businesses and work to create real economies.[46]

## *FEDERAL AND STATE ROLES*

Indians are American and state citizens, and these governments have the same responsibility to serve their Indian citizens as they do other citizens. Therefore, these governments must provide Indians with the same tools and assistance that they provide counties, cities, and other citizens to improve their economic conditions.

This role for state and federal governments is not just their duty, but it also presents them with a golden opportunity. If Indian citizens and reservation communities can be assisted to participate more fully in the U.S. economic system and create livable wage jobs and decent housing, then the national and state economies and social conditions as a whole will improve. These governments will also save the tax dollars that are now being spent on unemployment, food stamps, and various welfare services. The truth of this statement is demonstrated by the operations of ONABEN and its financial impact on state and federal economies. Studies conducted in 1998 and 2000 showed that the new businesses started by individual Indian ONABEN clients produced far more new tax revenues for the federal and state governments than these governments ever donated to assist ONABEN. This is graphic evidence for tribal, state, and federal governments that they will reap financial and social benefits from supporting tribal economies and individual Indian businesses.[47]

In addition, tribal and Indian economic developments clearly benefit state and federal governments in other ways. Tribal gaming is the perfect example. As of 2007, these endeavors employed about 670,000 people nationwide, and 75 percent of these tribal employees were non-Indians. In counties where tribes have opened gaming facilities, unemployment is way down. These new tribal employees pay state and federal taxes, although many of them were formerly unemployed and were on various types of public assistance before tribal governments provided them with jobs. Consequently, federal and state governments benefit from increased taxes on tribal employees and decrease governmental spending on social welfare problems. These kinds of statistics should give state and federal governments the motivation to assist tribes and individual Indians to engage in economic development.[48]

## The Federal Role

The United States plays a special role in Indian economic issues that is far beyond its duty to assist U.S. citizens in general. The federal government owes Indians and tribes a trust duty to care for their best interests. Under federal law, since at least 1831, the United States has voluntarily assumed a trustee's duties to care for tribes and Indians. The Supreme Court has stated that the United States has "charged itself with moral obligations of the highest responsibility and trust" which is to be "judged by the most exacting fiduciary standards."[49] Throughout many different eras of federal Indian policy, this trust duty has manifested itself in diverse ways. But today, in the Self-Determination Era of federal Indian policy, the United States expressly supports tribal economic development, self-determination, self-governance, and self-sufficiency.[50]

The United States also made numerous and specific economic promises in the 375 treaties the United States signed with tribal governments from 1778 to 1871. In most of these treaties, the United States asked for the exclusive power to regulate trade with the tribe and then promised to control the tribe's commerce for the tribe's protection and benefit. In many treaties, the United States expressly promised to provide the tribal nation and individual Indians with all sorts of specific kinds of economic assistance.[51]

The United States has not always fulfilled its trust duty to tribes nor even delivered on some specific treaty promises. The United States has also accidentally allowed and often even purposely caused many problems that seriously injured economic concerns and assets in Indian Country. It is time for the United States to live up to its trust and treaty responsibilities and do much more to assist tribal and individual Indian economic development.

## State Role

State governments can also play an important role in assisting economic development in Indian Country. As already mentioned, it makes perfect sense for state governments to help reservation residents to increase their economic activities, because that benefits tribal areas, the areas surrounding reservations, and a state's overall economy as well.

Some states recognize these facts and they support the development of reservation businesses because they understand the beneficial spillover effect of reservation economic activities. The Oregon Economic and Community Development Department has given extensive support to ONABEN to train Indians to start their own businesses, and Oregon has benefitted from increased tax revenues that more than covered its investments in ONABEN. In addition, Idaho gave a $500,000 rural community grant to the Coeur d'Alene Tribe to upgrade a plant in an attempt to spark local business development. Other states have undertaken similar efforts. It makes good business sense for states to help tribes and Indians when it also helps states increase their tax revenues and improve social issues for reservations and the states themselves.[52]

An additional long-range boost that state and federal governments can give tribes is to improve education for Indians generally. Many state and federal schools on and near reservations are in woeful condition in terms of building condition, maintenance, monetary support, and effectiveness. Educational attainment levels for reservation Indians are far below U.S. averages. While the numbers have improved, a 2005 report showed that 15 percent of Native American people 16 to 24 years of age were high school dropouts compared to 9.9 percent of Americans in general. Older statistics demonstrate that this has been a problem for a long time: a 1992 study found that 30 percent of American Indians dropped out of high school compared to 17 percent for Hispanics, 13 percent for blacks, and 9 percent for whites.[53]

State and tribal governments could also cooperate better with each other, to each other's benefit. These governments could enter more cooperative agreements on a wide range of issues including taxation, regulation, jurisdiction, law enforcement, and education. The range of options that states could pursue to help tribes, Indians, and the state itself is limitless. Such efforts would increase economic activities in Indian Country and in the state itself, demonstrating the win-win potential of these efforts.

## CONCLUSION

One of the most important and potentially powerful goals of tribal economic development is to create functioning reservation economies. An integrated and diverse community of tribally and privately owned large and small businesses is the best method to ensure that consumerism and business will occur in Indian Country. Then, the dollars that reservation residents and visitors have will stay on reservations to be spent and circulated between various businesses, employees, and activities to create the multiplier effect. Only then can beneficial employment and economic activities permanently support the building and preservation of tribal communities. Consequently, tribal leaders and Indians have the greatest incentives and motivations possible to work towards creating reservation economies.

Developing a reservation economy is only a means to an end. In no sense is it just about making money or making any particular individual rich. Instead, it is wholly about building and sustaining tribal communities. It is about developing a holistic approach to community development that can also help raise peoples and societies out of poverty. To the extent that tribal governments and Indians can create and sustain reservation-based businesses and attract non-Indian businesses and investors to Indian Country, then tribal communities can provide livable wage jobs and build adequate housing so that Indian families can live on their reservations if they desire. We are talking about tribal governments and their citizens working together to make their reservations more viable places to live and raise families, and to better preserve their governments, homelands, traditions, and cultures.

The truth of that last statement is established by a 1999 study of the Menominees of Wisconsin and the Metlakatlas of Alaska. In the 1880s, these tribal communities pursued economic development and wage labor jobs primarily in the timber and salmon industries. According to the professor who authored the study, these tribal peoples did not see economic development and business activities as a threat to their way of life. Instead, they saw these activities as a means of maintaining their "unity, independence, and indeed survival."[54] As one tribal economic planner puts it: "economic development is a tool to achieve cultural integrity and self-determination with tribal sovereignty."[55] Is there a better goal for tribal governments and Indian communities to work towards?

# CHAPTER 9

# *Conclusion*

There is nothing traditional about having the federal government take care of us. There is nothing cultural about that. ... My idea of tribal economic development is that sovereignty is economic independence. Until we get there, we are not independent.

—Clifford Lyle Marshall, Chairman, Hoopa Valley Tribe.[1]

If you own the economy, it won't hurt culture.

—Antone Minthorn, Chairman, Confederated Tribes
of the Umatilla Indian Reservation.[2]

**T**he most important issue facing tribal leaders and Indians today is to develop and expand the economies and business activities in Indian Country. It seems nearly impossible to overemphasize the importance of creating dramatic improvements in the economic conditions of Indian tribes and Indian peoples. This is true because without adequate housing, living wage jobs, and sustainable business activities, Indian families, cultures, and communities are not going to be able to continue to exist on many reservations. Without adequate jobs, housing, water, food, educational facilities, et cetera, Indian populations will continue to struggle with poverty and the accompanying social problems. The future of tribes, reservations, and Indian cultures depends to a great extent on the ability to sustain a reasonable level of life. Indian Country needs the kind of growth that creates real economies, businesses, and jobs so Indian families can support themselves. One proof of the obvious benefits tribal governments and cultures will enjoy from improving their economic situations is that many Indian families want to live near their relatives and on their reservations if they can find decent jobs and housing.[3]

The issues discussed in this book clearly demonstrate the importance and the potential of economic development in Indian Country. We examined history and saw that private property rights and Indian entrepreneurial economic activities are not new concepts to American Indian cultures. Instead, for hundreds and thousands of years, Indians and tribes supported themselves through activities in which individuals and families kept the "profits," that is, they retained the benefits and products of their labor and expertise. Tribal laws and governments protected the assets and rights people acquired from their labors. We then looked at how tribal governments and Indians lost most of their lands and assets and became dependent on the United States. The loss of the wealth, assets, and activities that tribes and communities used to support themselves historically not surprisingly led to dire conditions of poverty and need. Obviously, this situation has not worked out to the benefit of tribes and Indians economically, socially, or culturally.

We also discussed the modern-day economic and business activities of tribes in general and three specific tribes in particular and analyzed possible ways that Indian peoples and tribal governments can attract investments and develop functioning economies in Indian Country. The range of benefits available to tribal communities from tapping into, encouraging, and promoting their own citizens and governments to start and operate businesses are enormous. Keeping money circulating on reservations among reservation-based businesses, jobs, and activities will create even more economic activities and opportunities in those regions, and will create ever more new businesses and jobs. The opportunity to live and work on reservations will help more tribal citizens to move home to their reservations. That would be a win-win situation for tribes and Indians.

In addition, tribal governments have a responsibility to promote and foster economic security, development, and jobs. Helping to provide the necessities of life and resources for Indians to maintain their lives, families, health, and property is an important goal for tribal leaders. Currently, many tribal citizens do not have the tools or the opportunities to maintain their families at even minimal financial levels. If tribal governments and Indian peoples are to break out of the cycle of poverty and despair, and the absence of business activity on reservations, tribes need to use every possible economic and business tool, strategy, option, and resource at their disposal.

The potential from growing Indian-owned businesses and reservation economies is enormous. Even a modest increase in the number of Indian-owned business on reservations would go a long way towards creating viable economies. If reservation inhabitants could spend even a small amount of their money in reservation businesses then that money would circulate throughout the reservation to create even more economic activity, more businesses, and more employment. Beyond the benefits of increasing the income and standard of living for many

Indians, tribal governments themselves will benefit. Increasing economic activities and taxation opportunities on reservations is an extremely important part of tribes being able to govern, to assert self-determination and self-sufficiency, and to escape the paternalism of the United States.

Tribal governments play a major role in developing reservation economies in both the public and the private sector. As with all governments, tribes need to work to attract and promote private enterprise and to create business-friendly environments as much as is possible and prudent. Tribal governments can also emphasize and support privately owned Indian businesses by taking steps to foster their development and growth. Tribes need to fund and provide start-up loans; fund training and mentoring programs; enact and fairly enforce commercial laws, codes, and regulations; and develop bureaucracies that assist economic activities. In addition, tribal government employment and tribally owned businesses play a crucial role in encouraging economic development because they are the training ground for tribal citizens. Tribally owned businesses also assist in growing a diverse reservation economy where small privately owned businesses can be started. Tribal businesses add diversity to the reservation economy and they can also be clients of Indian-owned private businesses to help them get established and flourish. Furthermore, tribally owned businesses are appropriate vehicles for tribes to develop and market their own assets, such as natural resources and reservation tourism. By no means does the development of a private free market economy on reservations mean that tribes and federal and state governments are no longer important participants. It would be foolish to try to cut tribal governments out of reservation economic development. Instead, tribal governments help individual Indians and reservation inhabitants when they work to increase their own economic and sovereign authorities and abilities. As one Pequot citizen stated: "You need money to practice sovereignty."[4] And as the CEO of the Oneida Nation stated, economic success is "the crux of sovereignty and political power."[5]

## SELF-SUFFICIENCY IS SELF-DETERMINATION

The current era of federal Indian policy is called "Self-Determination." Many Indians, politicians, and commentators have rightfully put great hope in the promise of this policy to allow Indians and tribal governments to direct their own lives and affairs and to free themselves from the overbearing control of the federal government. In 1975, Congress stated that self-determination was to end the federal "domination" of Indian affairs. The main program under Self-Determination, which exemplifies the entire policy, is the right of tribal governments to contract from the United States the federal funding and programs that serve Indians. Hundreds of tribes now operate a wide variety of federal programs that were formerly operated by the BIA and the Indian Health Service.

Unquestionably, Self-Determination has improved the federal/tribal relationship and lessened federal and BIA control of Indians and tribal governments.

But the United States still has plenary power over Indian tribes and nearly unlimited control over many of the assets of tribal governments. In fact, tribes still rely on the United States for much of their governmental funding and services and are subject to the prevailing winds of Congress and annual appropriations. This extensive federal power and control raises the question whether tribal governments and Indians can ever be free of federal paternalism and their "Great White Father" if they remain tied to the federal purse strings? The answer to that question appears to be no. In fact, one of America's foremost historians on Indian affairs stated in 1982 that tribal governments can never be free of federal paternalism as long as they rely on federal funding for the majority of their needs.[6]

In addition, relying on the federal government to create economies and beneficial activities on reservations is a dead end. The federal government will never provide the amount of funding needed on a permanent basis to create economically healthy reservations for Indians and tribes. That is a fact of life for a federal government that is always faced with more demands and limited tax dollars and is perhaps not really motivated to fully address and solve tribal and individual Indian economic issues.

So what is the answer for tribal governments, Indians, and Indian Country? In my opinion, and the opinion of many tribal leaders and commentators, true self-determination will come when tribal governments and Indian people have created their own sustainable economic development. Then, Indian individuals and tribal economies and businesses will produce the wages and taxes that Indians and tribal governments need to operate and provide the programs they desire. Self-sufficiency, or doing it yourself, seems to be the only viable alternative. Who cares the most about the poverty, social problems, and suffering in Indian Country? Who will work the hardest and the smartest to address and solve these issues? The answers are obvious. Indians and tribal governments are the people and the entities that will address and solve their issues. The ability to take care of yourself creates the reality that you will do so. Self-sufficiency then becomes self-determination, because when Indian people can rely solely on themselves, their communities, and their governments to provide the majority of their needs, then tribes and Indians will have self-determination.

## INDIAN CULTURES AND ECONOMIC DEVELOPMENT

We have addressed at several points the important question of culture because it always arises in discussions of tribal economic development. I am well aware of the concerns that economic activities might have negative impacts on Indian cultures and also of the crucial importance of preserving Indian cultures, traditions, ceremonies, and ways of life. While I am a citizen of the Eastern Shawnee Tribe, I was not raised on a reservation or in a cultural or traditional way. Thus, in one sense, I am commenting on this subject as an outsider, but at the same time

I am a strong supporter of tribes and Indian communities fighting to maintain their languages, cultures, and religions.[7]

My main point on whether economic development can possibly injure tribal cultures is that this question raises a false conflict. History proves that there is little conflict between economic development and prosperity and traditional Indian cultures. Economic development and being able to support your family is not somehow the opposite or the antithesis of Indian cultures. It is not an "either/or" situation. You do not have to be poor to be Indian or to be a cultural person, and you do not stop being an Indian or a cultural person if you become materially well off. Studies and historians have noted that particular tribes at various times specifically participated in the capitalist business world, and Indian people voluntarily participated in wage labor jobs to survive. These tribes and Indians survived, and they did not stop being native or cultural peoples. Being prosperous and successful in business is not a contradiction or a sellout of Indian cultures. To the contrary, almost all Indian cultures throughout history pursued economic success and security. Those who produced surpluses (profits) were even honored for hosting potlatches, giveaways, and ceremonies, and for their generosity. Poverty was never a requirement nor was it seen as a good thing in any American Indian culture that I am aware of. Getting out of poverty cannot by itself injure Indian cultures.[8]

In contrast, economic development and success can support tribal cultures instead of injuring them. This is also proven by history, because many Indian cultures were financially successful enough that they had short "economic years." They were intelligent and so capable at economic activities that they earned, manufactured, grew, and captured all the necessities they needed to live for a year in four to five months of actual work. They then used their extra time to engage in cultural ceremonies and in arts and crafts. As a result, when Indians were prosperous and had extra leisure time they put it to use in practicing and strengthening their cultures.[9]

In the same way today, Indians and tribes with extra time and financial resources can use those assets to strengthen and perpetuate cultural practices and languages. It is clear that a certain level of prosperity helps modern-day Indians and tribal communities maintain their cultures, just as their ancestors did. And that is exactly what tribal governments and Indians are doing today, because they are using their extra resources to develop and support social welfare, cultural, and language programs; buy back land within their reservations; protect their first foods; and build cultural and community centers. The benefits to tribal cultures from these efforts are enormous and are only possible when Indians and tribal governments have produced economic surpluses.[10]

There is also no question that tribal cultures are improved when extra resources allow reservations and Indian communities to create significant improvements in children's health and educational levels. Many tribes have seen major gains in life expectancy rates and greatly reduced infant mortality rates. What culture, what government, what community would not consider these results to be great triumphs?[11]

In addition, when decent housing and jobs are available in Indian Country, then families can live on or near their reservations, near their relatives and elders, and they and their children can more easily practice tribal languages, learn ceremonies and beliefs, and help perpetuate them. This is truly a win-win situation for tribal families, governments, and cultures. Many Indian people want to live on or near their reservations and will do so when economic conditions allow. Some tribes are building a middle class and are experiencing severe housing shortages for citizens who want to live on their reservations. When Chief Phillip Martin of the Mississippi Choctaw was asked what economic development was doing to his tribe's culture, he said: "Well, it used to be that everyone moved away, but now they're all coming back."[12]

My second point is that most people do not identify any specific aspects of culture that they fear will be put at risk due to improved Indian and tribal economic conditions. Most commentators also fail to identify specific cultural issues, and they just discuss the topic in general terms. At ONABEN's Trading at the River conference on the Tulalip Reservation in May 2010, however, two persons mentioned the possible negative impacts of when a single or small group of entrepreneurs "capture" a reservation and acquire such power over tribal leadership that they can coerce or manipulate tribal politics to their advantage, or by their actions put at risk various issues of tribal sovereignty. I have no easy answer in response to these concerns. I suppose this type of issue can arise in Indian Country as easily as elsewhere and that such events just have to be dealt with on an issue-by-issue basis.[13]

A few writers have also mentioned the development of "greed" and the fact that economic development might bring many non-Indians to reservations as being possible problems. It appears that greed over the accumulation of material possessions would be solved in the same fashion that tribal cultures handled this issue for centuries. Potlatches, giveaways, paying for ceremonies and feasts, and helping to support the poor, for example, were ways in which richer individual Indians and families used their excess resources in culturally appropriate ways. These identical avenues are also available for modern-day Indians and tribal governments to appropriately and culturally use their excess material gains.[14]

The issue that numerous outsiders would visit reservations is a definite concern that I imagine would be factored into a tribal or entrepreneur's analysis before establishing a particular type of economic activity on a specific reservation. As mentioned, some tribal communities will not support or tolerate certain types of business activities, and the tribal government or entrepreneur that ignores this concern would doom their enterprise to failure from the start. It sounds like the tribal "market" or community would control these kinds of issues and protect reservations with concerns about having their cultures impacted in this fashion.

Finally, it has to be noted that there is no question that some and perhaps nearly all economic activities can have cultural impacts. Each individual tribal society has to determine whether to pursue and support particular types of activities. The approach of the Crow Nation and the Northern Cheyenne Tribe to coal mining is a good example of differences between reservations and tribal cultures. Even though their reservations abut each other, the Crow have avidly pursued coal mining while the Northern Cheyenne have worked vigorously to ban that activity on their reservation.[15]

But we must note that most tribal cultures throughout history have readily accepted many technological advances and new economic activities. Many tribes and individuals took up the European fur trade and became middlemen in the trade of European goods. Guns and horses also proved a perfect example of this fact. The Cayuse Tribe in eastern Oregon and many of the Plains Indian tribes eagerly adopted the horse, and it did change their cultures. Horses allowed many sedentary tribes to take up far more nomadic lifestyles. Was this a good or a bad thing? I am certain that most Cayuse and Plains peoples would say that these were good cultural changes. To my knowledge these tribes still honor the place of horses in their histories and in their modern-day lives. Almost all Indians were also happy to take up guns, as it made them more efficient hunters and better able to support their families. Subsistence Alaska Native hunters today make no apology for using snowmobiles and guns. Did that change their cultures? Perhaps. Do they think that was a bad thing?

As with horses and guns, some economic activities will cause cultural changes. Economic development can bring visitors and activities to reservations that some tribal communities might not desire. But it is up to each individual Indian society and tribe to determine for themselves whether to pursue development in general or whether to pursue only certain types of economic activities. Part of self-determination is for these societies and cultures to make these important decisions. And Indian societies have made these kinds of decisions throughout history. One historian writes about the Navajo Nation: "The Navajo accepted alterations selectively, as a means of enriching their lives without sacrificing cultural integrity."[16] Furthermore, a study of the Seminoles in the twentieth century says they have repeatedly chosen economic modernization as the best way "to preserve, not abandon, distinctive identities."[17] And Professor Loretta Fowler makes a very valid point that most Indian cultures had to change a lot in the past thousand years to survive. She argues that if we claim today that Indian cultures never changed, or should never change, then we make their very "success and survival become un-Indian."[18]

There is no doubt that concerns about the impacts of economic development on Indian culture raise very important questions that must be addressed and answered by each tribal community. But in my opinion, doing nothing about tribal and Indian economic conditions is not an option. That path might even be a betrayal of Indian cultures and communities, because allowing reservations and Indian families to continue to languish in poverty and for reservations to continue to be depopulated as families are forced to move away for jobs and housing will only lead to the eventual demise of those very cultures and communities. Letting tribal and reservation communities strangle on poverty is not an option.

* * * * * * * * * * * * * * * * * * * * * * * * * *

We have addressed an incredibly important and wide-ranging subject. This book could easily have been much longer. But my goal was not to try to cover every possible issue regarding American Indian economic development. Instead, I wanted to address some rarely noted points about historic tribal and American Indian economic activities and property rights. I wanted to look at why Indian economic systems and property rights regimes have been ignored and even falsely defined throughout U.S. history. I wanted to investigate how American Indians went from being fairly prosperous, self-sustaining communities for hundreds of years to now being the poorest people in the United States. And I wanted to highlight how Indians and tribal governments are pulling themselves out of that situation with intelligent hard work.

In addition, I wanted to address and suggest ways that tribal governments and Indian communities can attract investments to their reservations and create economies that will keep the assets and economic benefits of tribal and Indian business in Indian Country as much as possible. Reservation economies made up of a mix of tribal and Indian-owned businesses seem to be just about the only way to keep money circulating in Indian Country and to create lasting and sustainable economic development.

Today, Indian Country remains poor. Indian people, communities, and tribal governments need economic development and operating economies. They need capitalism, socialism, free market entrepreneurship; whatever you want to call it, Indian Country needs it. And only Indian people and their governments and communities can make this happen.

# *Notes*

## CHAPTER 1

1. Rich Lowry, *Detroit's real scandal isn't about Illicit sex*, The Oregonian, April 2, 2008, at E5.

2. Richard Read, *Economic Forecast: Gloomy*, The Oregonian, June 21, 2011, at A1.

3. Richard Read, *With 63% Unemployment, Oregon Tribe Clings to Hope*, The Oregonian, Dec. 5, 2009, at A1; U.S. Department of the Treasury, Community Development Financial Institutions Fund, *The Report of the Native American Lending Study* (Nov. 2001), 5, 11, 13–14, http://www.cdfifund.gov/docs/2001_nacta_lending_study.pdf; U.S. Census Bureau, U.S. Department of Commerce, *American Indian, Alaska Native Tables from the Statistical Abstract of the United States: 2004–2005* (124th ed. 2005), 441, 451, http://www.census .gov/statab/www/sa04aian.pdf; Bureau of Indian Affairs, *2003 Indian Labor Force Report* (2003), ii, http://www.bia.gov/idc/groups/public/documents/text/idc-001777.pdf; U.S. Comm'n on Civil Rights, *A Quiet Crisis: Federal Funding and Unmet Needs In Indian Country* (2003), 60–64; Housing Assistance Council, *Housing on Native American Lands* (2006), 1, http://www.ruralhome.org/storage/documents/nativeamerinfosheet2.pdf; Kenneth E. Robbins, *Reflecting on the Numbers: Media Hype Breeds Misperception*, Am. Indian Rep., Sept. 2000, at 22; U.S. Dept. of Housing and Urban Dev., *Assessment of Am. Indian Housing Needs and Program: Final Report* (May 1996), xii, 66–67, 76–78, 80.

4. Indian Country is defined under federal law to include all land within the boundaries of a reservation, no matter who owns it, and all other lands held by tribes and individual Indians if the United States has an ownership interest in the land. 18 U.S.C. § 1151.

5. *California's Largest Tribe Deploys 1st White Space Broadband*, News from Indian Country, June 2011, at 23; Jodi Rave, *U.S. Senators Seek $2B for Tribes*, Missoulian.com Dec. 11, 2008; U.S. Department of the Treasury, *The Report of the Native American Lending Study*, 5, 11, 14, 39–40; Brenda Norrell, *Clinton's New Market Focus on Indian Country*, Indian Country Today, May 3, 2000, at A1; U.S. Department of Energy, *Indian

*Energy Study* (Mar. 28, 2000); Michelle M. Taggart, *Challenging the Traditional View of Tribal Economics*, Am. Indian Rep., Oct. 1999, at 17.

6. Robert J. Miller, *Economic Development in Indian Country: Will Capitalism or Socialism Succeed?*, 80 Or. L. Rev. 757, 829–37 (2002); Mark Fogarty, *Many Indian Entrepreneurs, But Revenue Is Lagging*, Indian Country Today, Jan. 5, 2011 (Business magazine insert at 16); Felicia Fonseca, *Navajo Nation Reaches out to Entrepreneurs*, News from Indian Country, March 3, 2008, at 13; Gregg Paisley, *Economic Development: Defining It and Keeping Score*, Tribal Fin. Rev., Fall 1995, at 5–6; Beth Britton, *Tribes Seek Economic Salvation*, Great Falls Trib., June 1, 2001; Mark Fogarty, *Study: More Data Needed on Urban Indian Issues*, Indian Country Today, April 14, 2008; *Webster's Ninth New Collegiate Dictionary* (Springfield, MA: Merriam-Webster, 1985), 395.

7. Ericka Schenck Smith, *Meeting Spotlights Reservation Economies*, Billings Gazette (June 1, 2001); Presidential Commission on Indian Reservation Economies, *Report and Recommendations to the President of the United States* (Washington, DC: Gov't Printing Office, 1984); Amy Hsuan, *Success, Caring Infuse the Sacks Family Tradition*, The Oregonian, May 15, 2008, at D1.

8. Miller, 829; Paisley, 5–6; Kent Gilbreath, *Red Capitali$m: An Analysis of the Navajo Economy* (Norman: University of Oklahoma Press, 1973), 129; Ron Selden, *Economic Development Attitudes Must Change*, Indian Country Today, June 13, 2001 at A1 (observing that money normally circulates five times in local communities); Cathy Siegner, *Making and Keeping Dollars on Montana Reservations*, Am. Indian Rep., Feb. 1999, at 18 (claiming that money circulates seven times in communities).

9. Richard Cockle, *Jobs, Jobs, Jobs, But No Homes*, The Sunday Oregonian, April 20, 2008, at B4; Timothy Egan, *As Others Abandon Plains, Indians and Bison Come Back*, New York Times, May 27, 2001, at A1.

10. Richard H. White, *Tribal Assets: The Rebirth of Native America* (New York: Henry Holt 1990), 277.

11. Ray Halbritter & Steven Paul McSloy, *Empowerment or Dependence? The Practical Value and Meaning of Native American Sovereignty*, 26 N.Y.U. J. Int'l L. & Pol. 531, 568 (1994).

12. Antone Minthorn, Address at Trading at the River Conference (April 15, 2008).

13. *The History of ONABEN*, www.onaben.org; *ONABEN, 1999–2000 Bi-Annual Report*, at 6.

14. Ibid.

15. Stephen Cornell & Joseph P. Kalt, *Culture and Institutions as Public Goods: American Indian Economic Development as a Problem of Collective Action*, in Property Rights and Indian Economies, Terry L. Anderson, ed. (Lanham, MD: Rowman & Littlefield, 1992), 227; *accord* Joseph P. Kalt & Stephen Cornell, *The Redefinition of Property Rights*, in American Indian Reservations: A Comparative Analysis of Native American Economic Development, in American Indian Policy: Self-Governance and Economic Development, Lyman H. Legters & Fremont J. Lyden, eds. (1994), 121, 145.

16. Bill Yellowtail, *Meriwether and Billy and the Indian Business*, in Lewis and Clark Through Indian Eyes, Alvin M. Josephy, Jr., ed., (New York: Alfred Knopf, 2006), 73, 81–83.

17. Dean Howard Smith, *Modern Tribal Development: Paths to Self-Sufficiency and Cultural Integrity in Indian Country* (Walnut Creek, CA: Altamira Press, 2000), 3, 62, 71, 80, 89, 110–11.

18. Sam Deloria, *Obama Administration Indian Education Initiative*, The American Indian Graduate (Spring 2010), 7.

19. Smith, 3, 16, 71, 80, 111; *accord* Brian C. Hosmer, *American Indians in the Marketplace: Persistence and Innovation Among the Menominees and Metlakatlans, 1870–1920* (Lawrence: University of Kansas Press, 1999), 13–14, 16, 80, 219, 223.

20. Jim Shamp, *Cherokee Study: As Poverty Falls, So Do Psychiatric Problems*, Herald Sun, Oct. 14, 2003, http://www.heraldsun.com/tools/printfriendly.cfm?StoryID=402615; Peter J. Ferrara, *The Choctaw Revolution* (Washington, DC: Americans for Tax Reform Foundation, 1998), 13–14, 45–50, 64–66, 68–73, 80, 82, 84–85; Barbara Powell, Choctaws: *From Poverty to Prosperity in 40 Years*, Clarion-Ledger, June 26, 2003; Richard Cockle, *Reservation Shows No Signs of Slowing*, The Sunday Oregonian, April 20, 2008, at B4; Egan, at A1.

## CHAPTER 2

1. Leonard A. Carlson, *Learning to Farm: Indian Land Tenure and Farming Before the Dawes Act*, in Property Rights and Indian Economies, Terry L. Anderson, ed. (Lanham, MD: Rowman & Littlefield, 1992), 70–71.

2. Ibid.; Robert J. Miller, *Economic Development in Indian Country: Will Capitalism or Socialism Succeed?*, 80 Ore. L. Rev. 757, 764–95 (2001); Thomas R. Wessel, *Agriculture, Indians and American History*, 50 Agricultural Hist. 9–10, 14 (1976); *The Other Side of the Frontier: Economic Explorations into Native American History*, Linda Barrington, ed. (Boulder, CO: Westview Press, 1999), 70–71, 86.

3. Wilbur R. Jacobs, *Dispossessing the American Indian: Indians and Whites on the Colonial Frontier* (New York: Scribner, 1972), 111.

4. Wessel, 14.

5. Albert Memmi, *Attempt at a Definition*, in Dominated Man: Notes Toward a Portrait (New York: Orion Press, 1968), 185–95; *Other Side of the Frontier*, 17–18, 184–85, 236, 255; Boyce Richardson, *People of Terra Nullius: Betrayal and Rebirth in Aboriginal Canada* (Vancouver: Douglas & McIntyre, 1994), 28.

6. Fredrick Webb Hodge, *Handbook of American Indians North of Mexico*, vol. 2 (Washington, DC: Gov't Printing Off., 1910), 308.

7. Ibid.; Julian H. Steward, *Ethnography of the Owens Valley Paiute*, 33 Am. Archaeology & Ethnology 253 (1934); *American Encounters: Natives and Newcomers from European Contact to Indian Removal 1500–1850*, Peter C. Mancall & James H. Merrell, eds. (New York: Routledge, 2000), 176; Edward H. Spicer, *Cycles of Conquest* (Tucson: University of Arizona Press, 1962), 343; Terry L. Anderson, *Sovereign Nations or Reservations? An Economic History of American Indians* (San Francisco: Pacific Research Institute, 1995), 31.

8. *Other Side of the Frontier*, 5, 72, 74, 108; Clark Wissler, *Indians of the United States*, rev. ed. (New York: Doubleday, 1966), 37, 39–41; Richard White, *The Roots of Dependency: Subsistence, Environment, and Social Change among the Choctaws, Pawnees, and Navajos* (Lincoln & London: University of Nebraska Press, 1983), 184, 198; Wessel, 9–10, 14.

9. *American Encounters*, 5–6, 7–8, 9–10; Peter C. Mancall, *Valley of Opportunity: Economic Culture along the Upper Susquehanna, 1700–1800* (Ithaca, NY: Cornell University Press, 1991), 39–40, 125; Jacobs, 1, 5–9; 15 Smithsonian Inst., *Handbook of North*

*American Indians*, William C. Sturtevant, ed. (Washington, DC: Smithsonian Institution, 1978), 58, 162, 324; Spicer, 9–14, 119, 153, 541.

10. White, 20.

11. Ibid., 159, 200; Anderson, 8; Steward, 253; Melville J. Herskovits, *The Economic Life of Primitive Peoples* (New York: A.A. Knopf, 2d ed. 1952), 362.

12. Carlson, 71; 9 *Handbook of North American Indians* (Washington, DC: Smithsonian Institution, 1979), 554–57; *Food, Fiber, and the Arid Lands*, William G. McGinnies, ed., (Tucson: University of Arizona Press, 1971), 58.

13. 15 Smithsonian Handbook, 84.

14. Carlson, 70–71; Angie Debo, *A History of the Indians of the United States* (Norman: University of Oklahoma Press, 1970), 13–14; Anderson, 32–34.

15. Tome v. Navajo Nation, 4 Navajo Rptr. 159, 161 (Window Rock D. Ct. 1983).

16. Yazzie v. Jumbo, 5 Navajo Rptr. 75, 77 (Navajo S.Ct. 1986).

17. Begay v. Keedah, 19 Indian L. Rep. 6021, 6022 (Navajo S.Ct. 1991). *See also* Carlson, 71; Herskovits, 362.

18. Andrew P. Vayda, *Pomo Trade Feasts*, in Tribal and Peasant Economies, George Dalton, ed. (New York: Natural History Press, 1967), 498.

19. United States v. Washington, 384 F.Supp, 312, 353 (W.D. Wa. 1974), *aff'd*, 520 F.2d 676 (9th Cir. 1975), *cert den.*, 423 U.S. 1086 (1976).

20. Personal Interview, Clifford Lyle Marshall, Chairman, Hoopa Valley Tribe (March 19, 2009); *see also* Bruce L. Benson, *Customary Indian Law: Two Case Studies*, in Property Rights, 27; *The Other Side of the Frontier*, 71; Vayda, 495–96, 498.

21. John C. McManus, *An Economic Analysis of Indian Behavior in the North American Fur Trade*, 32 Tasks Econ. Hist. 36, 39 (1972). *See also* Anderson, 36–40; Eleanor Leacock, *The Montagnais' Hunting Territory and the Fur Trade*, 73 Am. Anthropologist 56 (1954); 15 Smithsonian Handbook, 84.

22. Phillip Drucker, *The Northern and Central Nootkan Tribes*, 144 Bureau Am. Ethnology Bull. 247 (1951).

23. Ibid.; Robert J. Miller, *Exercising Cultural Self-Determination: The Makah Indian Tribe Goes Whaling*, 25 Am. Indian L. Rev. 165 (2001); Alan D. McMillan, *Since the Time of the Transformers: The Ancient Heritage of the Nuu-chah-nulth, Ditidaht, and Makah* (Vancouver: UBC Press, 1999), 13–14, 16, 22; Kalervo Oberg, *The Social Economy of The Tlingit Indians* (Seattle: University of Washington Press, 1973), 35.

24. Anderson, xiv–xv, 24; Oberg, 55; 7 Smithsonian Inst., *Handbook of North American Indians*, William C. Sturtevant, et al., eds. (Washington, DC: Smithsonian Institution, 1990), 418; Drucker, 247; *The Other Side of the Frontier*, 71, 108; Elizabeth Colson, *The Makah Indians: A Study of an Indian Tribe in Modern American Society* (Minneapolis: University of Minnesota Press, 1953), 4; Carlson, 71; 9 Smithsonian Inst., 554–57; K. N. Llewellyn & E. Adamson Hoebel, *The Cheyenne Way: Conflict and Case Law in Primitive Jurisprudence* (Norman: University of Oklahoma Press, 1941), 213–14, 216–20, 233.

25. 7 Smithsonian Handbook, 418; *see also* Drucker, 247; Colson, 4; McMillan, 21, 33; Oberg, 55, 62–63, 79–83, 91–94; Benson, 34; Anderson, 40; Herskovits, 372–73, 376.

26. White, 180.

27. Personal Interview, Antone Minthorn, Chairman, Confederated Tribes of the Umatilla Indian Reservation (March 31, 2009); *The Cheyenne Way*, 223–25, 229, 233; Anderson, 41, 43, 62; Carlson, 71; Alan M. Klein, *Political Economy of the Buffalo Hide Trade: Race and Class on the Plains*, in The Political Economy of North American Indians,

John H. Moore, ed. (Norman: University of Oklahoma Press, 1993), 133, 141–42; Benson, 34; White, 187.

28. Colson, 4.

29. 1 Smithsonian Handbook, 315; Anderson, 41, 62; White, 180; Colson, 249–50; Oberg, 94–95; 10 Smithsonian Handbook, 714–15; Herskovits, 123–24.

30. Duane Champagne, *Economic Culture, Institutional Order, and Sustained Market Enterprise: Comparisons of Historical and Contemporary American Indian Cases*, in Property Rights, 196–98; 7 Smithsonian Handbook, 346, 493; Herskovits, 251, 478; Stephen H. Lekson et al., *The Chaco Canyon Community*, Sci. Am., July 1988, at 108; Oberg, 35, 56, 60–61, 132; 15 Smithsonian Handbook, 384; 9 Smithsonian Inst., 979.

31. Kenneth R. Philp, *John Collier's Crusade for Indian Reform, 1920–1954* (Tucson: University of Arizona Press, 1977), 239.

32. 7 Smithsonian Handbook, 493, 505, 540, 548, 551, 580, 591; Rick Rubin, *Naked Against the Rain: The People of the Lower Columbia River 1770–1830* (Portland: Far Shore Press, 1999), 27, 69, 71.

33. Robert Sullivan, *A Whale Hunt* (New York: Scribner, 2000), 67.

34. Champagne, 196–200; White, 180; Oberg, 35, 56, 60–61, 93–96, 98–99, 101, 132–33; 7 Smithsonian Handbook, 84–86, 469; McMillan, 13–14, 22, 42.

35. *Webster's Ninth New Collegiate Dictionary*, 9th ed. (Springfield: Merriam-Webster, 1985), 1118; *The Compact Oxford English Dictionary*, 2d ed. (Oxford: Oxford University Press, 1991), 494.

36. *Other Side of the Frontier*, 109; White, 187; Jacobs, 9; Ronald L. Trosper, *That Other Discipline: Economics and American Indian History*, in New Directions in American Indian History, Colin G. Calloway, ed. (Norman: University of Oklahoma Press, 1988), 210, 212; 15 Smithsonian Handbook, 84.

37. Michele Strutin, *Chaco: A Cultural Legacy* (Tucson, AZ: Southwest Parks & Monuments Assn., 1994), 34–35, 50–51; *see also* Lekson, 108; *Other Side of the Frontier*, 5.

38. Charles C. Mann, *1491: New Revelations of the Americas Before Columbus* (New York: Vintage Books, 2005), 41–42, 288–90; Lynda Norene Shaffer, *Native Americans Before 1492: The Mound Building Centers of the Eastern Woodlands* (New York: M. E. Sharpe, 1992), 3, 20–23, 25–26, 28, 33–34, 36–38, 40–42, 44–45; White, 193.

39. Mann, 27–28, 284–86, 291–97; Shaffer, 51, 53–54, 56–57, 62–67, 66, 75–76, 84–85; *Other Side of the Frontier*, 5, 86.

40. Salisbury, 5–10; *Other Side of the Frontier*, 86; Shaffer, 66; Debo, 13–14; 15 Smithsonian Handbook, 384.

41. David Murray, *Indian Giving: Economies of Power in Indian–White Exchanges* (Amherst: University of Massachusetts Press, 2000), 119–20; *Other Side of the Frontier*, 103; 15 Smithsonian Handbook, 83, 85, 202–06, 344–47, 430; 9 Smithsonian Handbook, 305; 7 Smithsonian Handbook, 125, 208–09; Klein, 148.

42. 7 Smithsonian Handbook, 119–20, 123–25, 131, 150; 15 Smithsonian Handbook, 85, 204–06, 344–47, 430; Klein, 148; *Other Side of the Frontier*, 9.

43. Salisbury, 13; 15 Smithsonian Handbook, 83; *Valley of Opportunity*, 47–48; 9 Smithsonian Handbook, 25–26, 71–72, 127–28, 149; Oberg, 105; Patricia C. Albers, *Symbiosis, Merger, and War: Contrasting Forms of Intertribal Relationship Among Historic Plains Indians*, in Political Economy, 94, 99, 101; 7 Smithsonian Handbook, 418.

44. 7 Smithsonian Handbook, 150, 208–09, 560, 580; 9 Smithsonian Handbook, 79, 201; Oberg, 105, 111–12; 10 Smithsonian Handbook, 712–13; 15 Smithsonian

Handbook, 45; John C. Ewers, *Plains Indian History and Culture* (Norman: University of Oklahoma Press, 1997), 24–25; Shaffer, 25.

45. Salisbury, 6, 10; 10 Smithsonian Handbook, 712–13; 15 Smithsonian Handbook, 763–64; Strutin, 50–51; Lekson, 108; Ewers, 24–25; 7 Smithsonian Handbook, 120–21; Spicer, 9, 147, 543; Paul VanDevelder, *Savages & Scoundrels: The Untold Story of America's Road to Empire Through Indian Territory* (New Haven, CT, & London: Yale University Press, 2009), 8.

46. *Valley of Opportunity*, 47–48.

47. Lekson, 108; Anderson, 63–64; Rubin, 69; Herskovits, 223–24.

48. James P. Ronda, *Lewis & Clark among the Indians* (Lincoln: University of Nebraska Press, 1998 ed.), 75–76, 88–89; Salisbury, 13; 9 Smithsonian Handbook, 189.

49. *The Cheyenne Way*, 228–29; Oberg, 36, 55, 105, 110; Herskovits, 86, 93–94; Trosper, 205; 7 Smithsonian Handbook, 119–20, 123–24, 131.

50. 10 Smithsonian Handbook, 721; Rubin, 69–71; Arthur J. Ray, *Indians in the Fur Trade: Their Role as Trappers, Hunters, and Middlemen in the Lands Southwest of Hudson Bay 1660–1870* (Toronto: University of Toronto Press, 1974), 51– 71, 125, 131–34, 138; 7 Smithsonian Handbook, 369, 585.

51. 7 Smithsonian Handbook, 123–25, 130, 153, 208, 282, 319–20, 407–08, 471; Colson, 5; 15 Smithsonian Handbook, 199, 204–06, 344–47, 430; 9 Smithsonian Handbook, 305; Wessel, 11–13; *Valley of Opportunity*, 50–51, 83, 91–94; Oberg, 106; Jacobs, 9; Ewers, 17, 28; Ray, 51–71, 125, 131–34, 138.

52. Jacobs, 9–10, 32–33; Ray, 51–71, 125, 131–34, 138; Oberg, 35, 56, 60–61, 132; 15 Smithsonian Handbook, 84; 7 Smithsonian Handbook, 119, 130; Klein, 143.

53. Murray, 119–20; 7 Smithsonian Handbook, 22, 369, 505, 537, 565; Strutin, 50–51; 9 Smithsonian Handbook, 149; Rubin, 71; 10 Smithsonian Handbook, 720–21; Vayda, 495–96; Oberg, 50–51, 112, 132; Marshall Sahlins, *Stone Age Economics* (Chicago: Aldine–Atherton, 1972), 219; 15 Smithsonian Handbook, 384.

54. Jacobs, 41.

55. 15 Smithsonian Handbook, 166, 202–03; Jacobs, 41, 48; Murray, 119–20; Oberg, 96, 152.

56. 7 Smithsonian Handbook, 29, 417, 493, 505, 537, 540, 548, 551, 562, 573, 580, 585, 591; Herskovits, 209, 251–53; Rubin, 27, 69, 71; Franz Boaz, *Physical Characteristics of the Indians of the North Pacific Coast*, Am. Anthropologist 4 (1891); Jacobs, 490, 609 n.61.

57. Delos Sackett Otis, *History of the Allotment Policy: Hearings on H.R. 7902 Before the House Comm. on Indian Affairs*, 73d Cong., 2d Sess. pt. 9, at 431 (1934).

## CHAPTER 3

1. *Foundations of Colonial America*, vol. 1, W. Keith Kavenagh, ed. (New York: Chelsea House, 1973), 23.

2. *Winthrop Papers*, Vol. 3, Malcolm Freiberg, ed. (Boston: Massachusetts Historical Society, 1931), 172.

3. Ibid.

4. David S. Jones, *Rationalizing Epidemics: Meanings and Uses of American Indian Mortality since 1600* (Cambridge, MA: Harvard University Press, 2004), 2.

5. 15 Cong. Globe 918 (1846).

6. Dee Brown, Bury My Heart at Wounded Knee, 218 (ed. 2007). *See also* Robert J. Miller, *Native America, Discovered and Conquered: Thomas Jefferson, Lewis & Clark, and Manifest Destiny* (Lincoln: University of Nebraska Press, 2008), 78–97, 115–21, 151–52, 160–61; Reginald Horsman, *Race and Manifest Destiny: The Origins of American Racial Anglo-Saxonism* (Cambridge, MA: Harvard University Press, 1981), 3, 5, 110, 195, 300–03.

7. Miller, *Native America*, 3–4, 39–45, 168–71.

8. Francis Paul Prucha, *Documents of United States Indian Policy*, 3rd ed. (Lincoln: University of Nebraska Press, 2000), 1–2.

9. Miller, *Native America*, 25–58, 77–98, 115–71; Gregory Evans Dowd, *Wag the Imperial Dog: Indians and Overseas Empires in North America, 1650–1776*, in A Companion to American Indian History, Philip J. Deloria & Neal Salisbury, eds. (Oxford: Blackwell Publishers, 2002), 122.

10. Richard White, *The Roots of Dependency: Subsistence, Environment, and Social Change among the Choctaws, Pawnees, and Navajos* (Lincoln: University of Nebraska Press, 1983), xv–xvii.

11. Magnus Blomstrom & Bjorn Hettne, *Development Theory in Transition: The Dependency Debate & Beyond: Third World Responses* (London: Zed Books Ltd., 1984), 1, 6, 56; David W. Murray, *Self-Sufficiency and the Creation of Dependency: The Case of Chief Isaac Inc.*, 16 Am. Ind. Q. 169 (Spring 1992).

12. Murray, 170–71; Blomstrom & Hettne, 66.

13. Murray, 171; White, xvi–xvii.

14. White, xvii–xix.

15. Ibid.

16. Brian C. Hosmer, *American Indians in the Marketplace: Persistence and Innovation Among the Menominees and Metlakatlans, 1870–1920* (Lawrence: University of Kansas Press, 1999), 1–13, 16.

17. Patricia Albers, *Labor and Exchange in American Indian History*, in A Companion to American Indian History, 279.

18. *Native Pathways: American Indian Culture and Economic Development in the Twentieth Century*, Brian Hosmer & Colleen O'Neill, eds. (Boulder: University Press of Colorado, 2004), 6–7, 11.

19. Charles C. Mann, *1491: New Revelations of the Americas Before Columbus* (New York: Vintage Books, 2005), 48–49; William H. McNeill, *Plagues and Peoples* (New York: Anchor Press, 1976); Richard H. Steckel & Joseph M. Prince, *Tallest in the World: Native Americans of the Great Plains in the Nineteenth Century*, 91 Am. Econ. Rev. 287, 287–94 (2001).

20. Russell Thornton, *Health, Disease, and Demography*, in A Companion to American Indian History, 69.

21. John E. Kicza, *First Contacts*, in A Companion to American Indian History, 33–34; White, 2.

22. Kicza, 34.

23. Mann, 107–09; White, 2, 3, 318; Kicza, 34–35.

24. Kicza, 31–33.

25. Dowd, 52, 128; Edward D. Castillo, *Short Overview of California Indian History*, (1998), http://ceres.ca.gov/nahc/califindian.html.

26. Kicza, 40–42.

27. White, 3–5, 43–48.

28. Kicza, 35–37.

29. Ibid., 35–38.
30. Ibid., 34–38.
31. Kicza, 38–39; Mann, 52.
32. *Foundations of Colonial America*, vol. 1, 23.
33. Kicza, 39–40; Mann, 33–34.
34. White, 57–58, 68.
35. White, 70, 93, 96–97; *The Other Side of the Frontier: Economic Explorations into Native American History*, Linda Barrington, ed. (Boulder, CO: Westview Press, 1999), 8.
36. White, 75, 78–79, 82–83.
37. Ibid., 96; Miller, *Native America*, 86–87.
38. *The Adams–Jefferson Letters*, Vol. 2, Lester J. Cappon, ed. (Chapel Hill: University of North Carolina Press, 1959), 308.
39. *A Companion to American Indian History*, 381; *see also* Miller, *Native America*, 39–40, 86–91.
40. Miller, *Native America*, 45.
41. *See generally* Robert A. Williams, Jr., *Linking Arms Together: American Indian Treaty Visions of Law and Peace, 1600–1800* (New York: Oxford University Press, 1997); *see also* Robert J. Miller, *Exercising Cultural Self-Determination: The Makah Indian Tribe Goes Whaling*, 25 Am. Indian L. Rev. 165, 189–99 (2001); Robert J. Miller, *Speaking with Forked Tongues: Indian Treaties, Salmon, and the Endangered Species Act*, 70 Or. L. Rev. 543, 551–63 (1991).
42. *A Companion to American Indian History*, 398–99.
43. Roger G. Kennedy, *Mr. Jefferson's Lost Cause: Land, Farmers, Slavery, and the Louisiana Purchase* (New York: Oxford University Press, 2003), 68, 251–52.
44. Miller, *Native America*, 90–91.
45. Ibid., 87.
46. Ibid., 45–46, 48, 86–89; Francis Paul Prucha, *The Great Father: The United States Government and the American Indians* (Lincoln: University of Nebraska Press, 1995), 116, 120; Ora Brooks Peake, *A History of the United States Indian Factory System 1795–1822* (Denver: Sage Books, 1954); Treaty with the Osage, Sept. 25, 1818, art. I, 7 Stat. 183; Treaty with the Choctaw, Nov. 16, 1805, art. II, 7 Stat. 98, 2 *Indian Affairs: Law and Treaties*, Charles J. Kappler, ed. (Washington, DC: Gov't Printing Off., 1904).
47. *A Companion to American Indian History*, 399; Cherokee Nation v, Georgia, 30 U.S. (8 Pet.) 1, 17 (1831).
48. Francis Paul Prucha, *The Indians in American Society: From the Revolutionary War to the Present* (Berkeley: University of California Press, 1985), 33–34, 36–39, 41, 43, 50.
49. Prucha, *Indians in American Society*, 24.
50. *A Companion to American Indian History*, 385, 401.
51. Prucha, *Indians in American Society*, 87–88.
52. *A Companion to American Indian History*, 402–03; Prucha, *Indians in American Society*, 73, 87–88.
53. White, 317, 321–22.
54. Craig H. Miner, *The Corporation and the Indian: Tribal Sovereignty and Industrial Civilization in Indian Territory, 1865–1907* (Columbia, MO: University of Missouri Press, 1976), 23–27, 58, 164; Sandra Faiman–Silva, *Multinational Corporate Development in the American Hinterland: The Case of the Oklahoma Choctaws*, in The Political Economy of North American Indians, John H. Moore, ed. (Norman: University of Oklahoma Press,

1993), 215, 218–19, 228; *Public Policy Impacts on American Indian Economic Development*, C. Matthew Snipp, ed. (Albuquerque: University of New Mexico, 1988), 2–3, 7.

55. *Chevron Agrees to $45 Million Settlement for Royalties*, News from Indian Country, Jan. 15, 2010, http://indiancountrynews.net/index.php?option=com_content&task=view&id=8166&Itemid=1 (Unocal, Texaco and others also paid to settle a False Claims Act suit and previously Burlington Resources, Inc. paid $105 million, Shell Oil paid $56 million, and Dominion Exploration paid $2 million for similar claims); Joseph Jorgensen, *Sovereignty and the Structure of Dependency at Northern Ute*, 10 Am. Ind. Culture & Research J. 75, 78, 83 (1986); *Public Policy Impacts*, 7–9.

56. U.S. Const. art. I, § 8; Cotton Petroleum Corp. v. New Mexico, 490 U.S. 163, 192 (1989).

57. Seminole Nation v. United States, 316 U S. 286, 296–97 (1942).

58. Cherokee Nation v. Georgia, 30 U.S. (5 Pet.) 1, 17 (1831).

59. 25 U.S.C. §§ 81, 84, 406, 464, 3501; Presidential Commission on Indian Reservation Economies, *Report and Recommendations to the President of the United States* (Washington, DC: Gov't Printing Off., 1984), 7, 921–24.

60. Trade and Intercourse Act of July 22, 1790, ch. 23, 1 Stat. 137, 137–38; Prucha, *The Great Father*, 18–19, 23–24, 26–27.

61. Prucha, *The Great Father*, 116–24, 130–34.

62. *American Indian Policy in the Twentieth Century*, Vine Deloria, Jr., ed. (Norman: University of Oklahoma Press, 1985), 243–44.

63. *See, for example*, Treaty with the Cherokee, Nov. 28, 1785, art. IX, 7 Stat. 18; Treaty with the Comanche, May 15, 1846, art. II, 9 Stat, 844; Treaty with the Makah, Jan. 31, 1855, art. XIII, 12 Stat. 939; *Indian Affairs: Laws and Treaties*, 10, 100, 225, 682.

64. General Allotment Act, ch. 119, 24 Stat. 388 (1887).

65. Prucha, *The Great Father*, 129, 139–51, 179–208, 283–92, 412, 465, 500, 510, 577–81, 609–10, 659, 661–62, 665, 689–92, 814–22, 864–65; Delos Sacket Otis, *The Dawes Act and the Allotment of Indian Lands* (Norman: University of Oklahoma Press, 1973), 11–12, 430–35; Montana v. United States, 450 U.S. 544, 560 n.9 (1981).

66. Prucha, *The Great Father*, 140–43, 659, 667–68, 873; Felix S. Cohen, *Handbook of Federal Indian Law*, Rennard Strickland et al., eds. (Charlottesville, VA: Michie, 1982 ed.), 128–34, 613, 617; 25 U.S.C. § 348.

67. Leonard A. Carlson, *Land Allotment and the Decline of American Indian Farming*, 18 Explorations in Econ. Hist. 128–54 (1981); Prucha, *The Great Father*, 42, 493, 609–10, 686, 895–96.

68. Prucha, *The Great Father*, 811, 873–74, 883, 896; Cohen, 137.

69. Carlson, 75; Prucha, *The Great Father*, 895.

70. Prucha, *The Great Father*, 650–51, 671–73, 738, 740, 887–89, 891, 894; 25 U.S.C. §§ 312, 319–320, 357, 403, 406–407; Paul VanDevelder, *Savages & Scoundrels: The Untold Story of America's Road to Empire Through Indian Territory* (New Haven, CT: Yale University Press, 2009), 24–25.

71. Pub. L. No. 73–383, 48 Stat. 984 (June 18, 1934); Prucha, *The Great Father*, 762, 808–10, 960–62; 25 U.S.C. §§ 461, 464.

72. 25 U.S.C. §§ 476–477; Graham D. Taylor, *The New Deal and American Indian Tribalism* (Lincoln: University of Nebraska Press, 1980), x, 120; Theodore H. Haas, *Ten Years of Tribal Government Under I.R.A.* (Chicago: U.S. Indian Service, 1947), 8.

73. 25 U.S.C. § 477.

74. Taylor, 27–30, 38, 66, 110, 120–24, 131–32, 136–37, 142–43; Cohen, 150.

75. Prucha, *The Great Father*, 958–60, 972, 994–96; 78 Cong. Rec. H11, 736 (daily ed. June 15, 1934) (Rep. Carter); Taylor, 123.

76. Taylor, 29.

77. Prucha, *The Great Father*, 1010; Taylor, 44–45, 60–65, 81; Cohen, 147.

78. 25 U.S.C. § 81 (the statute was extensively amended in 2000).

79. Taylor, 40, 93–94, 102–03; 25 U.S.C. § 81 (1994).

80. Lori Taylor, *Confederated Tribes of Grand Ronde Celebrate 25 Years of Restoration*, The Oregonian, Nov. 21, 2008, at B1.

81. Charles F. Wilkinson & Eric R. Biggs, *The Evolution of the Termination Policy*, 5 Am. Indian L. Rev. 139, 151–54 (1977).

82. Charles F. Wilkinson, *Blood Struggle: The Rise of Modern Indian Nations* (New York: W. W. Norton & Company, 2005), xii.

83. 25 U.S.C. §§ 450–450n.

84. Cohen, 189–90 n.100, 201, 712, 721–23; 25 U.S.C. §§ 1451, 1521–1524; 25 C.F.R. §§ 101.1–103.55; Prucha, *The Great Father*, 1091–1100.

# CHAPTER 4

1. The Harvard Project on American Indian Economic Development, *The State of the Native Nations: Conditions under U.S. Policies of Self-Determination* (New York: Oxford University Press, 2008), 7–8.

2. Robert H. White, *Tribal Assets: The Rebirth of Native America* (New York: Henry Holt & Co., 1990), 105, 211, 217; Personal Interview, Antone Minthorn, Chairman, Confederated Tribes of the Umatilla Indian Reservation (Jan. 2, 2009); Personal Interview, Gary George (Feb. 5, 2009); Harvard Project, 112.

3. Harvard Project, 162; Klaus Frantz, *Indian Reservations in the United States* (Chicago: University of Chicago Press, 1998), 264–72; 25 U.S.C. § 3101; http://www.itcnet.org.

4. White, 202, 208; Brian C. Hosmer, *American Indians in the Marketplace: Persistence and Innovation Among the Menominees and Metlakatlans, 1870–1920* (Lawrence: University of Kansas Press, 1999); Harvard Project, 166–67.

5. Harvard Project, 166–67.

6. Ibid.

7. 25 U.S.C. §§ 2101–2108; Judith V. Royster, *Practical Sovereignty, Political Sovereignty, and the Indian Tribal Energy Development and Self-Determination Act*, 12 Lewis & Clark L. Rev. 1065 (2008); Harvard Project, 161–62; Cohen's Handbook of Federal Indian Law (Newark: Matthew Bender, 2005 ed.), 965.

8. Harvard Project, 137; Ianthe Jeanne Dugan, *Indian Affairs: A Business Empire Transforms Life for Colorado Tribe*, Wall St. J., June 13, 2003, at A1; Melissa Campbell, *Bright Spots in Alaska Business*, Alaska Business Monthly, Mar. 2002, at 58.

9. Harvard Project, 167–68, 170–71; 25 U.S.C. § 415.

10. Frantz, 284–92; Ron Selden, *Tribes Attempt to Get Beyond Government Economies*, Billings Outpost, June 19, 2002; Dan Morse, *Tribal Pursuit: The Salish–Kootenai Tribe Has Succeeded Where Others Have Failed; Its Secret: Think Business, Not Bureaucracy*, Wall St. J., Mar. 27, 2002; White, 48, 253.

11. Peter J. Ferrara, *The Choctaw Revolution* (Washington, DC: Americans for Tax Reform Foundation, 1998), 45–50, 64–66, 68–73, 80, 82, 84–85; Barbara Powell, *Choctaws: From Poverty to Prosperity in 40 Years*, Clarion-Ledger, June 26, 2003.

12. Ferrara, 13–14, 45–50, 64–66, 68–73, 80, 82, 84–85; White, 57, 59, 61, 75–77, 83–85, 91, 93, 99.

13. Harvard Project, 167–70, 283; Frantz, 238–72; White, 160; Cohen, 965.

14. Harvard Project, 165; White, 105, 214, 217, 232–33.

15. Matthew B. Krepps, *Can Tribes Manage Their Own Resources? The 638 Program and American Indian Forestry*, in What Can Tribes Do?, Stephen Cornell & Joseph P. Kalt, eds. (Los Angeles: American Indian Studies Center, 1992), 182–83, 199.

16. *Summer Greater Than Others*, Indian Country Today, July 6, 2011, at 25 (American Indian Alaska Native Tourism Association 12-page advertisement).

17. Harvard Project, 10, 162; Susan Guyette, *Planning for Balanced Development: A Guide for Native American and Rural Communities* (Santa Fe: Clear Light Publishers, 1996), 171–204; White, 217.

18. Robert J. Miller, *Inter–tribal and International Treaties for American Indian Economic Development*, 12 Lewis & Clark L. Rev. 1103, 1114–15 (2008) (citing authorities).

19. Ibid., 1108–10 (citing authorities).

20. Ibid., 1106; http://www.indigenousnationstreaty.org/.

21. Harvard Project, 29, 78, 161–63.

22. *Trusteeship in Change: Toward Tribal Autonomy in Resource Management*, Richmond L. Clow & Imre Sutton, eds. (Boulder: University Press of Colorado, 2001), 72.

23. *Trusteeship in Change*, 9–11, 57–72, 265, 273–75; Frantz, 208–37.

24. Powell.

25. www.onaben.org; Robert J. Miller, *Economic Development in Indian Country: Will Capitalism or Socialism Succeed?*, 80 Or. L. Rev. 757, 829–32, 838–41, 844–45 (2001).

26. *wiyaxayxt * as days go by * wiyaakaa?awn, Our History, Our Land, and Our People: The Cayuse, Umatilla, and Walla Walla*, Jennifer Karson, ed. (Pendleton & Portland: Tamastslikt Cultural Institute & Oregon Historical Society Press, 2006), 97.

27. *Our History & Culture* (Part 2), http://www.umatilla.nsn.us/hist2.html; *as days go by*, 44–54, 61–89, 97–117, 174–75; Personal Interview, Bill Tovey (April 14, 2009).

28. *as days go by*, 110, 157–69, 175–82; *Our History & Culture* (Part 2).

29. *Our History & Culture* (Part 2); *as days go by*, 188, 194–96, 215–16.

30. *Our History & Culture* (Part 2); *as days go by*, 169–71, 198–202, 216–18, 223, 240.

31. *as days go by*, 204–07.

32. Gary George Interview.

33. *as days go by*, 210–11.

34. Richard Cockle, *Eastern Oregon Casino Powers Reservation*, The Oregonian, Feb. 28, 2011, at A1; *as days go by*, 181, 210–11; Wildhorse Resort & Casino Fact Sheet; Gary George Interview; Gary George Email (April 21, 2009).

35. Wildhorse Resort & Casino Fact Sheet; CTUIR: Facts and Figures (Jan. 2006); Bill Tovey Interview.

36. *McDonald's Big Draw for Arrowhead*, Confederated Umatilla J., April 2009, at 8.

37. Bill Tovey Interview; Confederated Umatilla J., April 2009, at 40.

38. *as days go by*, 165, 167, 185, 197–98, 212, 216, 226–27.

39. Ibid., 227, 236.

40. Ibid., 249–52; Bill Tovey Interview; http://www.umatilla.nsn.us/hist1.html #setting; Richard Cockle, *"First foods" Guide Tribes' Land Strategy*, The Sunday Oregonian, March 1, 2009, at C1.

41. CTUIR: Facts and Figures (Jan. 2006); Gary George Interview.

42. *as days go by*, 86–88.

43. Charles Callender, *Shawnee*, in 15 Handbook of North American Indians, William C. Sturtevant & Bruce G. Trigger, eds. (Washington, DC: Smithsonian Institution, 1978), 622–23, 630–32; R. David Edmunds, *The Shawnee Prophet* (Lincoln: University of Nebraska Press, 1983), 7–9; Jerry E. Clark, *The Shawnee* (Lexington: The University Press of Kentucky, 1993), 5–24; James H. Howard, *Shawnee! The Ceremonialism of a Native American Tribe and Its Cultural Background* (Athens, OH: Ohio University Press, 1981), 4–5, 11–15.

44. Callender, 624, 628.

45. Clark, 32; Howard, 43–46, 48–49, 109–10; Henry Harvey, *History of the Shawnee Indians* (Cincinnati: Morgan & Sons, 1855), 148; Thomas Wildcat Alford, *Civilization* (Norman: University of Oklahoma Press, 1936), 45.

46. Stephen Warren, *The Shawnees and Their Neighbors 1795–1870* (Chicago: University of Illinois Press, 2005), 17–18; Clark, 25–27; Callender, 632; William C. Sturtevant, *Oklahoma Seneca–Cayuga*, in 15 Handbook of North American Indians, 538; Howard, 15, 19–20.

47. Callender, 632; Sturtevant, *Oklahoma Seneca–Cayuga*, 538; Glenna J. Wallace, *From This Corner*, Shooting Star (March 2008), 4; Muriel H. Wright, *A Guide to the Indian Tribes of Oklahoma* (Norman: University of Oklahoma Press, 1951), 240, 244–25.

48. Chief George J. Captain, *Shooting Star* vol. 3 (1990), 1; Personal Interview, Charles Enyart (Feb. 21, 2009).

49. *Shooting Star* (Jan. 1978), 1.

50. *Shooting Star* (Sept. 1978), 3.

51. *Shooting Star* (June 1978), 3; (July 1978), 2; (Aug. 1978), 2, 7; (Sept. 1978), 4.

52. *Shooting Star* (Jan. 1978), 3; (Feb. 1979), 7.

53. *Shooting Star* (May 1985), 2; (April 1985), 3, 6–7.

54. *Shooting Star* (March 1986), 2–4; (Oct. 1996), 1; Personal Interview, Chief Glenna J. Wallace, Eastern Shawnee Tribe (Feb. 20, 2009).

55. *Shooting Star* (Dec. 1989), 1; (March 1987), 2; (Jan. 1987), 2; Glenna Wallace Interview; Personal Interview, Danny Captain (Feb. 21, 2009); Charles Enyart Interview.

56. Glenna Wallace Interview; Personal Interview, Second Chief Jack Ross, Eastern Shawnee Tribe (Feb. 22, 2009); Charles Enyart Interview; *Shooting Star* (June 2011), 38.

57. *Shooting Star* (June 2011), 1, 37, 48; (Mar. 2009), 1, 34; (Dec. 2008), 2; Glenna Wallace Interview; Jack Ross Interview.

58. *Shooting Star* (Nov. 2003), 8; (Oct. 2003), 9; (June 1998), 1; (May 1998), 1–2; (June 1997), 1; (Oct. 1996), 1; (May 1994), 1, 3; (Jan. 1994), 2; (Aug. 1993), 1; (1991, no. 1), 4–5; (1991, no. 2), 1; (March 1990), 1, 4, 6–7; (1990, no. 2), 6; (1990, no. 3), 4; (Dec. 1989), 1–2; (1988, no. 1, Spring), 1; (1988, no. 3), 3, 6; (1987, no. 8), 3; (Jan. 1987), 2; (Mar. 1987), 2, 4; (April 1986), 2.

59. *Shooting Star* (June 1997), 1; (Oct. 1996), 1; (May 1994), 1, 3.

60. *Shooting Star* (June 2011), 36; (July 1997), 3; (Oct. 1996), 1–3, 10; Glenna Wallace Interview; Personal Interview, Deron Burr, CEO, People's National Bank (Feb. 20, 2009).

61. *Shooting Star* (Feb. 2009), 8, 11; (Dec. 1989), 1–2; (June 1998), 1; (May 1998), 1–2; Jack Ross Interview; Deron Burr Interview; http://www.hoopa–nsn.gov/government/ statistics.htm.

62. *Shooting Star* (Mar. 1987), 2; Glenna Wallace Interview; Jack Ross Interview; Deron Burr Interview.

63. Personal Interview, Lora Nuckolls (Feb. 20, 2009).

64. *Shooting Star* (June 1997), 1; (Oct. 1996), 1; (July 1994), 1; (Mar. 1987), 4.

65. Glenna Wallace Interview; Personal Interview, Howard Birdsong (Feb. 21, 2009); Chief Glenna J. Wallace Emails (April 20 & 21, 2009); *Shooting Star* (June 2011), 38, 43.

66. *Hoopa Valley Tribe*, http://www.hoopa–nsn.gov/culture/history.htm.

67. Bugenig v. Hoopa Valley Tribe, 25 Indian L. Rep. 6139, 6141 (Hoopa Valley Ct. App. 1998).

68. http://www.hoopa–nsn.gov/culture/history.htm; Personal Interview, Clifford Lyle Marshall, Chairman, Hoopa Tribe (March 19, 2009); http://www.hoopa–nsn.gov/ government/statistics.htm.

69. http://www.hoopa–nsn.gov/culture/history.htm; http://www.hoopa–nsn.gov/ government/statistics.htm.

70. Clifford Marshall Interview.

71. Ibid.; Personal Interview, Danny Jordan (March 21, 2009).

72. Marshall Interview; Danny Jordan Interview; http://www.hoopa–nsn.gov/ enterprises/hfi.htm; http://www.xontahbuilders.com.

73. Clifford Marshall Interview; Danny Jordan Interview; http://www.hoopa–nsn.gov/ culture/art.htm; http://www.hoopa–nsn.gov/enterprises/businesses.htm.

# CHAPTER 5

1. Dave Palermo, *Tribal Gambling Revenues Fall for the First Time in History*, Indian Country Today, Apr. 21, 2010, at 2.

2. National Gambling Impact Study Commission Report 2–10, http://govinfo.library. unt.edu/ngisc/reports/2.pdf; U.S. General Accounting Office, *A Profile of the Indian Gaming Industry* (May 1997).

3. National Indian Gaming Association, *Indian Gaming Facts*, http://www .indiangaming.org/library/indian-gaming-facts/index.shtml; Alan Meister, *Indian Gaming Industry Report* (Newton, MA: Casino City Press Publication, 2006–2007 updated ed.), 2; ibid. (2004–2005), 1; Steven Andrew Light & Kathryn R. L. Rand, *Indian Gaming & Tribal Sovereignty: The Casino Compromise* (Lawrence: University Press of Kansas, 2005), 87–89.

4. Jeff Mayers, *Tribal Gaming in Wisconsin: An Emerging Political and Economic Force*, Wis. Int. (Spring 2003); Heidi L. McNeil, *Indian Gaming—Prosperity, Controversy, in the Gaming Industry on American Indian Lands*, 139, 157, PLI Corp. L. & Practice Course, Handbook Series No. B–872 (1994); Kathie Durbin, *Means to an End: Gambling Casinos Offer Oregon Tribes a Path Out of Poverty*, Or. Q., (2000), 21–22.

5. Richard Cockle, *Reservation Shows No Signs of Slowing*, The Sunday Oregonian, April 20, 2008, at B4; Timothy Egan, *As Others Abandon Plains, Indians and Bison Come Back*, New York Times, May 27, 2001, at A1.

6.  G. William Rice, *Tribal Governmental Gaming Law* (Durham, NC: Carolina Academic Press, 2006), 2–4; Kathryn Gabriel, *Gambler Way: Indian Gaming in Mythology, History and Archaeology in North America* (Boulder, CO: Johnson Books, 1996).

7.  Kathryn R. L. Rand & Steven Andrew Light, *Indian Gaming Law and Policy* (Durham, NC: Carolina Academic Press, 2006), 3–4.

8.  Matthew L. M. Fletcher, *Bringing Balance to Indian Gaming*, 44 Harvard J. Legislation, 39, 45 n.29 (2006); 132 Cong. Rec. S12,017–18 (Aug. 15, 1986) (Senator Andrews).

9.  Rand & Light, 6; http://www.nigc.gov/ReadingRoom/PressReleases/PressReleases Main/PR93062008/tabid/841/Default.aspx.

10.  Seminole Tribe of Florida v. Butterworth, 658 F.2d 310 (5th Cir. 1981).

11.  Ibid., 312–14; Bryan v. Itasca County, 426 U.S. 373 (1976).

12.  480 U.S. 202 (1987).

13.  Ibid., 215–17.

14.  Rand & Light, 30.

15.  Ibid., 29–30; Joseph M. Kelly, *Indian Gaming Law*, 43 Drake L. Rev. 501, 504 (1995).

16.  Rand & Light, 30–31; 25 U.S.C. §§ 2701–2721.

17.  25 U.S.C. § 2702.

18.  Robert N. Clinton, *Enactment of the Indian Gaming Regulatory Act of 1988: The Return of the Buffalo to Indian Country or Another Federal Usurpation of Tribal Sovereignty?*, 42 Arizona State L.J. 17 (2010).

19.  25 U.S.C. § 2703(6).

20.  25 U.S.C. § 2710(a)(1); Senate Rep. No. 446, 100th Cong., 2d Sess., at 11, reprinted in 1988 U.S.C.C.A.N. 3078; Conference of Western Attorneys General, *American Indian Law Deskbook* (Boulder: University Press of Colorado, 3rd ed., 2005), 429.

21.  25 U.S.C. § 2703(7) & 2703(7)(A); 25 C.F.R. §§ 502.3, 502.9; Senate Rep. 100–446, at 9.

22.  25 U.S.C. § 2717(a)(1); Senate Report, 100–446, at 9.

23.  25 U.S.C. § 2710(b)(1)(A).

24.  25 U.S.C. § 2710(c)(5)(A).

25.  25 U.S.C. § 2703(7)(A)(ii)(II).

26.  25 U.S.C. § 2710(b)(1)(A); *Indian Law Deskbook*, 432; Light & Rand, 8.

27.  25 U.S.C. §§ 2703(7)(a)(i), (B)(ii).

28.  Senate Rep. 100–446.

29.  United States v. 103 Electronic Gambling Devices, 223 F.3d 1091 (9th Cir. 2000); United States v. 162 MegaMania Gambling Devices, 231 F.3d 713 (10th Cir. 2000); Rand & Light, 49, 84–89.

30.  Rand & Light, 87; 70 Fed. Reg. 23,011 (May 4, 2005); 25 U.S.C. § 2711(c)(1)–(2).

31.  25 U.S.C. § 2703(8).

32.  25 U.S.C. § 2710(d)(1)(B).

33.  25 U.S.C. §§ 2710(d)(1), 2710(d)(7)(B)(vii); 25 C.F.R. pts 522, 523.

34.  25 U.S.C. § 2710(b)(2)(B), (d)(2)(A); http://www.thecommunityfund.com/; Dean Rhodes, *Community Fund Surpasses $54 Million in Giving*, Smoke Signals, July 1, 2011, at 3.

35.  25 U.S.C. § 2710(b)(3); http://www.indiangaming.org/library/indian-gaming -facts/index.shtml; Stephen Cornell et al, *Per Capita Distributions of American Indian Tribal Revenues: A Preliminary Discussion of Policy Considerations*, http://www.arizonanativenet

.com/pdf/2007-11-09_NNI_Per_caps_paper_for_NCAI—FINAL.pdf; Timberly Ross, *Tribes Buy Back Thousands of Acres of Land*, News from Indian Country, Jan. 15, 2010, at 7.

36. Rumsey Indian Rancheria v. Wilson, 41 F.3d 421 (9th Cir. 1994), *amended*, 64 F.3d 1250 (9th Cir. 1994) and 99 F.3d 321 (9th Cir. 1996).

37. 25 U.S.C. § 2710(d); Senate Rep., 100–446, at 13.

38. 25 U.S.C. § 2710(d)(3)(C)(i)–(vii).

39. 25 U.S.C. §§ 2710(d)(7)(A)(i)–(ii), (d)(7)(B)(ii); Mashantucket Pequot Tribe v. Connecticut, 913 F.2d 1024 (2d Cir. 1990).

40. 25 U.S.C. §§ 2710(d)(3)(A), (d)(7)(B).

41. Seminole Tribe of Florida v. Florida, 517 U.S. 44, 72–73 (1996); Light & Rand, 50.

42. 25 U.S.C. § 2710(d)(7)(B)(vii); Seminole Tribe v. Florida, 11 F.3d 1016, 1029 (11th Cir. 1994), *aff'd*, 517 U.S. 44 (1996).

43. 25 C.F.R. part 291; Texas v. United States, 497 F.3d 491 (5th Cir. 2007), *cert. denied*, 129 S.Ct. 32 (2008); Rand & Light, 102–03.

44. Light & Rand, 125.

45. 25 U.S.C. §§ 2701(4), 2702, 2710(d)(3)(C)(iii), 2710(d)(4), 2710(d)(7)(B)(iii)(II); Light & Rand, 69–73, 86–87.

46. Fletcher, 43.

47. *In re Indian Gaming Related Cases*, 331 F.3d 1094, 1111, 1114–15 (9th Cir. 2003); Sault Ste. Marie Tribe of Chippewa Indians v. Engler, 271 F.3d 235 (6th Cir. 2001); Fletcher, 42–43; Rand & Light, 151–52 & n.47; Rincon Band of Luiseno Mission Indians v. Schwarzenegger, 602 F3d. 1019 (9th Cir. 2010), *cert. den.*, 79 U.S.L.W. 3142 (9–2–2010).

48. Rand & Light, 157–58, 161, 167–71; Rice, 379; Justin Juozapavicius, *Officials Describe New Gaming Policy That Opens Doors to Potential Off-Reservation Casino Construction*, News from Indian Country, June 2011, at 4.

49. Rand & Light, 157.

50. *Indian Law Deskbook*, 452; Catawba Indian Tribe of South Carolina v. State, 642 S.E.2d 751, 754–55 (S.C. 2007).

51. National Gaming Impact Study Commission, *Final Report* (1999), 8–1 to 8–5, http://govinfo.library.unt.edu/ngisc/reports/finrpt.html; Light & Rand, 81–82, 88, 97 & n.70; Rand & Light, 142.

52. Jonathan B. Taylor, Matthew B. Kreps, & Patrick Wang, *The National Evidence on the Socioeconomic Impacts of American Indian Gaming on Non-Indian Communities* (Cambridge, MA: Harvard Project on American Indian Economic Development, 2000), 1, 4, 26–27, http://www.ksg.harvard.edu/hpaied/pubs/pub_006.htm.

53. Light & Rand, 81–83, 91–92, 98–104; Cockle, B4; Egan, A1; Gary George Interview (Feb. 5, 2009).

54. Jim Shamp, *Cherokee Study: As Poverty Falls, Psychiatric Problems Decline*, Herald Sun, Oct. 14, 2003; Peter J. Ferrara, *The Choctaw Revolution* (Washington, DC: Americans for Tax Reform Foundation, 1998), 13–14, 45–50, 64–66, 68–73, 80, 82, 84–85; Barbara Powell, *Choctaws: From Poverty to Prosperity in 40 Years*, Clarion-Ledger, June 26, 2003.

55. U.S. Census Bureau, DP–3, Profile of Selected Economic Characteristics, Census 2000 (SF–3): Barona Reservation, CA; Kirk Johnson, *Gambling Helps Tribe Invest in Education and the Future*, New York Times, Feb. 21, 1995, at A5; Meister, (2006–2007), 2.

56. National Indian Gaming Association, *Indian Gaming Facts*, http://www.indian gaming.org/library/indian-gaming-facts/index.shtml; McNeil, 157.

57. National Indian Gaming Assoc., Indian Gaming Facts, at http://www.indian gaming.org/library/indian-gaming-facts/index.shtml; *Research in Human Capital and Development: American Indian Economic Development*, Carol Ward & C. Matthew Snipp, eds. (Greenwich, CT: Jai Press, Inc., 1996), 89.

58. Ray Halbritter & Steven Paul McSloy, *Empowerment or Dependence? The Practical Value and Meaning of Native American Sovereignty*, 26 N.Y.U. J. Int'l L. & Pol. 531, 568 (1994).

59. *Drugs, Alcohol Worsening Problems for Seminoles*, Indian Country Today, Oct. 8, 2008, at 14.

60. Jessica R. Cattelino, *High Stakes: Florida Seminole Gaming and Sovereignty* (Durham, NC: Duke University Press, 2008), 2–4, 9, 62, 112–17, 200, 204.

61. Quair v. Sisco, 2007WL1490571 (E.D. Cal. 2007); Quair v. Sisco, 359 F.Supp.2d 948 (E.D. Cal. 2004); Lewis v. Norton, 424 F.3d 959 (9th Cir. 2005); Lamere v. Superior Court, 31 Cal. Rptr. 3d 880 (Cal. Ct. App. 2005); Patrice H. Kunesh, *Banishment as Cultural Justice in Contemporary Tribal Legal Systems*, 37 N.Mex. L. Rev. 85, 119–35 (2007). In 2006, one commentator estimated that "more than 1,500 people from 23 tribes have been disenrolled in recent years, often for speaking out." Rachel Dornheim, *Tribes' Riches Increase Membership Battles* (July 7, 2006), http://www.marketplace.org/topics/ tribes-riches-increase-membership-battles.

62. Rand & Light, 143–44 & n.10; Dean Gerstein et al., *Gambling Impact and Behavior Study: Report to the National Gambling Impact Study Commission* (Chicago: National Opinion Research Center, April 1, 1999), 16–19.

63. Gerstein et al., *Gambling Impact and Behavior Study*; Rand & Light, 143; Light & Rand, 93–96.

64. National Indian Gaming Association, Media Release, http://www.indiangaming .org/info/pr/presskit/PROCEEDS.pdf.

# CHAPTER 6

1. Videotape: 3rd Annual ATNI Economic & Planning Summit (James Parker, Inc., March 20, 2008).

2. Hunter R. Clark & Amanda Velazquez, *Foreign Direct Investment in Latin America: Nicaragua—A Case Study*, 16 Am. U. Int'l L. Rev. 743, 759 (2001).

3. David D. Haddock, *Foreseeing Confiscation by the Sovereign*, in The Political Economy of the American West, Terry L. Anderson & Peter J. Hill, eds. (Lanham, MD: Rowman & Littlefield, 1994), 129.

4. Stock W. Corp. v. Taylor, 942 F.2d 655, 657 (9th Cir. 1991), *rev'd en banc on other grounds*, 964 F.2d 912 (9th Cir. 1992).

5. Santa Clara Pueblo v. Martinez, 436 U.S. 49, 58 (1978); Sokaogon Gaming Enterp. Corp. v. Tushie-Montgomery Assoc., 86 F.3d 656, 659 (7th Cir. 1996); United States v. Oregon, 657 F.2d 1009, 1012 (9th Cir. 1981).

6. Griffin v. Tri-County Metro. Transp. Dist., 870 P.2d 808 (Or. 1994); Nevada v. Hall, 440 U.S. 410, 412–13 n.2, 417 n.13 (1979).

7. 28 U.S.C. §§ 1346, 1491, 2402, 2672, 2674–75; 1 Lester S. Jayson & Robert C. Longstreth, *Handling Federal Tort Claims*, 2–4 & § 2.01 (New York: Matthew Bender, 2003); Or. Rev. Stat. § 30.270 (2001); Cal. Gov. Code §§ 850, 850.2, 850.4.

8. 25 U.S.C. §§ 81, 177, 415, 466, 2103(b), 3104(b); 25 C.F.R. § 166.300.

9. Confederated Tribes of the Grand Ronde Community of Oregon, Tribal Tort Claims Ordinance, Tribal Code § 255.6 (1988), http://www.narf.org/nill/Codes/grcode/gr2556tort.htm; Duran v. Confederated Tribes of the Grand Ronde Cmty., No. C–99–08–003 (Apr. 18, 2000), http://www.grandronde.org/court/PublishedOpinions/DURAN.PDF (last visited on Jun. 30, 2004); Mashantucket Pequot Tribal Nation, http://narf.org/nill/Codes/mpcode/title_4.pdf.

10. Craig J. Dorsay, Address, Oregon State Bar Indian Law Conference (Nov. 1, 2002).

11. 523 U.S. 751, 753–54 (1998).

12. 532 U.S. 411, 414–15, 418–20, 423 (2001).

13. Ibid.

14. Ibid.

15. *Sokaogon Gaming*, 86 F.3d at 659–60; Ninigret Dev. Corp. v. Narragansett Indian Wetuomuck Hous. Auth., 207 F.3d 21 (1st Cir. 2000).

16. 25 U.S.C. § 458cc(c); Dept. of Interior and Related Agencies Appropriations Act, Pub. L. No. 103–138, § 308, 107 Stat. 1379, 1416 (1993); 25 C.F.R. § 900.180–.210; Confederated Tribes of the Grand Ronde Community of Oregon, Tribal Tort Claims Ordinance, Tribal Code § 255.6(c), (e) (1998), http://www.narf.org/nill/Codes/grcode/gr2556tort.htm; Mashantucket Pequot Tribal Nation, Tribal Laws and Rules of Court, tit. IV.

17. 25 U.S.C. § 1302(8). *See also* Kaighn Smith, Jr., *Labor and Employment Law in Indian Country* (Boulder, CO: Native American Rights Fund, 2011), 107–31.

18. James C. McKinley, Jr., *Mohawk Tribe Is Rethinking Land Accord with Albany*, New York Times, Oct. 31, 2003, at B5; Rosebud Sioux Tribe v. McDivitt, 286 F.3d 1031 (8th Cir. 2002), *cert. denied*, 537 U.S. 1188 (2003).

19. Frank Pommersheim, *Braid of Feathers* (Berkeley: University of California Press, 1995), 170.

20. John C. Mohawk, *Indian Economic Development*, Akwe:kon J. (Summer 1992), 42, 46–48.

21. John J. Miller, *Off the Rez*, National Review, Dec. 31, 2002, at 28.

22. U.S. Const. art. I, § 10, cl. 1.

23. Elmer R. Rusco, *Civil Liberties Guarantees Under Tribal Law: A Survey of Civil Rights Provisions in Tribal Constitutions*, 14 Am. Ind. L. Rev. 269, 289 (1990); Constitution of the Snoqualmie Tribe of Indians, art. XI, § 1(9), http://www.snoqualmienation.com/organic%20documents.htm.

24. Robert J. Miller, *Inter–tribal and International Treaties for American Indian Economic Development*, 12 Lewis & Clark L. Rev. 1103 (2008).

25. Rosebud Sioux Tribe v. McDivitt, 286 F.3d 1031, 1035 (8th Cir. 2001).

26. Ibid.; Rain Archambeau, Note, Rosebud Sioux Tribe v. McDivitt, 286 F.3d 1031, *Hog Farm Corporation in Indian Country Lacks Standing in Federal Court to Challenge BIA Action Voiding Land Lease*, 7 Great Plains Nat. Res. J. 243, 249, n.37 (2002).

27. David Melmer, *Courts No Help Against Hog Farm*, Indian Country Today, June 18, 2003, at B1.

28. Steve Miller, *Judge Says Hog–Farm Lease Valid*, Rapid City J., June 10, 2003, http://rapidcityjournal.com/news/local/judge-says-hog-farm-lease-valid/article_e76579da-0124-5127-8256-91771dc33337.html.

29. *Rosebud Sioux Tribe*, 286 F.3d at 1035, 1040; Sun Prairie v. Martin, No. CIV 02–3030 RHB (D.S.D. June 5, 2003); *Rosebud Hog Farm Back in Court*, http://www.redorbit.com/news/science/176069/rosebud_hog_farm_back_in_court/.

30. Sangre de Cristo Dev. Co. v. United States, 932 F.2d 891, 893 (10th Cir. 1991), *cert. denied*, 503 U.S. 1004 (1992).

31. *Sangre de Cristo*, 932 F.2d at 892–95.

32. United Nuclear Corp. v. United States, 912 F.2d 1432, 1433–37 (Fed. Cir. 1990).

33. Dean Howard Smith, *Modern Tribal Development: Paths to Self-Sufficiency and Cultural Integrity in Indian Country* (Walnut Creek, CA: Altamira Press, 2000), 131.

34. Sac & Fox Tribe of the Miss. v. United States, 264 F. Supp. 2d 830, 833–34 (N.D. Iowa 2003); *Iowa Tribal Dispute Shuts Casino*, New York Times, May 24, 2003, http://college3.nytimes.com/guests/articles/2003/05/24/1090757.xml (last visited on Jul. 9, 2004).

35. Felicia Fonseca, *Hopi Lawmakers Suspend Tribe's Appellate Court in Continuing Turmoil*, News from Indian Country, Nov. 24, 2008, at 4.

36. Iowa Mutual Ins. Co. v. LaPlante, 480 U.S. 9, 18 (1987).

37. Nell Jessup Newton, *Tribal Court Praxis: One Year in the Life of Twenty Indian Tribal Courts*, 22 Am Indian L Rev 285, 285–87, 351–52 (1998) (analyzing 85 cases in tribal courts and concluding that they demonstrated fairness to non–Indian litigants).

38. April Schwartz & Mary Jo B. Hunter, *United States Tribal Courts Directory* (Buffalo: W.S. Hein, 2002), 73; Santa Clara Pueblo v. Martinez, 436 U.S. 49, 66 n.22 (1978); Mary Ann Glendon et al., *Comparative Legal Traditions* (St. Paul, MN: West Publishing, 2d ed., 1999), 61–66, 198–200.

39. Ron Selden, *Economic Development Attitudes Must Change*, Indian Country Today, June 13, 2001, http://www.indiancountry.com/367&style=printable; Robert J. Miller, *Economic Development in Indian Country: Will Capitalism or Socialism Succeed?*, 80 Or. L. Rev. 757, 847–48 & n.338 (2001).

40. *What Tribes Can Do: An Interview with Joseph P. Kalt*, Am. Indian Rep., Mar. 1999, at 18.

41. Stephen Cornell & Joseph P. Kalt, *Culture and Institutions as Public Goods: American Indian Economic Development as a Problem of Collective Action*, in Property Rights and Indian Economies, Terry L. Anderson, ed. (Lanham, MD: Rowman & Littlefield, 1992), 215, 227, 235, 237; Stephen Cornell & Joseph P. Kalt, *Reloading the Dice: Improving the Chances for Economic Development on American Indian Reservations*, in What Can Tribes Do? Strategies and Institutions in American Indian Economic Development (Los Angeles: American Indian Studies Center, 1992), 25–26.

42. Grand Ronde Constitution, art. IV, § 3.

43. Tribal Court Promulgation of Tribal Court Rules for the Confederated Tribes of the Grand Ronde Community of Oregon (December 21, 1998); http://www.tribalresource center.org/legal/opfolder/default.asp (last visited on Jul. 2, 2004); http://www.grandronde.org/court/index.html (last visited on Jul. 2, 2004).

44. Clark & Velazquez, 760; *Vlad the Impaler*, Economist, Nov. 1, 2003, at 13, 45, 69; Sabrina Tavernise, *Glimmers of an Investor-Friendly Russia*, New York Times, February 15, 2003, at C1.

45. Stephen Cornell, *Sovereignty, Prosperity and Policy in Indian Country Today*, 5 Cmty. Reinvestment 5, 5–7, 9–13 (1997); Matthew B. Krepps, *Can Tribes Manage Their Own*

*Resources? The 638 Program and American Indian Forestry*, in What Can Tribes Do?, 182–83, 199.

46. *BIA Replaces Blackfeet Police*, Indian Country Today, Apr. 30, 2003, at A1; Miller, National Review, 28–30.

47. Marley Shebala, *Tax Credit for Coal Companies OK'd*, Navajo Times, Aug. 9, 2001.

48. Tribal Employment Rights Ordinance, Hoopa Valley Indian Reservation, Ord. No. 2–80, §§ 13.4, 13.5 (1995); Red Lake Band of Chippewa Indians, Tribal Employment Rights Organization, http://www.redlakenation.org/jtpa/tero/html.

49. United States v. Shoshone Tribe of Indians, 304 U.S. 111, 115 (1938); 25 U.S.C. §§ 81, 415; Miller, *Economic Development*, 804–06.

50. John Stromnes, *Indian Housing Woes Outlined*, Missoulian, June 13, 2003, http://missoulian.com/news/state-and-regional/indian-housing-woes-outlined/article_c0ab9ab2-bb47-584e-b0a5-9cf735224edb.html; Mark Fogarty, *Title Insurance Getting Off the Ground in Indian Country*, Indian Country Today, May 14, 2003, at B1; Sally Willett, *An Overview of Indian Probate Past and Present* (Mar. 2002).

51. Stock W., Inc. v. Confederated Tribes of the Colville Reservation, 873 F.2d 1221, 1222–24 & nn.4–6 (9th Cir. 1989); 25 U.S.C. § 81; Indian Tribal Economic Development and Contract Encouragement Act of 2000, Pub. L. No. 106–179, § 2, 114 Stat. 46 (2000).

## CHAPTER 7

1. *The History of ONABEN*, www.onaben.org; *ONABEN, 1999–2000 Bi–Annual Report*, 6.

2. Kathleen Ann Pickering, *Lakota Culture, World Economy* (Lincoln: University of Nebraska Press, 2000), 5, 14; Videotape: 2008 3rd Annual ATNI Economic & Planning Summit, Reno, Nevada (James Parker, Inc.), Day 1, Tape 2, March 20, 2008.

3. The Harvard Project on American Indian Economic Development, *The State of the Native Nations: Conditions under U.S. Policies of Self-Determination* (New York: Oxford University Press, 2008), 135.

4. Richard H. White, *Tribal Assets: The Rebirth of Native America* (New York: Henry Holt, 1990), 277; Kent Gilbreath, *Red Capitali$m: An Analysis of the Navajo Economy* (Norman: University of Oklahoma Press, 1973), 7, 59, 92, 105–07, 116–17, 136.

5. Frank Pommersheim, *Braid of Feathers: American Indian Law and Contemporary Tribal Life* (Berkeley: University of California Press, 1995), 183–84.

6. Ibid., 185.

7. Karin Mika, *Private Dollars on the Reservation: Will Recent Native American Economic Development Amount to Cultural Assimilation?*, 25 New Mex. L. Rev. 23, 31–34 (1995). *See also* Aaron Drue Johnson, Comment, *Just Say No (to American Capitalism): Why American Indians Should Reject the Model Tribal Secured Transactions Act and Other Attempts to Promote Economic Assimilation*, 35 Amer. Indian L. Rev. 107 (2011).

8. Ron Selden, *Economic Development Attitudes Must Change*, Indian Country Today, June 13, 2001, at A1.

9. Robert J. Miller, *Economic Development in Indian Country: Will Capitalism or Socialism Succeed?*, 80 Ore. L. Rev. 757, 767–98 (2001); Bill Yellowtail, *Meriwether and Billy and the Indian Business,* in Lewis and Clark Through Indian Eyes, Alvin M. Josephy, Jr., ed. (New York: Alfred A. Knopf, 2006), 81–83.

10. Stephen Cornell & Joseph P. Kalt, *Culture and Institutions as Public Goods: American Indian Economic Development as a Problem of Collective Action,* in Property Rights and Indian

Economies, Terry L. Anderson, ed. (Lanham, MD: Rowman & Littlefield, 1992), 227; Joseph P. Kalt & Stephen Cornell, *The Redefinition of Property Rights in American Indian Reservations: A Comparative Analysis of Native American Economic Development*, in American Indian Policy: Self-Governance and Economic Development, Lyman H. Legters & Fremont J. Lyden, eds. (Westport, CT: Greenwood, 1994), 145.

11. Yellowtail, 83.

12. Dean Howard Smith, *Modern Tribal Development: Paths to Self-Sufficiency and Cultural Integrity in Indian Country* (Walnut Creek, CA: Altamira Press, 2000), 3, 62, 68, 71, 80, 110–11.

13. Ibid.

14. Ibid.

15. Miller, *Economic Development*, 767–98; Robert J. Miller, *Exercising Cultural Self-Determination: The Makah Indian Tribe Goes Whaling*, 25 Am. Ind. L. Rev. 165, 171–75, 178–84 (2001).

16. Cornell & Kalt, 245–46; Raymond Cross, *De-Federalizing American Indian Commerce: Toward a New Political Economy for Indian Country*, 16 Harv. J.L. & Pub. Pol'y 445, 486–87 & n.186 (1993); Klaus Frantz, *Indian Reservations in the United States: Territory, Sovereignty, and Socioeconomic Change* (Chicago: University of Chicago Press, 1999), 171–74, 182.

17. Frantz, 171; Miller, *Economic Development*, 855; Curt Wolters, *Social Jealousy: Its Role in Slowing Socioeconomic Transformation, Growth and Development*, http://cwedasllc .net/?p=277; *Panel on Culture*, Trading at the River Conference, April 15, 2008, Portland, OR.

18. *Panel on Culture* (Midwest Indian's comment); Frantz, 164–67, 182; *What Can Tribes Do?, Strategies and Institutions in American Indian Economic Development*, Stephen Cornell & Joseph P. Kalt, eds. (Los Angeles: American Indian Studies Center, 1992), 19–20, 43, 46–47; Miller, *Economic Development*, 855.

19. Miller, *Economic Development*, 841.

20. White, 111; U.S. Dept. of Housing & Urban Development, *Assessment of American Indian Housing Needs and Programs: Final Report* (May 1996), 146, 190–91, 229–30.

21. Federal Financial Institutions Examination Council, *Nationwide Summary Statistics for 2002* (2003), http://www.ffiec.gov/hmcrpr/hm_fs02.htm.

22. Pickering, 23; *Red Capitali$m*, 7, 59, 92, 105–07, 116–17, 136; Frantz, 138–48; *Public Policy Impacts on American Indian Economic Development*, C. Matthew Snipp, ed. (Albuquerque, NM: Institute for American Indian Development, 1988), 40, 129, 151.

23. Miller, *Economic Development*, 837–38; *Red Capitali$m*, 7, 59, 92, 105–07, 116–17, 136.

24. *Native American Death Rates Rise*, The Oregonian, March 31, 2009, at B3; Harvard Project, 219–31; Indian Health Service, *Indian Health Disparities* (2008), http://info.ihs. gov/Disparities.asp; *Public Policy Impacts*, 40, 151.

25. *On Capitalism*, Victor Nee & Richard Swedberg, eds. (Stanford, CA: Stanford University Press, 2007), 305; Cornell & Kalt, 227; Sabrina Tavernise, *Glimmers of an Investor–Friendly Russia*, New York Times, February 15, 2003, at C1.

26. 25 U.S.C. § 1302; Elmer R. Rusco, *Civil Liberties Guarantees Under Tribal Law: A Survey of Civil Rights Provisions in Tribal Constitutions*, 14 Am. Ind. L. Rev. 269, 289 (1990).

27. Robert J. Miller, *Inter-tribal and International Treaties for American Indian Economic Development*, 12 Lewis & Clark L. Rev. 1103, 1110–14 (2008).

28. Felicia Fonseca, *Navajo Nation Reaches Out to Entrepreneurs*, News from Indian Country, March 3, 2008, at 13; John J. Miller, *Off the Rez*, National Review, Dec. 31, 2002, at 28–30; David D. Haddock & Robert J. Miller, *Can a Sovereign Protect Investors from Itself? Tribal Institutions to Spur Reservation Investment*, J. Small & Emerging B. 173, 210 (2004).

29. Smith, 63, 68, 96; Fonseca, 13.

30. Fonseca, 13; Mark Fogarty, *Fractionation Fixed?*, American Indian Report 18–19 (April 2005).

31. Merrion v. Jicarilla Apache Tribe, 455 U.S. 130 (1982); Kenneth E. Robbins, *State Support for Healthy Reservation Economies: A Win–Win Strategy for All!*, Am. Indian Rep., June 1999, at 18; Brenda Norrell, *Catching the Dream of Free Enterprise*, Indian Country Today, May 23, 2001, at C1.

32. U.S. Const. art. I, § 8; Treaty with the Cherokee, Nov. 28, 1785, art. IX, 7 Stat. 18; Treaty with the Choctaw, Jan. 3, 1786, art. VIII, 7 Stat. 21; *reprinted in* 2 *Indian Affairs: Laws and Treaties*, Charles J. Kappler, ed. (Washington, DC: Gov't Printing Office, 1904), 10, 13, 15–16; United States v. Shoshone Tribe of Indians, 304 U.S. 111, 115 (1938); Cherokee Nation v. Georgia, 30 U.S. (5 Pet.) 1, 17 (1831); Presidential Commission on Indian Reservation Economies, *Report and Recommendations to the President of the United States* (Washington, DC: Gov't Printing Office, 1984), 31, 34.

33. John Stromnes, *Indian Housing Woes Outlined*, Missoulian, June 13, 2003; Mark Fogarty, *Title Insurance Getting Off the Ground in Indian Country*, Indian Country Today, May 14, 2003, at B1.

34. *Public Policy Impacts*, 8–9. *See also* George Pierre Castile, *North American Indians: An Introduction to the Chichimeca* (New York: McGraw–Hill, 1979), 272–73; Presidential Commission, 34.

35. Haddock & Miller, 212–13.

36. 25 U.S.C. §§ 261–264; Francis Paul Prucha, *The Great Father: The United States Government and the American Indians* (Lincoln: University of Nebraska Press, 1995 ed.), 91–93.

37. *The Poorest Part of America*, The Economist, Dec. 8, 2005, at 14; Timothy Egan, *As Others Abandon Plains, Indians and Bison Come Back*, New York Times, May 27, 2001, at A1.

38. *What Tribes Can Do: An Interview with Joseph P. Kalt*, Am. Indian Rep., March 1999, at 16.

39. U.S. Census, *Survey of Business Owners – American Indian- and Alaska Native-Owned Firms: 2002*, http://www.census.gov/csd/sbo/aiansummaryoffindings.htm; U.S. Department Commerce, *Am. Indians and Alaska Natives: 1997 Econ. Census Survey of Minority–Owned Business Enterprises* (May 2001), http://www.census.gov/prod/ec97/e97cs-6.pdf.

40. http://www.census.gov/csd/sbo/aiansummaryoffindings.htm.

41. *Harvard: Self-Government Leads to Large Gains for Native Americans*, Native American Report 1–3 (Jan. 22, 2005).

42. 25 U.S.C. §§ 1451, 1461, 1521–1524; 25 C.F.R. §§ 101.1–103.55; Miller, 842–43.

43. Zander v. Zander, 720 N.W.2d 360, 369 (Minn. Ct. App. 2006); *Silver Covenant Chain of Friendship Scholarship Program*, http://oneidanationfoundation.org/covenant.html (last visited on Nov. 20, 2008).

44. Chairman Antone Minthorn, Board of Trustees, Confederated Tribes of the Umatilla Indian Reservation, *Address at Trading at the River* (April 15, 2008).

45. Rob Capriccioso, *Colleges Help Communities*, Indian Country Today, March 16, 2011, at 18; Pickering, 31; American Indian Higher Education Consortium, http://www. aihec.org/colleges/TCUroster.cfm; American Indian College Fund, *Did You Know?*, http:// info.ihs.gov/Disparities.asp; U.S. Dept. of Educ., Nat'l Ctr. for Educ. Statistics, *Bachelor's Degrees Conferred by Degree-Granting Inst. by Race/Ethnicity and Sex of Student: Selected Years, 1976–77 Through 2005–06* (Jun. 2007), http://nces.ed.gov/programs/digest/d07/ tables/dt07_274.asp; http://www.dinecollege.edu/about/history.php.

46. David H. Getches, Charles F. Wilkinson, & Robert A. Williams, Jr., *Federal Indian Law*, 5th ed. (St. Paul: West Publishing, 2005), 21; Billie Jo Kipp, *Clinical Psychology*, The American Indian Graduate (March 2010), 19; George Blue Spruce, Jr., *One Man's Destiny*, The American Indian Graduate (March 2010), 20–21; Ken Lucero, *The Need for More Native Healthcare and Dental Professionals*, The American Indian Graduate (March 2010), 34–35.

47. Matthew B. Krepps, *Can Tribes Manage Their Own Resources? The 638 Program and American Indian Forestry, in* What Can Tribes Do?, 182–83, 199; White, 77, 84–85, 105, 214, 217, 248.

48. *Native American Death Rates Rise*, The Oregonian, March 31, 2009, at B3; U.S. Department of Health and Human Services, *Indian Health Service Fact Sheets*, http://info. ihs.gov/Population.asp; Robert J. Miller & Maril Hazlett, *The "Drunken Indian": Myth Distilled into Reality Through Federal Indian Alcohol Policy*, 28 Ariz. St. L. J. 223, 226 n.9 (1996); Indian Health Service, *Facts Sheets* (2008), http://info.ihs.gov/Diabetes.asp.

49. Theresa Julnes, *Economic Development as the Foundation for Self-Determination, in* American Indian Policy, 151.

50. *Cheyenne River First Tribe to Adopt State Business Code*, Indian Country Today, Jan. 17, 2001, at D1; *Compact between Crow Tribe of Indians/Apsaalooke Nation and Office of the Montana Secretary of State for a Joint Sovereign Filing System*, http://www.nccusl.org/Shared/ Docs/MTSTA/Final%20UCC%20Compact.pdf; Johnson, *Crow Sign Historic Pact*, http:// sos.mt.gov/News/archives/2008/February/2–6–08.htm (last visited on Nov. 17, 2008).

51. Miller, *Inter–tribal*, 1110–14.

52. Ibid.; Miller, *Economic Development*, 842–43; *Interview with Joseph P. Kalt*, 16.

53. Krepps, 182–83, 199; White, 77, 214, 217, 248; Peter J. Ferrara, *The Choctaw Revolution: Lessons for Federal Indian Policy* (Washington, DC: Americans for Tax Reform Foundation, 1998), 52–53, 142.

54. Caxsep Xununikga, *Indianpreneurship Course Graduates*, Hocak Worak (Ho-chunk Nation newspaper), March 27, 2009, at 5; *ONABEN: A Native American Business Network*, http://www.onaben.org; ONABEN, *1998 Annual Report* 7–8 (1998); ONABEN, *1999–2000 Bi–Annual Report* 6 (2000); http://www.indianpreneurship.com/ (last visited on Jan. 22, 2012).

55. Mark Fogarty, *Cheyenne River Loan Fund Seeded For "Economic Sovereignty,"* Indian Country Today, Jan. 31 2001, at B1; Cate Montana, *Business Consultants Expand Operations*, Indian Country Today, Jan. 24 2001, at B1.

56. Ron Selden, *Blackfeet Bank Keeps Dollars Circulating on the Reservation*, Indian Country Today, Dec. 1, 1999, at C2; Mark Fogarty, *Beyond the Jewelry Booth*, Am. Indian Rep., July 1999, at 16–17; David A. Benson, Aaron Lies, Albert A. Okunade & Phanindra V. Wunnava, *Small Business Economics of the Lakota Fund on the Native American Indian*

*Reservation*, IZA Discussion Paper No. 3933 (Jan. 2009), 1–3, at http://papers.ssrn.com/sol3/papers.cfm?abstract_id=1329571.

57. Ernie Stevens Speech, Trading at the River Conference, Tulalip Reservation (May 4, 2010); Gabriel S. Galanda, *Buy Indian. What Are We Waiting For?*, Indian Country Today, Mar. 17, 2010; Harold Monteau, *Is Indian Preference Dear?*, Indian Country Today, Feb. 24, 2010, at 5 & http://www.indiancountrytoday.com/internal?st=print&id=84771487 &path=/opinion (Indian vendors to the multibillion-dollar Indian gaming industry comprise less than 5%); Personal Interview, Roberta Conner, Tamastslikt Cultural Institute (April 14, 2009); Personal Interview, Gary George, Wildhorse Resort Casino (June 10, 2004); ONABEN, *Trading at the River* (April 15, 2008) (Midwestern audience member commented it is hard for Indian entrepreneurs to sell on their reservations); Dennis Thayer & Deborah Warren, *What Kind of Message Do Tribes Give to American Indian Businesses?*, Indian Country Today, Aug. 4, 2004, at A5; Kenneth E. Robbins, *Gaming: A Good Bet for Tribal Economical Development?*, Am. Indian Rep., Apr. 1999, at 20.

58. Miller, *Economic Development*, 830–31; Randall G. Holcombe, *Entrepreneurship and Economic Growth, in* Making Poor Nations Rich: Entrepreneurship and the Process of Economic Development, Benjamin Powell, ed. (Stanford, CA: Stanford University Press, 2008), 55–56, 61, 71–74.

59. Ron Selden, *Economic Development Attitudes Must Change*, Indian Country Today, June 13, 2001, at A1; *see also* Cathy Siegner, *Making and Keeping Dollars on Montana Reservations*, Am. Indian Rep., Feb. 1999, at 18.

60. *Interview with Joseph P. Kalt*, 16.

61. U.S. Small Business Administration, Office of Native American Affairs, *Mission*, http://www.sba.gov/aboutsba/sbaprograms/naa/index.html; Oregon Economic Community Development Department, *Government to Government 2003 Activity Report*, http://www.leg.state.or.us/cis/gov_to_gov/OECDD_2003.pdf.

62. http://www.nccusl.org/Shared/Docs/MTSTA/Final%20UCC%20Compact.pdf; Judy Zelio, *Piecing Together the State-Tribal Tax Puzzle* (April 2005), http://www.ncsl.org/programs/fiscal/sttribe_tax.htm.

63. Prucha, 1091–1100; Nick Wakeman, *Top 8(a)s Show Wide Range of Information Technology Skills as ANCs Continue Their Dominance*, Washington Technology, Sept. 17, 2007, http://www.washingtontechnology.com/print/22_17/31439-1.html.

64. GSA, *2009 Agency Financial Report* http://www.gsa.gov/AFR/afr_1201_finanalysis2.html; *see also* Presidential Commission, 57.

65. James J. Chrisman, *The Economic Impact of ONABEN's Counseling Activities in Oregon: 1998*, at 2, 11; James J. Chrisman, *The Economic Impact of ONABEN's Counseling Activities of the Oregon Native American and Entrepreneurial Network: 2000*, at 2, 15.

66. Selden, Siegner, 18; Castile, 273.

67. Smith, 3, 62, 71, 80, 110–11; Miller, *Economic Development*, 832–53.

68. Richard Cockle, *Jobs, Jobs, Jobs, But No Homes*, The Sunday Oregonian, April 20, 2008, at B4; Kenneth E. Robbins, *Doing Business Since 1941*, Am. Indian Rep., Apr. 2001, at 20; Egan, A1; Babette Herrmann, *Suquamish Tribe Debuts Community House*, Indian Country Today, March 18, 2009, at 7.

69. *Public Policy Impacts*, 159; Richard Cockle, *Reservation Shows No Signs of Slowing*, The Sunday Oregonian, April 20, 2008, at B4.

70. Minthorn speech.
71. Yellowtail, 73.

## CHAPTER 8

1. Paul A. Samuelson & William D. Nordhaus, *Economics* (New York: McGraw-Hill, 14th ed., 1992), 31, 439–42, 477.

2. Kent Gilbreath, *Red Capitali$m: An Analysis of the Navajo Economy* (Norman: University of Oklahoma Press, 1973), 129; Ron Selden, *Economic Development Attitudes Must Change*, Indian Country Today, June 13, 2001, at A1; Cathy Siegner, *Making and Keeping Dollars on Montana Reservations*, American Indian Report, Feb. 1999, at 18.

3. *Indian Self-Rule: First-Hand Accounts of Indian-White Relations from Roosevelt to Reagan*, Kenneth R. Philp, ed. (Salt Lake City: Howe Bros., 1986), 224.

4. *Economic Development in American Indian Reservations*, Roxanne Dunbar Ortiz, ed. (Albuquerque: University of New Mexico, 1979), 114, 116. *See also* Rodger J. Boyd, Executive Director, Division of Economic Development, Navajo Nation, April 7, 1994, Federal Bar Association Indian Law Conference, Albuquerque, NM; Ron Selden, *Blackfeet Bank Keeps Dollars Circulating on the Reservation*, Indian Country Today, December 1, 1999, at C2.

5. Siegner, 18; Selden, A1. *See generally* C. K. Prahalad, *The Fortune at the Bottom of the Pyramid* (Upper Saddle River, NJ: Wharton School Publishing, 2006).

6. Gregg Paisley, *Economic Development: Defining It and Keeping Score*, Tribal Finance Review, 1995, at 5–6; Kenneth E. Robbins, *Doing Business since 1941*, American Indian Report, April 2001, at 20.

7. Presidential Commission on Indian Reservation Economies, *Report and Recommendations to the President of the United States* (1984); The Harvard Project on American Indian Economic Development, *The State of the Native Nations: Conditions under U.S. Policies of Self-Determination* (New York: Oxford University Press, 2008), 135; David A. Benson, Aaron Lies, Albert A. Okunade, & Phanindra V. Wunnava, *Small Business Economics of the Lakota Fund on the Native American Indian Reservation* (Jan. 2009), 1, at http://papers.ssrn.com/sol3/papers.cfm?abstract_id=1329571.

8. Dean Howard Smith, *Modern Tribal Development: Paths to Self-Sufficiency and Cultural Integrity in Indian Country* (Walnut Creek, CA: Altamira Press, 2000), 53.

9. Harvard Project, 117; *Public Policy Impacts on American Indian Economic Development*, C. Matthew Snipp, ed. (Albuquerque: University of New Mexico, 1988), 135, 147–48; *Research in Human Capital and Development: American Indian Economic Development*, Carol Ward & C. Matthew Snipp, eds. (Greenwich, CT: Jai Press, Inc., 1996), 51; Robert H. White, *Tribal Assets: The Rebirth of Native America* (New York: Henry Holt & Co., 1990), 105, 217, 274; Kathleen Ann Pickering, *Lakota Culture, World Economy* (Lincoln: University of Nebraska Press, 2000), 16.

10. Stephen Cornell & Joseph P. Kalt, *Reloading the Dice: Improving the Chances for Economic Development on American Indian Reservations*, in What Can Tribes Do? Strategies and Institutions in American Indian Economic Development, Stephen Cornell & Joseph P. Kalt, eds. (Los Angeles: American Indian Studies Center, 1992), 29–31, 36–37; *American Indian Policy: Self-Governance and Economic Development*, Lyman H. Legters & Fremont J. Lyden, eds. (Westport, CT: Greenwood Press, 1994), 121, 126, 131–33;

*Navajo Ag Tops List of Federal Agricultural Farm Subsidy Payments for 2000*, Indian Country Today, Sept. 19, 2001, at D1.

11. Harvard Project, 123.

12. Richard Cockle, *Reservation Shows No Signs of Slowing*, The Sunday Oregonian, April 20, 2008, at B4; *see also* Gilbreath, 116–17.

13. Jaime Arsenault & Stephanie Carroll Rainie, *Tribal Management Key to Improved Health Services*, Indian Country Today, July 22, 2009, at 5; Harvard Project, 126–30; What Can Tribes Do?, 183, 199–200.

14. Harvard Project, 121–22, 126–30.

15. Ibid., 121–25; Gilbreath, 40, 42–45.

16. Robert J. Miller, *Economic Development in Indian Country: Will Capitalism or Socialism Succeed?*, 80 Or. L. Rev. 757, 829–37, 859 (2002); Harvard Project, 122–25.

17. Harvard Project, 125–26.

18. Harvard Project, 128; Stephen Cornell & Joseph P. Kalt, *Where's the Glue? Institutional Bases of American Indian Economic Development*, Journal of Socio–Economics, vol. 29 (2000), at 16–19.

19. Felicia Fonseca, *Hopi Lawmakers Suspend Tribe's Appellate Court in Continuing Turmoil*, News from Indian Country, Nov. 24, 2008, at 4.

20. *See, for example, Energy Development for Indians: Harvesting the Air*, The Economist, Mar. 31, 2010, at http://www.economist.com/world/united–states/PrinterFriendly.cfm ?story_id=15819117; *Mohawks Vote to Create Electric Utility*, News from Indian Country, July 20, 2009, at 7; *New Biomass Plant Up and Running in Shakopee*, News from Indian Country, July 20, 2009, at 7; Navajo Tribal Utility Authority, http://www.ntua .com/; *Concerns about Power Plant on Umatilla Indian Reservation*, http://www .accessmylibrary.com/coms2/summary_0286-7776993_ITM.

21. 25 U.S.C. §§ 47, 450e(b); Cohen's Handbook of Federal Indian Law (Newark: Matthew Bender, 2005 ed.), 1331.

22. Ernie Stevens Speech, Trading at the River Conference, Tulalip Reservation (May 4, 2010); Gabriel S. Galanda, *Buy Indian. What Are We Waiting For?*, Indian Country Today, Mar. 17, 2010; Harold Monteau, *Is Indian Preference Dear?*, Indian Country Today, Feb. 24, 2010, at 5 & http://www.indiancountrytoday.com/internal?st=print&id=84771487 &path=/opinion; Dave Palermo, *Rebuilding Tradition of Trade Has Not Been a Smooth Ride*, Indian Country Today, July 22, 2009, at 5; Tom Thayer & Debra Warren, *What Kind of Message Do Tribes Give to American Indian Businesses?*, Indian Country Today, Aug. 4, 2005, at A5; Oregon Native American Business & Entrepreneurial Network, *Trading at the River* (April 15, 2008); Personal Interview, Gary George, Chief Operating Officer, Wildhorse Resort Casino, Portland, OR (June 10, 2004 & Feb. 5, 2009).

23. U.S. Dept. of Housing & Urban Development, *Assessment of American Indian Housing Needs and Programs: Final Report* (May 1996), 229; Mark Fogarty, *Building More Than Houses: Meeting Indian Country's Housing Needs Fuels Other Industries*, American Indian Report, July 2000, at 20.

24. Robert J. Miller & Dean B. Suagee, *The New Indian Housing Act and Some of Its Environmental Implications* (1997), at 1–2; U.S. Dept. of Housing & Urban Development, *Final Report*, xii, 66–67, 76.

25. U.S. Dept. of Housing & Urban Development, *Final Report*, 146, 190–91, 229–30; Miller & Suagee, 2–5; Cohen, 189, 707–12.

26. Pickering, 7.

27. Ibid., 8.

28. Ibid., 7–9.

29. 25 U.S.C. §§ 4101–4243 (2006); Fogarty, *Building More Than Houses*, 20; *Family Closes First Loan on Pueblo with Help of Rural Housing Service*, Native American Report, June 1, 2001, at 107; *Fannie Mae Aided 104 Families on Trust Land*, Indian Country Today, June 13, 2001 at C2.

30. Jerry Reynolds, *Indian Housing Continues Despite Grim National Setting*, Indian Country Today, Apr. 11, 2008, http://www.indiancountry.com/content.cfm?id=10964 17024.

31. U.S. Department of the Treasury, Community Development Financial Institutions Fund, *The Report of the Native American Lending Study* (Nov. 2001), http://www.cdfifund .gov/docs/2001_nacta_lending_study.pdf, 5, 11, 14, 39–41.

32. James MacPherson, *Turtle Mountain See Private Indian Owned Bank Opened*, News from Indian Country, Jan. 17, 2008, http://indiancountrynews.net/index.php?option =com_content&task=view&id=2484&Itemid=1.

33. Ibid.

34. Ibid.

35. http://www.nabna.com/about.shtml; Ron Selden, *Blackfeet Bank Keeps Dollars Circulating on the Reservation*, Indian Country Today, Dec. 1, 1999, at C2; Mark Fogarty, *When Credit Is Due: The Debate Over the Direction of Indian Banking*, Am. Indian Rep., Nov. 1999, at 18.

36. Joanna Wagner, *Improving Native American Access to Federal Funding for Economic Development Through Partnerships with Rural Communities*, 32 Am. Indian L. Rev. 525 (2007/2008); *Challenges for Rural America in the 21st Century*, David L. Brown & Louis Swanson, eds. (University Park: The Pennsylvania State University Press, 2003), 48; Joseph Jorgensen, *Sovereignty and the Structure of Dependency at Northern Ute*, 10 Am. Ind. Culture & Research J. 75, 91–92 (1986).

37. Dave Palermo, *Rebuilding Tradition of Trade Has Not Been a Smooth Ride*, Indian Country Today, July 22, 2009, at 5; Robert J. Miller, *Inter-Tribal and International Treaties for American Indian Economic Development*, 12 Lewis & Clark L. Rev. 1103, 1114–15 (2008).

38. http://www.atnitribes.org/2008%20Summit%20DRAFT%20Agenda.pdf (last visited on Mar. 20, 2008). Miller, *Inter–Tribal*, 1110–14 & Appendix B.

39. 15 U.S.C. § 637; 13 C.F.R. § 124.

40. Vernon Loeb, *Alaskan Ventures Land Big Technology Contract*, Wash. Post, June 14, 2001, at A41; Kenneth E. Robbins, *Department of Defense Legislative Changes Promote Native-to-Native Business*, Am. Indian Rep., July 1999, at 18.

41. *ONABEN: A Native American Business Network*, at http://www.onaben.org; ONABEN, *1999–2000 Bi-Annual Report* 6, 8, 15 (2000); Mark Fogarty, *Cheyenne River Loan Fund Seeded for "Economic Sovereignty*," Indian Country Today, Jan. 31 2001, at B1; Cate Montana, *Business Consultants Expand Operations*, Indian Country Today, Jan. 24, 2001, at B1; Eric J. Greene, *Blackfeet Bank Builds Community as Well as Profits*, News from Indian Country, Late Aug. 1999, at 10.

42. Susan Guyette, *Planning for Balanced Development: A Guide for Native American and Rural Communities* (Santa Fe: Clear Light Publishers, 1996), 135, 137, 167.

43. Randall G. Holcombe, *Entrepreneurship and Economic Growth, in* Making Poor Nations Rich: Entrepreneurship and the Process of Economic Development, Benjamin Powell, ed. (Stanford, CA: Stanford University Press, 2008), 55–56, 61, 71–74.

44. Gilbreath, 96, 134.

45. Miller, *Economic Development*, 835.

46. Klaus Franz, 175–76; Gilbreath, 7, 28, 50, 96, 134.

47. James J. Chrisman, Ph.D., *The Economic Impact of ONABEN's Counseling Activities in Oregon: 1998*, at 2, 11; James J. Chrisman, Ph.D., *The Economic Impact of ONABEN's Counseling Activities of the Oregon Native American and Entrepreneurial Network: 2000*, at 2, 15, 16.

48. Harvard Project, 76, 119–20, 138, 154; National Indian Gaming Association, *Indian Gaming Facts*, http://www.indiangaming.org/library/indian-gaming-facts/index.shtml.

49. Seminole Nation v. United States, 316 U S. 286, 297 (1942).

50. Morton v. Mancari, 417 U.S. 535, 551–52 (1974); Cherokee Nation v. Georgia, 30 U.S. (5 Pet.) 1, 17 (1831).

51. *See, for example*, Treaty with the Cherokee, Nov. 28, 1785, art. IX, 7 Stat. 18; Treaty with the Wyandot, Etc., Aug. 3, 1795, art. V & VIII, 7 Stat. 49; Treaty with the Osage, Nov. 10, 1808, art. 10, 7 Stat. 107; *Indian Affairs: Laws and Treaties*, vol. 2, Charles J. Kappler, ed., (Washington, DC: Gov't Printing Office, 1904), 10, 42–43, 97.

52. Becky Kramer, *State Grants Provide Money to Boost Jobs*, Spokesman–Review, Aug. 7, 2001; ONABEN, *1999–2000 Bi-Annual Report*, 6, 8, 15.

53. Harvard Project, 202–04, 208; Michelle Tirado, *Left Behind: Are Public Schools Failing Indian Kids?*, Am. Indian Rep., Sept. 2001, at 12; *Public Policy*, 147–48.

54. Brian C. Hosmer, *American Indians in the Marketplace: Persistence and Innovation Among the Menominees and Metlakatlans, 1870–1920* (Lawrence: University of Kansas Press, 1999), 16, 219, 224.

55. Smith, 3, 111; *accord* Gilbreath, 129.

# CHAPTER 9

1. Personal Interview, Clifford Lyle Marshall, Chairman, Hoopa Valley Tribe (March 19, 2009).

2. Personal Interview, Antone Minthorn, Chairman, Confederated Tribes of the Umatilla Indian Reservation (April 14, 2009).

3. Richard Cockle, *Jobs, Jobs, Jobs, But No Homes*, The Sunday Oregonian, April 20, 2008, at B4; Carson Walker, *Reservations Revive as Native Americans Return to Roots*, The Oregonian, Apr. 11, 2001, at A3; Diane Brooks, *Tribes Once Crippled by Poverty Now Realizing American Dream: Tulalips Roll Dice, Hit Jackpot with Casino*, Seattle Times, July 13, 2000, at A8.

4. Naomi Mezey, Note, *The Distribution of Wealth, Sovereignty, and Culture Through Indian Gaming*, 48 Stan. L. Rev. 711, 727 (1996).

5. Ray Halbritter & Steven Paul McSloy, *Empowerment or Dependence? The Practical Value and Meaning of Native American Sovereignty*, 26 N.Y.U. J. Int'l L. & Pol. 531, 564 (1994); *see also* Frank Pommersheim, *Braid of Feathers* (Berkeley: University of California Press, 1995), 168.

6. Francis Paul Prucha, *The Indians in American Society: From the Revolutionary War to the Present* (Berkeley: University of California Press, 1985), 101–03.

7. *See, for example*, Robert J. Miller, *Exercising Cultural Self-Determination: The Makah Indian Tribe Goes Whaling*, 25 Am. Indian L. Rev. 165 (2001); Robert J. Miller, *Speaking with*

*Forked Tongues: Indian Treaties, Salmon, and the Endangered Species Act*, 70 Or. L. Rev. 543 (1991).

8. *Native Pathways: American Indian Culture and Economic Development in the Twentieth Century*, Brian Hosmer & Colleen O'Neill, eds. (Boulder: University Press of Colorado, 2004), 7, 10, 15; Robert H. White, *Tribal Assets: The Rebirth of Native America* (New York: Henry Holt, 1990), 277; Brian C. Hosmer, *American Indians in the Marketplace: Persistence and Innovation Among the Menominees and Metlakatlans, 1870–1920* (Lawrence: University of Kansas Press, 1999), 16, 219, 221, 223–24; Kent Gilbreath, *Red Capitali$m: An Analysis of the Navajo Economy* (Norman: University of Oklahoma Press, 1973), 87–88, 91; *Native Americans and Wage Labor*, Alice Littlefield and Martha C. Knack, eds. (Norman: University of Oklahoma Press, 1996), 5, 13–14, 67, 245–47, 260–61.

9. Robert J. Miller, *Economic Development in Indian Country: Will Capitalism or Socialism Succeed?*, 80 Or. L. Rev. 757, 776–77 (2001).

10. Dean Rhodes, *Tribal Government Day Honors Native First Foods*, Smoke Signals, June 1, 2011, at 10; Dave Palermo, *Native Stewards of the Land, Once Again*, Indian Country Today, Feb. 10, 2010 (Gaming Magazine insert), at 28; Timberly Ross, *Tribes Buy Back Thousands of Acres of Land*, News from Indian Country, Jan. 14, 2010, at 7; Babette Herrmann, *Suquamish Tribe Debuts Community House*, Indian Country Today, March 18, 2009, at 7; *wiyaxayxt * as days go by * wiyaakaa?awn, Our History, Our Land, and Our People: The Cayuse, Umatilla, and Walla Walla*, Jennifer Karson, ed. (Portland: Tamastslikt Cultural Institute & Oregon Historical Society Press, 2006), 210–11, 214; *Tulalips Buy Piece of Their Property Back*, Spokesman-Review (Spokane, WA), Feb. 18, 2001; Kit Miniclier, *Indians Buy Back Ancestral Lands*, Denver Post, Dec. 20, 2000, at B1; *1997 BIA Self-Governance Tribes Population and Labor Force Report*, http://www.hoopa -nsn.gov/documents/97BIAReport.pdf

11. Jim Shamp, *Cherokee Study: As Poverty Falls, So Do Psychiatric Problems*, Herald Sun, Oct. 14, 2003, http://www.heraldsun.com/tools/printfriendly.cfm?StoryID =402615; Peter J. Ferrara, *The Choctaw Revolution* (Washington, DC: Americans for Tax Reform Foundation, 1998), 13–14, 45–50, 64–66, 68–73, 80, 82, 84–85; Barbara Powell, *Choctaws: From Poverty to Prosperity in 40 Years*, Clarion-Ledger, June 26, 2003, http://www.clarionledger.com/news/0306/26/m08.html; The Harvard Project on American Indian Economic Development, *The State of the Native Nations: Conditions under U.S. Policies of Self-Determination* (New York: Oxford University Press, 2008), 112.

12. Cockle, *Job, Jobs, Jobs*; Edward Sifuentes, *More Indians Living Off Reservation*, North County Times.Net (Escondido, Cal.) (May 24, 2001); Walker, at A3; Address given at Harvard University, September 29, 1998.

13. Personal notes, Trading at the River Conference (May 4, 2010) (on file with author).

14. Kathleen Ann Pickering, *Lakota Culture, World Economy* (Lincoln: University of Nebraska Press, 2000), 7, 38–39.

15. *Research in Human Capital and Development: American Indian Economic Development*, Carol Ward & C. Matthew Snipp, eds. (Greenwich, CT: Jai Press, Inc., 1996), 132; Al Gedicks, *Liberation Sociology and Advocacy for the Sokaogon Ojibwe*, 467 (2004), http://oae. sagepub.com/cgi/reprint/17/4/449.pdf; *Crow Tribe Wants to Exploit Coal*, http://lawlib .lclark.edu/blog/native_america/?p=1722.

16. Robert S. McPherson, *Naalyehe Ba–Hooghan—"House of Merchandise": The Navajo Trading Post as an Institution of Cultural Change, 1900–1930*, in American Nations: Encounters in Indian Country, 1850 to the Present, Frederick E. Hoxie et al., eds. (New York: Routledge, 2001), 81.

17. *The Hidden Half: Studies of Plains Indian Women*, Patricia Albers & Beatrice Medicine, eds. (New York: University Press of America, 1983), 70.

18. Loretta Fowler, *Shared Symbols* (Ithaca: Cornell University Press, 1987), 8; *see also* Hosmer, *American Indians*, 13–14; McPherson, 84–85, 95; *The Hidden Half*, 118, 220.

# Selected Bibliography

Only my primary sources are listed here. Please refer to the chapter endnotes for citations to all the materials I relied on.

## ARTICLES

Haddock, David D., & Robert J. Miller, *Can a Sovereign Protect Investors from Itself? Tribal Institutions to Spur Reservation Investment*, 8 J. Small & Emerging Bus. L. 173 (2004).

Jorgensen, Joseph, *Sovereignty and the Structure of Dependency at Northern Ute*, 10 Am. Ind. Culture & Research J. 75–94 (1986).

Miller, Robert J., *American Indian Entrepreneurs: Unique Challenges, Unlimited Potential*, 40 Arizona St. L.J. 1297 (2008).

Miller, Robert J., *Inter-tribal and International Treaties for American Indian Economic Development*, 12 Lewis & Clark L. Rev. 1103 (2008).

Miller, Robert J., *Economic Development in Indian Country: Will Capitalism or Socialism Succeed?*, 80 Oregon L. Rev. 757 (2001).

Pascal, Vincent J., & Daniel Stewart, *The Effects of Location and Economic Cluster Development on Native American Entrepreneurship*, 9 Entrepreneurship and Innovation 121–131 (2008).

## BOOKS

*American Encounters: Natives and Newcomers from European Contact to Indian Removal, 1500–1850*, Peter C. Mancall & James H. Merrell, eds. (New York: Routledge, 2000).

*American Indian Policy in the Twentieth Century*, Vine Deloria, Jr., ed. (Norman: University of Oklahoma Press, 1985).

*American Indian Policy: Self-Governance and Economic Development*, Lyman H. Legters & Fremont J. Lyden, eds. (Westport, CT: Greenwood, 1994).

Anderson, Terry L., *Sovereign Nations or Reservations? An Economic History of American Indians* (San Francisco: Pacific Research Institute, 1995).

Blomstrom, Magnus, & Bjorn Hettne, *Development Theory in Transition: The Dependency Debate & Beyond: Third World Responses* (London: Zed Books Ltd., 1984).

*Challenges for Rural America in the 21st Century*, David L. Brown & Louis Swanson, eds. (University Park: The Pennsylvania State University Press, 2003).

De Soto, Hernando. *The Mystery of Capital: Why Capitalism Triumphs in the West and Fails Everywhere Else* (New York: Basic Books, 2000).

*Economic Development in American Indian Reservations*, Roxanne Dunbar Ortiz, ed. (Albuquerque: University of New Mexico, 1979).

Ferrara, Peter J., *The Choctaw Revolution: Lessons for Federal Indian Policy* (Washington, DC: Americans for Tax Reform Foundation, 1998).

Frantz, Klaus, *Indian Reservations in the United States: Territory, Sovereignty, and Socioeconomic Change* (Chicago: University of Chicago Press, 1999).

Guyette, Susan, *Planning for Balanced Development: A Guide for Native American and Rural Communities* (Santa Fe, NM: Clear Light Publishers, 1996).

Haberfeld, Steven, *A Self-Help Manual for Tribal Economic Development* (Boulder, CO: Native American Rights Fund, 1982).

The Harvard Project on American Indian Economic Development, *The State of the Native Nations: Conditions under U.S. Policies of Self-Determination* (New York: Oxford University Press, 2008).

*The Hidden Half: Studies of Plains Indian Women*, Patricia Albers & Beatrice Medicine, eds. (New York: University Press of America, 1983).

Hosmer, Brian C., *American Indians in the Marketplace: Persistence and Innovation Among the Menominees and Metlakatlans, 1870–1920* (Lawrence: University of Kansas Press, 1999).

*Jobs and Economic Development in Minority Communities*, Paul Ong & Anastasia Loukaitou-Sideris, eds. (Philadelphia: Temple University Press, 2006).

Mancall, Peter C., *Valley of Opportunity: Economic Culture along the Upper Susquehanna, 1700–1800* (Ithaca, NY: Cornell University Press, 1991).

Miller, Robert J., *Native America, Discovered and Conquered: Thomas Jefferson, Lewis & Clark, and Manifest Destiny* (Lincoln: University of Nebraska Press, 2008).

Miner, H. Craig, *The Corporation and the Indian: Tribal Sovereignty and Industrial Civilization in Indian Territory, 1865–1907* (Columbia, MO: University of Missouri Press, 1976).

*Native Americans and Wage Labor*, Alice Littlefield and Martha C. Knack, eds. (Norman: University of Oklahoma Press, 1996).

*Native Pathways: American Indian Culture and Economic Development in the Twentieth Century*, Brian Hosmer & Colleen O'Neill, eds. (Boulder: University Press of Colorado, 1988).

*New Directions in American Indian History*, Colin G. Calloway, ed. (Norman: University of Oklahoma Press, 1988).

*The Other Side of the Frontier: Economic Explorations into Native American History*, Linda Barrington, ed. (Boulder, CO: Westview Press, 1999).

Pickering, Kathleen, Mark H. Harvey, Gene F. Summers, & David Mushinski, *Welfare Reform in Persistent Rural Poverty* (University Park: The Pennsylvania State University Press, 2006).

*The Political Economy of North American Indians*, John H. Moore, ed. (Norman: University of Oklahoma Press, 1993).

*Property Rights and Indian Economies*, Terry L. Anderson, ed., (Lanham, MD: Rowman and Littlefield, 1992).

Prucha, Francis Paul, *The Great Father: The United States Government and the American Indians* (Lincoln: University of Nebraska Press, 1995).

*Public Policy Impacts on American Indian Economic Development*, C. Matthew Snipp, ed. (Albuquerque: University of New Mexico Press, 1988).

Sahlins, Marshall, *Stone Age Economics* (Chicago: Aldine-Atherton, 1972).

Samuelson, Paul A., & William D. Nordhaus, *Economics*, 14th ed. (New York: McGraw-Hill, 1992).

Smith, Dean Howard, *Modern Tribal Development: Paths to Self-Sufficiency and Cultural Integrity in Indian Country* (Walnut Creek, CA: AltaMira Press, 2000).

Smithsonian Institution, Handbook of North American Indians, vols. 1–15, William C. Sturtevant, ed. (Washington, DC: Smithsonian Institution, 1978–2008).

*What Can Tribes Do? Strategies and Institutions in American Indian Economic Development*, Stephen Cornell & Joseph P. Kalt, eds. (Los Angeles: University of California, 1992).

White, Richard, *The Roots of Dependency: Subsistence, Environment, and Social Change among the Choctaws, Pawnees, and Navajos* (Lincoln: University of Nebraska Press, 1983).

White, Robert H., *Tribal Assets: The Rebirth of Native America* (New York: Henry Holt, 1990).

*wiyaxayxt * as days go by * wiyaakaaʔawn, Our History, Our Land, and Our People: The Cayuse, Umatilla, and Walla Walla*, Jennifer Karson, ed. (Portland: Tamastslikt Cultural Institute & Oregon Historical Society Press, 2006).

# Index

91, 177 n.2, 179 n.51; negative effects, 85–86, 88–91; pathological and problem gambling and definitions, 90; positive effects for tribes and non-Indians, 86–88; revenues, 71–72, 74; Seminole Tribe bingo, 73; *Seminole Tribe of Florida v. Butterworth*, 74–76; *Seminole Tribe of Florida v. Florida*, 82, 84; state gaming, 74–76; state opposition, 74. *See also* Indian Gaming Regulatory Act

Gas, 38, 51

Genesis 1:28, 26

Georgia, 1802 compact with United States to remove Cherokee Nation, 35

Golf courses, 54, 59

Grand Traverse Tribe, tort claims act waiver of sovereign immunity, 98

Greed, 162

The Harvard Project on American Indian Economic Development, 5, 108, 114; Cornell, Stephen, 106; gaming study, 86; Kalt, Joseph, 106–7; keys to successful tribal economic development, 140–42; small businesses have no chance without "independent tribal court systems," 131; tribal cultures do not oppose economic development, 142; value of impartial, independent courts and separation of powers, 142

Hatcheries, 54–55

Havasupai Tribe, 13; private property principles, 13

Head Start program, 59

Health issues, 7, 29, 119–20, 141

Hidatsa Nation, 23

Hohokam, 13

Honey bee trees, individually owned, 63

Hoopa Valley Tribe, 50, 57, 68–70; acorns, 68; allotment, 68; casino, 69; contracting for federal programs, 69–70; Hoopa Forest Industries, 69; Hoopa Roads Aggregate and Ready Mix, 69; modern-day private fishing rights, 14; treaty, 68; unemployment, 68; Xontah Builders, 69

Hopewell culture, 19; astronomical knowledge, 19

Hopi Nation, 13, 105; coal, 38

Horses, 15–16, 163; inheritable, leasable, and private property, 16

Hosmer, Brian C.: *American Indians in the Marketplace: Persistence and Innovation Among the Menominees and Metlakatlans, 1870–1920*, 28, 156

Hotels, 54, 59

Housing, 2, 55, 146–48; inadequate reservation housing, 2, 162

Hualapai Nation, 138

Hunting, 18, 53; private property rights, 62–63; tribal permits, 53

Huron Tribe, 31; diseases, 31; middlemen in trade, 31

Indian Civil Rights Act, 101, 107; tribes required to give equal protection and due process to all, 101

Indian Country, 166 n.3

Indian Gaming Regulatory Act, 76–83; annual audits, 78; background checks, 78; bingo, 78; blackjack, 80; class I gaming, 77–78; class II gaming, 78–79; class III gaming, 80–82; computer and electronic gaming, 79; defining "such gaming," 81; National Indian Gaming Commission, 78–80, 85, 105; negotiate compacts in good faith, 81–82; off-reservation casinos, 84–85; revenue-sharing agreements, 83; secretarial class III procedures, 82–84; *Seminole Tribe of Florida v. Florida*, 82, 84; slot machines, 80; state control and veto power, 78–79, 81–83; Tiguas Tribe lawsuit regarding secretarial procedures, 84; tribal-state compacts, 80–82

Indian Health Service, 53, 64, 69, 159

Indian/Interstate Commerce Clause, 39

Indian Reorganization Act, 37, 44–46; called communism and socialism, 45–46; section 16 tribal governments, 46; section 17 tribal corporations, 46; tribal constitutions, 45